I see maths
Teaching resources

Book 2

Sue Jennings and Richard Dunne

www.letts-education.com

Published by Letts Educational
The Chiswick Centre
414 Chiswick High Road
London W4 5TF
☎ 020 8996 3333
📠 020 8742 8390
🖳 mail@lettsed.co.uk
🌐 www.letts-education.com

Letts Educational Limited is a division of Granada Learning Limited, part of Granada plc.

© Sue Jennings and Richard Dunne 2003

First published 2003

ISBN 184 085 6939

The authors assert the moral right to be identified as the authors of this work.

British Library Cataloguing in Publication Data
A catalogue record for this book is available from the British Library.

Commissioned by Helen Clark
Project management by Vicky Butt
Designed and edited by Topics · The Creative Partnership, Exeter
Diagrams by Tony Wilkins
Production by PDQ
Printed and bound by Ashford Colour Press, Gosport

Contents

Introduction

Who are these books for?

This series of three Student's Books and three Teaching Resources covers the content of Key Stage 3 of the National Curriculum for Mathematics (England and Wales) and satisfies the requirements of the National Strategy *Framework for Teaching Mathematics*. These Teaching Resources support Student's Book 2. The books are designed for students at all levels of attainment.

How to use the Student's Book

Student's Book 2 begins with ten sets of Reviews to revise work that students are likely to have covered previously. Depending on the class you are working with, these may need extensive teaching before students attempt the exercises.

The second part is divided into four sections on Number and Algebra; Shape and Space; Handling Data; and Using and Applying Mathematics. There are forty-eight pairs of double pages, each consisting of a lesson with demonstrations and a set of exercises.

The third part of the book has practice sheets for tests.

Each of these parts is supported by dedicated pages in these Teaching Resources.

The final part of the Student's Book is a glossary of important mathematical vocabulary used within the text.

What are the lesson pages?

Each **Lesson** focuses on a 'teachable chunk' of work. It does not necessarily fit an exact timetabled lesson but may span over a series of lessons. You will need to use your professional judgement about how much time you spend on each chunk of work. This will depend on your students' present attainment level.

Lesson plan

The first double-page spread is divided into the three-part lesson structure recommended in the Framework. The **Goals** specify what students will be able to do on completion of the lesson. Prior knowledge for the lesson is practised in the **Starter**. Two **Demonstrations**

represent visually the crucial points of learning. In some cases a **Worked example** clarifies how the ideas are applied to typical test items. **Key words** pinpoint the organising language. The **Plenary** returns to the Goals to ensure they have real meaning for each student.

Exercise bank

A spread of **Exercises** indicates and practises the significance of the work. These are grouped as **Essential exercises**, **Challenging exercises** and **Problem-solving exercises**.

The **Exercises** provide opportunities for students to model what has been demonstrated. **Essential exercises** focus on content sufficient to progress through the book. **Challenging exercises** make greater demands on students in interpreting the questions (often using a form of words not necessarily specifically taught) but they should not be reserved for the most confident. Omitting the challenging exercises for some students is a practical problem of teacher time, not a question of student ability. This is true also of **Problem-solving exercises**; these practise the important emphasis on context (outside mathematics and within mathematics).

The underlying rationale of each lesson is explained in these Teaching Resources so that the lessons can be most effectively engaged. The exercises are discussed so their purpose is clear.

What is a Demonstration?

Effective teaching involves demonstration by the teacher and modelling by the students. The teacher demonstrates (with direct teaching) how to do mathematics and how to think about mathematics. This always includes some means of representing the mathematics visually. The students model this with a range of appropriate examples.

In the Student's Books each lesson includes **Demonstration 1** and **Demonstration 2**. These visual representations focus on the main aspects of the direct teaching. They are more than an *aide-mémoire*. Students should study each demonstration and articulate the detailed meaning of what they are learning. These visual demonstrations are not designed to do the teaching on their own. They summarise what is available in the teaching. Pages 13–129 of these Teaching Resources provide support in how to demonstrate the mathematics.

How to use the Teaching Resources

This pack of fully photocopiable Teaching Resources is designed to help you use *I See Maths* Student's Book 2 effectively with your students.

What are the Teacher's Notes?

The main section of this pack (pages 13–129) is made up of structured advice for you, the teachers of *I See Maths*. The Teacher's Notes work through each lesson in the Student's Book (relevant page numbers are provided) from Goals to Plenary.

Wherever possible, the notes provide:
- advice on classroom organisation
- advice on differentiation
- advice on preparation and delivery
- additional worked examples
- an indication of where and how to use the worksheets (see below).

Lesson scripts

I See Maths gives special emphasis to the teaching of mathematics through visualisation and the precise use of mathematical vocabulary. The Teacher's Notes provide back-up for all staff on the delivery of this focus. Within the Teacher's Notes, you will notice a number of shaded boxes like the one below. These are 'lesson scripts'. They provide examples of the kind of wording that could be used in the classroom.

> *Text in italics, like this, is designed to be spoken out loud by you, as you address the class.*
>
> [Text in plain type and square brackets, like this, gives instructions (rather like stage directions) on what you should be doing as you speak the words.]

This feature is of particular benefit to non-specialist teachers. However, the scripts also provide invaluable support for all teachers on delivering the demonstration sections of the Student's Book.

Worksheets

The final section of this pack (pages 130–176) is made up of photocopiable worksheets. Advice is given on how to integrate these into the delivery of the Student's Book, although many of them could also be used as free-standing tasks for:
- homework
- cover lessons
- 'finished early' tasks.

What is unique about this series?

There are two important features for a significant impact on the quality of students' learning. Firstly, four **big ideas** in mathematics are identified: Operations; Equivalence; Comparison; Classification. These provide a framework for thinking about mathematics to enable students to make sense of their work.

Secondly, detailed and deliberate **whole-class interactive** teaching underpins the work to secure the benefits of consistent mathematical treatment. The most important aspect of this is the idea of visualisation. It is the emphasis on visualisation that prompted the title *I See Maths*.

Big ideas in mathematics

Proficient students do not memorise large numbers of unrelated items. They categorise their developing knowledge so that many things are understood as being of the same type. Recall is facilitated, instinctively, by searching for a category and then within a category. Proficient students also build up a vast repertoire of examples (within categories) so that a 'new problem' is rarely completely new.

Less proficient students do not instinctively think in categories. Sometimes, however, they do have a quite astonishing ability to memorise many individual things. These students are usually successful but not proficient. Other students, with only normal memories (or worse), become neither proficient nor successful.

All students need to be taught how to categorise; and they need to be taught categories that efficiently represent mathematics. They also need help to build up a repertoire of examples within those categories.

Four appropriate categories (or 'big ideas in mathematics') are identified in *I See Maths*. They do not constitute a 'new mathematics'. It is the manner in which they are taught and used that makes them especially useful.

The following is a brief introduction to the 'big ideas', and an illustration of how they are relevant to Student's Book 2.

1. **Operations**

   The big idea of 'operations' includes $+$, $-$, $\times$, $\div$ (and, of course, they are often referred to as 'the four operations'). However, in *I See Maths,* operations also include solving equations, drawing graphs, constructing geometric shapes, proving, comparing distributions, and so on. Each set of operations has its own accepted laws and conventions. When teaching ensures these become 'second nature', the students make progress.

2. Equivalence

Equivalence is one of the most powerful ideas in mathematics. It is familiar in the ubiquitous '=' sign. In *I See Maths* it is given greater significance by using the phrase, **'same value: different appearance'** in relation to expressions such as:

325 and 300 + 20 + 5 $\frac{1}{5}$ and 0·2

3. Comparison

It is surprising how much mathematics involves making comparisons. Clearly, ratio and proportion are explicitly comparisons, and so is scale factor. However, each time you use a fraction you are implicitly making a comparison. All measurement, whether of length or angle or anything else, is a comparison (including probability and standard deviation). Measurement involves comparison with an accepted standard (or denomination).

4. Classification

The idea of classification permeates mathematics. Specified as a 'big idea' it helps students recognise its different forms. For example, we can use the categories 'implicit information' and 'explicit information' to focus our attention on a diagram, graph or word problem. Similarly, we can examine lines and line segments, and classify them as parallel, perpendicular, or coincident.

Operations: an illustration

Most students are well rehearsed in using +, −, ×, and ÷ with at least some types of number. Indeed, students may become so familiar with +, −, × and ÷ that they pay little attention to what the symbols mean. This familiarity prevents them from applying the operations to new types of number. They do not see the connection between, say, the division of whole numbers and the division of fractions and of negative numbers. The big idea of 'operation' has passed them by.

Consider the expression 3 + 2 = 5 for example. It implies starting with 3 and then applying a transformation to turn it into 5. The object 3 is transformed into the image 5. This is generally thought of as being achieved by the operation 'add 2'. This is correct but there is a much more effective way of thinking about it.

Look again at the equation 3 + 2 = 5. In *I See Maths* we pay detailed attention to 'add 2' by looking separately at the plus sign and the 2. The operation 'add', standing alone, is to be thought of as an imperative verb: 'get ready to get some more'. This is explained further below.

1. Addition

Arrange two tables at the front of the class. Tell students that the one on their left is the 'resource table' and the one on their right is the 'maths table'. Place paper cups on the resource table.

> *When I show you 3 + 2 = 5 you read from left to right. You look at the 3 and start by putting three cups on the maths table. You look at the + and get ready to get some more [move to the resource table and act 'readiness' by raising hands over the cups]. You look at the 2 and you get 2 more [carry them to the maths table]. You look at the = and recognise this as an instruction to look at the maths table and count the cups. You see 5 cups.*

Notice that + and = are treated as imperative verbs; but 3 and 2 and 5 are treated as nouns. It is this idea of imperative verbs and nouns that underpins the idea of 'operations'.

An important part of this teaching process is using physical objects to convey the meaning of + (this makes it possible to visualise 3 + 2 = 5). To capitalise on this we need further physical objects to continue the use of the imperative verb. For this reason, the fraction $\frac{1}{5}$ should be written on large display cards. Then $\frac{3}{5}$ (three of those things called fifths) is visualised as three of the appropriate cards. $\frac{3}{5} + \frac{4}{5} = \frac{7}{5}$ is understood as:

> *You look at the $\frac{3}{5}$ and start by putting three of those things called fifths on the maths table. You look at the + and get ready to get some more; you look at $\frac{4}{5}$ and get four of those things called fifths. You look at = and recognise this as an instruction to look at the maths table and count the cups. You see $\frac{7}{5}$.*

This **process** remains true for:

3 + ⁻2 =   3 + $\frac{2}{5}$ =   3 + 200 =
3 + ·2 =   3 + 2x =   3x + 2y =

The general idea of operations as a 'noun / imperative verb' combination is used consistently. We need to indicate its use with the operations +, −, ×, and ÷.

2. Subtraction

The resource table and maths table are used universally in *I See Maths* (not always physically – sometimes they are visualised). The 'equals' sign always requires attention to be given to the quantity on the maths table. Then the symbol '−' means 'get ready to take some away' (move to the maths table and indicate readiness to remove some from the maths table).

> *3 − 2 = 1 requires putting three cups on the maths table; getting ready to take some away; take away two cups; look at the maths table; one cup.*

3. Multiplication

× means 'do the same thing lots of times'.

> $\frac{2}{5} \times 4 = \frac{8}{5}$ *requires putting $\frac{2}{5}$ on the maths table; doing the same thing lots of times (i.e. immediately pick up another $\frac{2}{5}$ and walk to the maths table); do it four times altogether; looking at the maths table; $\frac{8}{5}$.*

4. Division

÷ means 'look at it and wonder how many piles of …' so that:

> $\frac{6}{5} \div \frac{2}{5} = 3$ *requires putting $\frac{6}{5}$ on the maths table; looking at it and wondering how many piles of $\frac{2}{5}$; [make piles of $\frac{2}{5}$]; there are 3 piles.*

Big ideas in teaching

It has become fashionable to teach mathematical concepts through real-life experience or contexts. However, in order to establish mathematical concepts as powerful categories we first need to avoid their identification with particular contexts.

Let us take the example of addition. You will see that, in *I See Maths* lessons, addition ('get ready to get some more') is taught with paper cups. This is vitally important. The cups are carefully selected objects that are used for thinking with, not for thinking about. They are a half-way house between symbolism and reality. Their physical existence is important, but they themselves are not important. The cups provide a tangible object that, widely used, can be visualised (and that is the main point about using physical objects).

Important topics in mathematics are introduced with these tangible objects so that they provide a clear, known reference when, later, students cannot accurately recall a topic. The underlying 'big idea' here is that visualisation, supported by careful articulation and prompted by symbols, needs a concrete reference point. You will see how this is relentlessly developed in the lessons; and you will see how each of the demonstrations strengthens this.

Whole-class interactive teaching

Whole-class interactive teaching involves demonstration, modelling and summarising. The Teacher's Notes for each lesson, provided in these Teaching Resources, support this.

Each lesson is introduced by the teacher who demonstrates how to do mathematics and how to think about mathematics. This involves detailed attention to language and conventions, and focuses on enabling students to visualise the implications of the Goals.

Students' individual or group work in doing the exercises involves them in modelling how to do mathematics and how to think about mathematics. This will not happen easily: students are likely to have a learnt preference only to 'do' the exercises rather than think about them. The necessity of ensuring students *think* is a priority supported by 'summarising' how to do mathematics and how to think about mathematics in the Plenary. This is why the plenary session must put an emphasis on examining the Goals in relation to Demonstration 1 and Demonstration 2 (these appear in each lesson in the Student's Book).

Of course, 'examining the Goals' means students must articulate their understanding of what they have been doing. They need to come to the board, talk through a specific goal or demonstration and respond to your supportive and searching questions. Careful and accurate use of technical vocabulary, phrases and expressions must be central to students' summarising in the plenary.

Many schools lack a tradition of students articulating their emergent understanding. The necessary willingness, confidence, thoughtfulness, sensitivity and competence (for the speaker and the audience) must be a key aim in teaching mathematics. Mathematics teaching cannot be effective without it.

Differentiation by assistance

The National Curriculum (England and Wales) is an entitlement curriculum (an insistence on all students being offered the same programme of study). One way of doing this is by representing the content so that it is accessible to all students. This is why we focus on 'big ideas in mathematics'. These ideas are persistently revisited so all students can appreciate the clarifying coherence of mathematics. An individual's progress will require different levels of support. The appropriate maxim is: 'Differentiate as a last resort, not as a first principle. Differentiate principally by support, not by outcome or task'.

Using the Content and Levels grid

The grid on pages 9–12 provides references to the Strategy and to the National Curriculum. The levels of assistance that you offer will depend upon the class you are teaching and the students' present levels of attainment.

For those students who struggle with any of the exercises, do not omit the work but provide sufficient assistance for the students to gain some access to the learning. Invite students to write solutions on the board following your instructions, or get them to help you with the demonstrations. Eventually, these students will gain familiarity with the work, and the success they get with assistance will transform into success without assistance.

For any average class, you might expect to offer the following levels of assistance:

☺ – little or no assistance

☊ – some assistance

✪ – maximum assistance

Key to the Content and Levels grid

U = Using and applying mathematics to solve problems

N = Numbers and the number system

C = Calculations

A = Algebra

S = Shape, space and measure

H = Handling data

Objectives are numbered consecutively within each topic as laid out in the *Framework for Teaching Mathematics*, pages 6–11.

We believe that the approach to mathematics learning that is used in *I See Maths* is both effective and stimulating for students. They will be able to achieve mastery and understanding of mathematical concepts and apply these in everyday contexts. We hope that you and your students will enjoy using *I See Maths*.

SUE JENNINGS AND RICHARD DUNNE

Answers

The answers to the student book and to the worksheets from this book can be found at:

www.letts-education.com/iseemaths

The fastest way to access the files is to:
1. Right-click on the relevant section.
2. Follow the instruction to 'Save Target As'. This will download the file to your computer.
3. Open and print the file from your computer.

Download time is approximately 15 seconds for each file with a non-Broadband connection.

Lesson	Differentiation		Using and applying mathematics to solve problems	Numbers and the number system	Calculations	Algebra	Shape, space and measure	Handling data
Book 1 Review								
Addition and subtraction 1	Essential	☺		N4, N8 Lev 4–5	C1, C4 Lev 4–5			
	Challenge	◑	U1 Lev 4–5	N4, N8 Lev 4–5	C1, C4 Lev 4–5	A4 Lev 4–5		
	Problems	☺	U1 Lev 4–5	N4, N8 Lev 4–5	C6, C10 Lev 4–5			
Addition and subtraction 2	Essential	☺		N4	C1–C3 Lev 4–5			
	Challenge	◑		N4	C1–C4 Lev 4–6	A4 Lev 5–6		
	Problems	☺	U1 Lev 4–5	N4	C6, C10 Lev 4–6			
Multiplication and division 1	Essential	☺		N4, N8	C1–C4, C7 Lev 4–5			
	Challenge	◑			C1, C3, C4 Lev 4–6	A4 Lev 5–6		
	Problems	☺	U1 Lev 4–6		C10 Lev 4–5		S11 Lev 4–6	
Multiplication and division 2	Essential	☺		N4, N8	C1, C3, C7, C10 Lev 4–5			
	Challenge	◑			C1, C3 Lev 4–6	A4 Lev 4–5		
	Problems	☺	U1 Lev 4–6	N4, N8 Lev 4–5	C1, C3 Lev 4–5			
Equivalence	Essential	☺		N7, N9 Lev 4–5	C3 Lev 4–5			
	Challenge	◑		N7, N9 Lev 4–5	C3 Lev 4–5			
	Problems	☺	U1 Lev 4–5	N7, N9 Lev 4–5	C3 Lev 4–5			
Proportion	Essential	☺		N9, N10 Lev 4–5	C3, C4 Lev 4–5			
	Challenge	◑		N9, N10 Lev 5–6	C3, C4 Lev 5–6	A4 Lev 4–5		
	Problems	☺	U1 Lev 4–5					
Algebra	Essential	☺				A1, A2, A4, A6 Lev 5–6		
	Challenge	◑				A6, A11 Lev 5–6	S11 Lev 5–6	
	Problems	☺	U1 Lev 4–5				S11 Lev 4–5	
Angles, lines and triangles	Essential	☺					S1, S2 Lev 5–6	
	Challenge	◑					S1, S2 Lev 5–6	
	Problems	☺	U1 Lev 5–6				S1, S2 Lev 5–6	
Shapes	Essential	☺					S2, S9 Lev 5–6	
	Challenge	◑					S2, S9 Lev 5–6	
	Problems	☺	U1 Lev 5–6				S2, S9 Lev 5–6	
Handling data	Essential	☺		N9 Lev 4–5				H5, H7, H10, H11 Lev 4–5
	Challenge	◑						H3, H6 Lev 5–6
	Problems	☺	U1 Lev 4–6					H5 Lev 5–6
Number and Algebra								
Laws of arithmetic	Essential	◑		N5 Lev 5–6	C1, C2, C10 Lev 4–5			
	Challenge	✪			C1, C2, C10 Lev 5–6	A2 Lev 5–6		
	Problems	◑	U1 Lev 4–5					
Order of operations	Essential	◑		N5 Lev 4–5	C1, C2 Lev 4–5			
	Challenge	✪			C1, C2 Lev 5–6	A2 Lev 5–6		
	Problems	◑	U1 Lev 4–5		C1, C2 Lev 4–5			
Making connections 1	Essential	◑		N6 Lev 4–5	C3, C7 Lev 5–6			
	Challenge	✪		N6 Lev 4–5		A2 Lev 5–6		
	Problems	☺	U1, U2, U4 Lev 4–5					
Equivalence	Essential	◑			C3, C7 Lev 4–5			
	Challenge	✪			C3, C7 Lev 5–6	A2, A4 Lev 6–7		
	Problems	☺	U1 Lev 4–5		C3, C7 Lev 4–5			
Making connections 2	Essential	◑			C3, C7 Lev 4–5			
	Challenge	✪			C3, C7 Lev 6–7	A2, A4 Lev 6–7		
	Problems	☺	U1, U4 Lev 4–5		C3, C7 Lev 4–5			

continued

Key: ☺ little or no assistance   ◑ some assistance   ✪ maximum assistance

 I See Maths Book 2

Lessons: Content and Levels

Lesson	Differentiation		Using and applying mathematics to solve problems	Numbers and the number system	Calculations	Algebra	Shape, space and measure	Handling data
Powers and roots	Essential	♁		N1, N6 Lev 5–6	C4, C8 Lev 4–5			
	Challenge	✿		N1, N6 Lev 6–8	C4, C8 Lev 6–8	A2, A9 Lev 6–8		
	Problems	☺	U1–U3 Lev 5–6	N1, N6 Lev 5–6	C4, C8 Lev 6–8	A9 Lev 6–8	S11 Lev 4–5	
Conventions for answers	Essential	♁		N3 Lev 5–6	C5, C10 Lev 5–6			
	Challenge	✿		N3 Lev 7–8	C5, C8, C10 Lev 7–8			
	Problems	☺	U1 Lev 5–6	N3, N9 Lev 5–6	C5, C8, C10 Lev 5–6		S11 Lev 5–6	
Decimal fractions	Essential	♁		N2, N7 Lev 5–6	C3, C4 Lev 5–6			
	Challenge	✿		N2, N7 Lev 7–8	C3, C4 Lev 7–8			
	Problems	☺	U1 Lev 5–6	N2, N7 Lev 5–6	C3, C4 Lev 5–6			
Reasoning with negative numbers	Essential	♁			C1, C2, C9 Lev 5–6			
	Challenge	✿			C1, C2, C9 Lev 6–7	A3, A4 Lev 6–7		
	Problems	☺	U1 Lev 5–6		C1, C2 Lev 5–6			
Reasoning with fractions 1	Essential	♁		N8 Lev 5–6	C4 Lev 5–6			
	Challenge	✿		N8 Lev 7–8	C4 Lev 7–8	A2 Lev 7–8		
	Problems	☺	U1, U4 Lev 5–6	N8 Lev 5–6	C4 Lev 5–6			
Reasoning with fractions 2	Essential	♁		N8 Lev 5–6	C4 Lev 5–6			
	Challenge	✿		N8 Lev 6–7	C4, C9 Lev 6–7	A2 Lev 7–8		
	Problems	♁	U1 Lev 5–6	N8 Lev 5–6	C4, C9 Lev 5–6		S6 Lev 5–6	
Percentages 1	Essential	♁		N9 Lev 5–6	C4, C7–C9 Lev 5–6			
	Challenge	✿		N9 Lev 6–7	C4, C8, C9 Lev 6–7			
	Problems	♁	U1 Lev 5–6	N9 Lev 5–6	C4, C5, C8, C9 Lev 5–6			
Percentages 2	Essential	♁		N9 Lev 5–6	C4, C8, C9 Lev 5–6			
	Challenge	✿		N9 Lev 6–7	C4, C8, C9 Lev 6–7			
	Problems	♁	U1, U4 Lev 5–6	N9 Lev 5–6	C4, C8, C9 Lev 5–6			
Sequences	Essential	☺				A7, A8 Lev 5–6		
	Challenge	♁				A7–A9 Lev 6–7		
	Problems	♁	U1–U4 Lev 5–6			A7, A8 Lev 5–6 A9 Lev 6–7		
Algebraic expressions	Essential	♁				A1–A3 Lev 5–6		
	Challenge	✿				A1–A3 Lev 6–7		
	Problems	♁	U1–U4 Lev 5–6			A1–A3, A6, A9 Lev 5–6		
Formulae	Essential	♁	U1 Lev 5–6			A6 Lev 5–6	S11, S13 Lev 5–6	
	Challenge	✿	U1 Lev 5–6			A6 Lev 6–7	S11, S13 Lev 6–7	
	Problems	♁	U1 Lev 5–6			A6 Lev 5–6	S11, S13 Lev 5–6	
Solving equations 1	Essential	☺				A1–A4 Lev 5–6		
	Challenge	✿				A3, A4, A11 Lev 6–7		
	Problems	☺	U1 Lev 5–6			A3, A4, A10 Lev 5–6		
Linear graphs	Essential	☺	U1 Lev 5–6			A11 Lev 5–6		
	Challenge	♁	U1 Lev 6–7			A11 Lev 6–7		
	Problems	☺	U1 Lev 5–6			A11 Lev 5–6		
Solving equations 2	Essential	♁				A1–A5 Lev 5–6		
	Challenge	✿				A3 Lev 6–7 A4 Lev 6–8		
	Problems	☺	U1 Lev 5–6			A4 Lev 5–6		
Proportion	Essential	♁	U1 Lev 5–6			A1, A2, A5, A11 Lev 5–6		
	Challenge	✿	U1 Lev 5–6			A5, A11 Lev 5–6		
	Problems	☺	U1 Lev 5–6			A11, A12 Lev 5–6		

continued

Key: ☺ little or no assistance ♁ some assistance ✿ maximum assistance

Lesson	Differentiation		Using and applying mathematics to solve problems	Numbers and the number system	Calculations	Algebra	Shape, space and measure	Handling data
Interpreting graphs	Essential		U1 Lev 5–6			A11, A12 Lev 5–7	S11 Lev 5–6	
	Challenge		U1 Lev 6–8			A11, A12 Lev 6–8		
	Problems		U1 Lev 5–6			A11, A12 Lev 5–6		
Investigating graphs	Essential		U1–U3, U5 Lev 5–6			A11 Lev 5–7		
	Challenge		U1–U3, U5 Lev 8			A11 Lev 8		
	Problems		U1–U3, U5 Lev 7–8			A11 Lev 8		

Shape and Space

Lesson	Differentiation		Using and applying mathematics to solve problems	Numbers and the number system	Calculations	Algebra	Shape, space and measure	Handling data
Measures and scales	Essential			N3, N10 Lev 5–6	C6, C10 Lev 5–6		S11 – S13 Lev 5–6	
	Challenge			N3, N10 Lev 6–7	C10 Lev 6–7	A12 Lev 6–7	S11, S12 Lev 6–7	
	Problems		U1, U2 Lev 5–6	N3, N10 Lev 5–6	C10 Lev 5–6		S11 Lev 5–6	
Angles and parallel lines	Essential		U1, U2, U4 Lev 5–6				S1, S9 Lev 5–6	
	Challenge		U1, U2, U4 Lev 6–7				S1, S9 Lev 6–7	
	Problems		U1, U2, U4 Lev 5–6				S1, S9 Lev 5–6	
Angles in polygons	Essential		U1, U2, U4, U5 Lev 5–6				S1, S2 Lev 5–6	
	Challenge		U1, U2, U4, U5 Lev 5–6				S1, S2 Lev 5–6	
	Problems		U1, U2, U4, U5 Lev 5–6				S1, S2 Lev 5–6	
Geometrical reasoning	Essential		U1–U5 Lev 5–6				S2, S4 Lev 5–6	
	Challenge		U1–U5 Lev 5–6				S2, S4 Lev 5–6	
	Problems		U1–U5 Lev 5–6				S2, S4 Lev 5–6	
Geometrical deduction	Essential		U1–U5 Lev 5–6				S2, S4 Lev 5–6	
	Challenge		U1–U5 Lev 5–6				S2, S4 Lev 6–7	
	Problems		U1–U5 Lev 5–6				S2, S4 Lev 5–6	
Constructions and loci	Essential		U1 Lev 5–6				S1, S2, S9, S10 Lev 5–6	
	Challenge		U1 Lev 5–6				S1, S2, S9, S10 Lev 5–6	
	Problems		U1 Lev 5–6				S1, S2, S9, S10 Lev 5–6	
Transformation geometry 1	Essential		U1 Lev 5–6				S3, S5, S6 Lev 5–6	
	Challenge		U1 Lev 5–6				S5, S6 Lev 5–6	
	Problems		U1 Lev 5–6				S3, S5, S6 Lev 5–6	
Transformation geometry 2	Essential		U1 Lev 5–6	N10 Lev 5–6			S3, S6, S7 Lev 5–6	
	Challenge		U1 Lev 5–6	N10 Lev 5–6			S3, S6, S7 Lev 5–6	
	Problems		U1 Lev 5–6	N10 Lev 5–6			S3, S6, S7 Lev 5–6	
Visualisation	Essential		U1–U5 Lev 5–6				S2, S4 Lev 5–6	
	Challenge		U1–U5 Lev 5–6				S2, S4 Lev 5–6	
	Problems		U1–U5 Lev 5–6				S2, S4 Lev 5–6	
Area and volume	Essential		U1 Lev 5–6				S2, S4, S13, S14 Lev 5–7	
	Challenge		U1 Lev 5–6				S2, S4, S13, S14 Lev 5–7	
	Problems		U1–U5 Lev 5–6				S2, S4, S13, S14 Lev 5–7	
Circles	Essential		U1 Lev 5–6		C6 Lev 5–6		S10, S13 Lev 5–6	
	Challenge		U1 Lev 5–6		C6 Lev 5–6		S10, S13 Lev 5–6	
	Problems		U1–U5 Lev 5–6		C6 Lev 5–6		S10, S13 Lev 5–6	

Key: ☺ little or no assistance   ☊ some assistance   ✪ maximum assistance

Teacher's Notes Teacher's Notes Teacher's Notes Teacher's Not
acher's Notes Teacher's Notes Teacher's Notes
Lessons: Content and Levels

Lesson	Differentiation		Using and applying mathematics to solve problems	Numbers and the number system	Calculations	Algebra	Shape, space and measure	Handling data
Handling Data								
Theoretical probability	Essential	☺	U1, U2 Lev 5–6					H10, H11 Lev 5–6
	Challenge	♁	U1, U2 Lev 5–6					H10, H11 Lev 5–6
	Problems	☺	U1, U2 Lev 5–6					H10, H11 Lev 5–6
Probability from experimental data	Essential	♁	U1, U2 Lev 5–6					H10–H13 Lev 5–6
	Challenge	✪	U1, U2 Lev 5–6					H10–H13 Lev 6–7
	Problems	♁	U1, U2 Lev 5–6					H10–H13 Lev 5–6
Successive events	Essential	♁	U1, U2 Lev 5–6					H10–H13 Lev 7–8
	Challenge	✪	U1, U2 Lev 5–6					H10–H13 Lev 7–8
	Problems	♁	U1, U2 Lev 5–6					H10–H13 Lev 7–8
Descriptive statistics 1	Essential	☺	U1, U2 Lev 5–6					H5, H7–H8 Lev 5–6
	Challenge	✪	U1, U2 Lev 5–6					H5, H7–H8 Lev 7–8
	Problems	☺	U1, U2 Lev 5–6					H5, H7–H8 Lev 5–6
Descriptive statistics 2	Essential	♁	U1, U2 Lev 5–6					H5, H7 Lev 5–6
	Challenge	✪	U1, U2 Lev 5–6					H5, H7 Lev 7–8
	Problems	♁	U1, U2 Lev 5–6					H5, H7 Lev 5–6
Interpreting data 1	Essential	♁	U1, U2 Lev 5–6					H5, H7–H8 Lev 5–6
	Challenge	✪	U1, U2 Lev 5–6					H5, H7–H8 Lev 7–8
	Problems	♁	U1, U2 Lev 5–6					H5, H7–H8 Lev 5–6
Interpreting data 2	Essential	♁	U1, U2 Lev 5–6					H5, H7–H8 Lev 5–6
	Challenge	✪	U1, U2 Lev 5–6					H5, H7–H8 Lev 7–8
	Problems	♁	U1, U2 Lev 5–6					H5, H7–H8 Lev 5–6
Planning an enquiry	Essential	☺	U1–U3 Lev 5–6					H1–H3 Lev 5–6
	Challenge	♁	U1–U3 Lev 5–6					H1–H3 Lev 7–8
	Problems	☺	U1–U3 Lev 5–6					H1–H3 Lev 5–6
Collecting data	Essential	☺	U1–U3 Lev 5–6					H1–H4 Lev 5–6
	Challenge	♁	U1–U3 Lev 5–6					H1–H4 Lev 7–8
	Problems	☺	U1–U3 Lev 5–6					H1–H4 Lev 5–6
Representing data	Essential	☺	U1, U2 Lev 5–6					H6–H9 Lev 5–6
	Challenge	♁	U1, U2 Lev 5–6					H6–H9 Lev 7–8
	Problems	☺	U1, U2 Lev 5–6					H6–H9 Lev 5–6
Communicating results	Essential	☺	U1, U2 Lev 5–6					H7–H9 Lev 5–6
	Challenge	♁	U1, U2 Lev 5–6					H7–H9 Lev 7–8
	Problems	☺	U1, U2 Lev 5–6					H7–H9 Lev 5–6

Using and Applying Mathematics								
Using maths in everyday life		☺	U1, U2 Lev 5–6	N1, N3, N9, N10 Lev 5–6	C1, C4, C9 Lev 5–6			
Using maths to investigate		♁	U1–U5 Lev 4–8			A9 Lev 4–8		
Working like a detective		♁	U1–U5 Lev 4–8				S1, S2, S4, S9, S13, S14 Lev 4–8	
Maths across the curriculum		☺	U1, U2 Lev 5–6				S7, S11 Lev 5–6	

Key: ☺ little or no assistance ♁ some assistance ✪ maximum assistance

 I See Maths Book 2

Book 1 Review

Introduction

Why the Review section is important

The exercises in this section revise earlier topics. It is important for all students to do this work for smooth transition from one book to the next.

In some cases, students will have insecure knowledge of previous work that will be clarified by this revision. In other cases, with high attaining students, their previous knowledge is often intuitive and needs some formalisation.

In a small number of cases, students will not have covered the work in these *Reviews* prior to this course and a substantial teaching programme will be needed before attempting the exercises.

When and how to use the Review section

We recommend that, for the majority of students, you use the complete section as a 'transition module' in the early weeks of the course. This will give students a fairly intensive induction into the ways of working that they will meet later in the book.

For those students who have very insecure knowledge you may wish to use each *Review* separately as you introduce a new topic. This may help the students to make links and connections with previous work.

It would not be appropriate to use the *Review* section only as independently worked tests or homework. It is designed so that the 'big ideas' in maths (see page 5) are taught in relation to topics that have been previously covered. The notes for each *Review*, on pages 14–33 of this book, indicate how the emphasis on 'big ideas' can be maintained.

The way in which the exercises are introduced must depend upon close monitoring and assessment of the students. For those students who are assessed as needing maximum assistance there will be a need for substantial demonstrations for students to model, and regular summarising to consolidate learning.

Algebra as a continuing theme

The use of symbols is central to maths. It is a substantial part of the language of maths. It needs to become natural language for all students. For this reason, algebraic notation is introduced and used at every opportunity throughout *I See Maths*. This is not done in the expectation that students are already familiar with algebra as a 'topic'. It is done so that all students become fearless users of the marvellous economy that is offered by symbols.

One example of this is in the grids that are a regular feature in the book. For example, the following grid contains all the information necessary for students to know what is required.

x	429	24·6		$\frac{44}{5}$
y	863		4·25	
$x + y$		35·9	7·63	$\frac{127}{5}$

The need to teach the Book 1 Review section

The note above about using algebraic notation provides a straightforward example of why it is important to teach the work in the *Reviews*. Students who can add and subtract decimals may not have been expected to inspect a grid, or symbols, to deduce what is required.

Any demonstration of the grid should include an explanation of how x can be any number and y can be any number and how the expression $x + y$ is an instruction to add the number x to the number y.

Many students will look at the third column and intuitively see that 3·38 has to be added to 4·25 to get the result 7·63. In order to progress to the next stage of learning they need to formalise their thinking and recognise that the missing number can be calculated by performing the inverse operation $7·63 − 4·25 = 3·38$. At first students should explain orally how they work out their answers, and then they formalise this in writing.

The *Demonstrations* in the main sections of the Student's Book and the related explanations in these Teaching Resources provide support and ideas for teaching that you may wish to study before teaching this *Review* section.

Book 1 Review

 Page 4 Addition and subtraction 1

Content for revision

- **Addition and subtraction of whole numbers, fractions, decimals and negative numbers.**
- **Addition and subtraction as inverse operations.**
- **Making connections with algebra.**
- **Solving word problems.**

This *Review* revises work on the operations of addition and subtraction completed in Book 1, pages 4–5, 8–9, 24–35, 52–63 (see the description of how to teach these operations on pages 5–7 of this book). Students should be encouraged to do questions mentally, but they also need to have secure written methods that they set out neatly.

It is important that all students begin to make connections between number operations and algebra. Do not avoid the questions containing algebra with unsuccessful students but provide them with sufficient assistance to be able to do the questions successfully.

Starter

Place a selection of number cards on the resource table using numbers that are appropriate for the students in the class. Ask students to act out the operations of addition and subtraction using the resource table and the maths table. Invite one student to act out the operation as you speak it and ask another student to write the symbols on the board. Invite students to make up their own examples of addition and subtraction for other students to act and write. Provide sufficient assistance for all students to be successful.

Demonstration

See Book 1, pages 24–35. Use the resource and maths tables and cards to demonstrate the actions for addition and subtraction of fractions, decimals and negative numbers:

$\frac{3}{5} + \frac{4}{5} = \frac{7}{5}$

Place three fifths on the maths table. Get some more. Get four more fifths. Look at the maths table. There are seven fifths.

$1\frac{3}{5} - \frac{4}{5} = \frac{4}{5}$

Place eight fifths on the maths table. Get ready to take some away. Take four fifths away. Look at the maths table. There are four fifths.

Extend the concept through use of language to:

*Three **hundred** fifths add four **hundred** fifths is seven **hundred** fifths and eight **thousand** fifths take away four **thousand** fifths is four **thousand** fifths.*

Extend further by using cards with decimals. Demonstrate how to read the number 4·2:

This number 4 tells us that there are four ones. This point is telling us to start thinking about those things called tenths. There are two tenths. The number is four point two.

4·2 + 1·7 = 5·9. Place four and two tenths on the maths table. Go and get some more. Get one and seven tenths. Look at the maths table. There are five and nine tenths.

Place four point two on the maths table. Go and get some more. Get one point seven. Look at the maths table. There is five point nine. Four point two and one point seven equals five point nine.

Extend by using cards with negative numbers. Tell the garden story (see Book 1, pages 52–63) as you act out the operations with cards:

$3 + ^-3 = 0$
When I look in my garden, I can see three lumps of earth and I can see three holes. I can put the three lumps of earth into the three holes and I have zero lumps of earth. Three and negative three has the same value as zero.

Essential exercises

All of these exercises could be done as mental and oral starters. Invite students to come to the board to complete Exercise 1. Ask them to explain how they worked out their answers. For example, the question 568 + 246 can be done mentally in many different ways. Here are three:

(1) 500 + 200 = 700, 60 + 40 = 100, 8 + 6 = 14, Answer 814
(2) 6 + 8 = 14, 560 + 240 = 800, Answer 814
(3) 568 + 2 + 30 = 600, 600 + 214 = 814, Answer 814

It is possible that some students may never have thought of these methods. Inviting students to explain their methods when giving answers will assist the rest of the class. There will be different methods demonstrated depending on the problem. Students who are very competent with mental arithmetic complete questions like this instinctively and find it very difficult to unpack their methods. Take care not to interpret this as inability to do the questions.

Students also need a written method to call on at any time.

$$
\begin{array}{r}
5\,6\,8 \\
+\,2\,4\,6 \\
\hline
8\,1\,4 \\
\tiny{1\,\,1}
\end{array}
$$

Questions like $520 - 246$ are straightforward when done mentally. However, the written method requires the knowledge of how to partition numbers. This introduces the idea of *equivalence:*

> *520 has the same value as 400 + 120*
> *which has the same value as 400 + 110 + 10.*
>
> $$
> \begin{array}{ccc}
> 5\,2\,0 & 4\,{}^1 2\,0 & 4\,{}^1 1\,{}^1 0 \\
> -\,2\,4\,6 & -\,2\,4\,6 & -\,2\,4\,6 \\
> \hline
> & & 2\,7\,4
> \end{array}
> $$

Before completing the questions with fractions, decimals and negative numbers, demonstrate how to do them using cards on the resource and maths tables (See pages 24–35 in Book 1).

Exercises 2 and 3 can be done orally with you reading the questions and the students writing their answers down. This makes students listen carefully to what you are saying. Invite students to write the calculations on the board as you say them, to ensure that everyone knows the meaning of the language for **operations.** Students can make up their own questions to ask a partner.

Demonstrate how to complete the tables in Exercise 4. You may need to do more work with whole numbers before moving on to decimals. Extend to harder questions for more confident students.

For example, formalise the problems:
$$
\begin{aligned}
x - 33{\cdot}3 &= 18{\cdot}4 \\
x &= 18{\cdot}4 + 33{\cdot}3 \\
&= 51{\cdot}7
\end{aligned}
$$

Challenging exercises

Students who can do the *Essential exercises* alone or with a little assistance should be able to attempt these exercises. Emphasise the idea of equivalence. For students who need practice with addition and subtraction, use **Worksheet 1.** Some students will benefit from discussing the questions in pairs, completing them together in class and then repeating them for homework.

Exercise 5 formalises questions like those in Exercise 4. Teach the students how to set out the solution to an equation. Solutions of equations were covered in Book 1, pages 76–87.

Number pyramids and magic squares in Exercises 6 and 7 should be familiar to students who completed Book 1 but they may need reminding what to do. Ensure that the students inspect the diagrams carefully to decide how to begin the questions.

> *In the pyramid, add two consecutive numbers to get the answer above. $3{\cdot}4 + 5{\cdot}7 = 9{\cdot}1$ There are no more straightforward additions in the bottom row at present. Look at $5{\cdot}7 + ? = 7{\cdot}4$ and $8{\cdot}2 + ? = 10{\cdot}1$. How do you find the missing numbers? [subtract] Enter $1{\cdot}7$ and $1{\cdot}9$. Now you can complete the pyramid.*

Magic squares are so called because each vertical, horizontal and diagonal line adds to the same total. Notice that the total is always three times the number in the centre. Invite the students to look for this rule and ask them to make up their own magic squares.

Problem-solving exercises

Read the questions in Exercises 8, 9 and 10 with the students. Read them for a second time and make notes of the key facts. Students are often tempted to 'do arithmetic' without thinking about the problem.

> *Micky saves £42 each month for June, July, August, September, October and November.*
> *That is 6 months.* $£42 \times 6 = £252$
> *He saves £252.*
> *He already has £600.*
> *How much altogether?* $£600 + £252 = £852$
> *£852*
> *Is that enough to buy the*
> *computer at £899·98?* $£899{\cdot}98 - £852 = £47{\cdot}98$
> *No. He needs another £47·98.*

Plenary

Invite students to come to the front to complete questions like those in the exercises and explain how they worked out their answers. Record how much assistance the students still need for this work. If the majority of students need a lot of assistance plan to do more of this work next lesson.

Homework

Making up real-life stories for maths stories is not easy. Demonstrate examples like these before setting homework.

> $83 + 25 - 41 = 67$
> *Danny is working in an office. He counts out eighty-three sheets of paper and sees that the packet is empty. He opens a new packet and counts out a further twenty-five sheets of paper. One of the secretaries comes along and takes forty-one sheets of paper leaving sixty-seven.*

Book 1 Review

Book 1 Review

 # Addition and subtraction 2

Content for revision

- **How new facts can be derived from known facts.**
- **Addition and subtraction as inverse operations.**
- **Using standard column procedures for addition and subtraction.**
- **Making connections with algebra.**
- **Solving word problems.**

Students need to be able to derive new facts from known facts. Without this facility they see maths as a collection of thousands of discrete things to learn. We have to assist them in making the vital connections between things that they know or are given, and new facts.

We begin to make use of words that prompt students to think logically. For example, we say 'given the fact that' to prompt students to know that they have to look at what is 'given' and use it to work out (derive) something new. They need to learn to spend time inspecting the new question to see how it relates to the 'given' fact.

Another way of prompting the same thinking is to say 'if this, then this'. This is a shorthand for 'if this is true then it follows that this is true'. For example, if $79 + 86 = 165$, then it follows that $165 - 86 = 79$. The reason that the second fact follows from the first is that subtraction is the inverse of addition. The addition that is given is an **explicit** fact and the facts that can be derived from it are **implicit** facts. They are known implicitly because of some property or convention that is known about the explicit fact.

The same logic will be used again and again in maths. Geometrical reasoning and statistical inference depends upon such logic.

Starter

Write the sum $3 + 4 = 7$ on the board.
Ask students to write down the answers to a range of linked questions such as:

$300 + 400$, $3000 + 4000$, $^-3 + ^-4$, $\frac{3}{5} + \frac{4}{5}$, $\cdot3 + \cdot4$,
$\cdot03 + \cdot04$, £3 + £4, 3 birds plus 4 birds, 3 cm + 4 cm, etc.

Students can volunteer to come and write the answers on the board, write the answers in their books, or write answers on white boards to show when asked.

Demonstration

This first demonstration shows students how to derive new facts from given facts where the operation remains the same but the denomination of the number changes. In other words, we can use an addition of, say, two-digit numbers to work out the addition of six-digit numbers, fractions, decimals, negative numbers, measures such as centimetres or dollars and the addition of objects such as marbles.

$65 + 37 = 102$
This is a given fact. We can use this fact to derive new facts.
For example: $6500 + 3700 = 10\,200$
This is the same sum written in hundreds. Sixty-five **hundred** *plus thirty-seven* **hundred** *equals one hundred and two* **hundred**.
Six thousand five hundred plus three thousand seven hundred equals ten thousand two hundred.

Similarly we can use the given fact to derive another new fact.
$6\cdot5 + 3\cdot7 = 10\cdot2$
This is the same sum written in tenths. Sixty-five **tenths** *plus thirty-seven* **tenths** *equals one hundred and two* **tenths**.

Six point five plus three point seven equals ten point two.

And we can derive another new fact using negative numbers.
$^-65 + ^-37 = ^-102$
Negative *sixty-five plus* **negative** *thirty-seven equals* **negative** *one hundred and two.*

Invite students to make up their own new facts using the given fact. Encourage them to use large numbers, fractions, decimals and negative numbers. Ask them to write them on the board.

This second demonstration shows students how to use a given fact to derive another fact based on knowledge of inverse operations.

$32 + 14 = 46$
This is a given fact. We can use this fact to derive new facts. We know that subtraction is the inverse of addition and so:
$46 - 14 = 32$ and $46 - 32 = 14$

Letts I See Maths Book 2

We can use the three facts to derive new facts:
3200 + 1400 = 4600
4600 − 1400 = 3200
4600 − 3200 = 1400

Invite students to make up their own new facts using the given facts.

Essential exercises

The first two exercises provide practice of the work done in the demonstrations above, using the language 'Given that…'. Exercise 3 focuses on inverse operations and uses the language 'If … then…'.

Exercise 4 provides further practice in making connections but this time the table is used to make the link with algebra.

Exercise 5 may require some further demonstration work. Begin with positive numbers and demonstrate that the way of working with negative numbers uses exactly the same principles. It is important that you continue to use the idea of logic rather than looking for different models for these questions such as the number line. A change of model will give the students more to learn rather than less.

Given that $3 + 8 = 11$ *then using inverse operations we know that:*
$11 − 8 = 3$ *and* $11 − 3 = 8$.
We also know that:
$300 + 800 = 1100$
$1100 − 800 = 300$
$1100 − 300 = 800$
And we also know that:
$^-3 + {}^-8 = {}^-11$
$^-11 − {}^-8 = {}^-3$
$^-11 − {}^-3 = {}^-8$

Challenging exercises

Exercises 6 and 7 continue the idea of making links and connections using algebra. They formalise the work done in the *Essential exercises* and make the vital link between number and algebra. Get all the students to work in pairs on these questions, and invite them to write the answers on the board whilst explaining their thinking. For those who struggle with algebra this regular articulation of thinking will be of great help. It is important not to deny students the opportunity to do these exercises but to give them sufficient help to be able to do them successfully. The more students see algebra in use, the more familiar it will become, and the more confident they will get at doing it.

Exercise 8 extends the work to three numbers and again links this with algebra. Invite pairs of students to make up their own examples to present to the class.

Problem-solving exercises

These exercises practise the same ideas but expressed in words and using the denomination of different measures. Insist that the students use the given fact and do not merely work out the answers each time. Ask them to present answers on the board and get them to explain how they used the given facts each time. Do not allow students to use calculators.

Plenary

Summarise the work done and set a sample of questions. If you have confident students you may wish to set these questions as a test, to see how many questions students can do unassisted. However, you may wish to invite students to present answers on the board, to monitor their progress and record the levels of assistance required.

Discuss the words 'given', 'derive' and 'inverse operation'.

Homework

Demonstrate how to make up stories for the given fact. Show how to use all the ideas covered in the lesson. For example, show how you would use the given fact to make up stories using hundreds, decimals, fractions or negative numbers. Also, show how you would use inverse operations.

Alternatively use **Worksheet 2** to provide further practice in this work. It is important that students get a good grasp of these ideas to help them in future work.

Book 1 Review

Multiplication and division 1

Content for revision

- **Multiplication tables.**
- **Words associated with multiplication and division.**
- **Multiplication and division as inverse operations.**
- **Making connections with algebra.**
- **Solving word problems.**

At this stage students should see multiplication as an operation in its own right rather than as repeated addition. They should also recognise that division is the inverse of multiplication. See Book 1, pages 10–11, 14–15, 36–39, 64–67. For those who struggle with these ideas demonstrate the following.

$3 \times 4 = 12$

I put three cups on the maths table. I need to do this lots of times. I need to do this four times altogether. I have done it one time. I do it two times, three times, four times. I look at the maths table. I see twelve cups.

$12 \div 3 = 4$

I put twelve cups on the maths table. I look and wonder how many piles of three cups I can see. [Make piles of three cups.] I see four piles.

Multiplication tables need regular practice. For those students who quickly forget the tables (and this is most students) spend a few moments during each lesson practising them. Chant the tables together (from posters on the wall) until they become familiar, before asking individuals to chant them. Provide table squares for students to complete in a given time. Do not put the digits in order because the students will complete them by following the number patterns. Instead, jumble up the digits as in **Worksheet 3** (we humorously call these 'torture squares').

When students are confident with chanting the tables extend the tables to hundreds, thousands, fifths, tenths etc. Show how knowing just one fact means you actually know many more. For example knowing $3 \times 4 = 12$ means that you also know $300 \times 40 = 12\,000$, $3000 \times 4000 = 12\,000\,000$, $\cdot3 \times \cdot4 = \cdot12$, and so on.

You may need to do lots of practice with this sort of work before the students complete the exercises on this page. A few moments every day is better than spending whole lessons

revising this work. Students do forget what they have done before, but they easily lose their motivation if we merely repeat whole lessons that they received in earlier years. We need to acknowledge that they have done the work before and treat it as revision. Meanwhile, in the main part of the lesson, you can introduce the students to new ideas by using exercises from future pages that do not depend on new knowledge. In this way you can show the students they are moving on and making progress in their learning.

Starter

Display the seven-times table. Invite students to act out the seven-times table using bags of seven beads. Chant the table as written. Work in the imagination. Chant the seven**ty**-, seven **hundred**-, seven **thousand**-, seven-**tenths**-, and seven-**hundredths**-times tables. Invite students to act these out using imaginary bags of beads. Ask students to write the answers to questions using the seven-times table and its extensions. You can get them to write the answers in their books, on the board or on white boards to 'show'.

Use this activity to determine how extensive your demonstration will need to be for students to complete the exercises. The *Starter* is always an excellent opportunity to monitor pupils' prior knowledge. Some classes will demonstrate sufficient expertise at this work to be able to complete the exercises with the minimum of help, whilst others will need more practice like this *Starter* activity before attempting any of the exercises.

Demonstration

For a first demonstration draw tables like those in Exercise 1 on the board. Complete the first multiplication example yourself, explaining your working as you write in the answers. Invite students to come to the board to complete the rest of the tables. Either get them to explain their working at the board or ask the class for a volunteer to explain. Complete the first division example yourself, and again get students to complete the rest. The explanations are crucial in assisting all members of the class with the examples.

With some classes you may need to demonstrate how you work out each answer using cups or cards. This may take time but will enable the students to understand what they are doing rather than completing the grid mechanically.

For a second demonstration use cups and/or cards to show students how to do several operations working from left to right.

> $4 \times 2 \times 3$
>
> *I put four cups on the maths table. I have to do it lots of times. I have to do it two times. I have done it one time and now I have done it two times. I see eight cups. I now have to do that lots of times. I have to do it three times altogether. I have done it one time, two times, three times. I look at the maths table. I see twenty-four cups.*
>
> $12 \div 3 \times 5$
>
> *I put twelve cups on the maths table. I look at them and wonder how many piles of three cups I can see. Four. I have to do that lots of times. I do it five times altogether. I see twenty cups.*

Essential exercises

Exercises 1, 3 and 4 are practice in the work done in the demonstrations.

Exercise 2 is practice in using the words connected with multiplication and division. Invite students to rephrase each question using different words. This will help them to see how economical words like 'product' and 'difference' can be.

Students often think that mathematicians have concocted a language to make the subject difficult. We need to demonstrate how technical words are used to save time and to provide clarity. Mathematics is economical, efficient and elegant. It is unfortunate that national tests often make questions unnecessarily difficult by refusing to use the correct technical language and replacing single words with long complicated phrases.

Challenging exercises

Whenever possible we connect arithmetic with its formal algebraic representation. When students have completed several numerical examples based on division being the inverse of multiplication they can easily see the connection with algebra. Exercise 5 provides practice in applying this knowledge.

You can demonstrate an example using twin maths tables and cards:

> $9x = 540$
>
> [Two students work at the two maths tables. One student puts an 'x' card on the first table nine times. The other student puts the number 540 on the second table. They each look at their tables and wonder how many nines they can see.]

> Replace 540 with 9×60
>
> $9 \times x = 9 \times 60$
>
> So $x = 60$

Exercise 6 should be completed by all students. It is fairly straightforward and can be regarded as a puzzle to be solved.

Problem-solving exercises

The most difficult part of solving word problems in different contexts is deciding on which operation is required. Get students to read the questions and write down whether they have to multiply or divide. This could be done as a whole-class activity before the students complete the exercises themselves.

The exercises in this section should be used to give the students practice in setting out their working correctly. Do not let them write answers only, and do not let them use a calculator.

Plenary

Summarise the work covered and set a sample of questions to check what the students can do, and how much assistance they need.

Discuss the words 'product' and quotient'.

Discuss 'inverse operations' and review work done on this involving addition and subtraction.

Homework

Demonstrate how to make up real-life stories for multiplication and division questions before setting the examples for homework.

Book 1 Review

Multiplication and division 2

Content for revision

- **Multiplication tables.**
- **Using known multiplication and division facts to derive new facts.**
- **Making connections with algebra.**
- **Solving word problems.**

This *Review* continues the work done previously but, as with the work on addition and subtraction, it introduces the logic of using given facts to derive new facts.

If we had to learn and memorise every separate multiplication and division fact then all but a small minority of us would be unsuccessful. Most of us succeed by linking what is new to what we already know. We work out new facts from known facts. Some people are able to make these connections without much help, but most people need the links and connections to be made explicit. Teachers who are able to teach students how to make these links and connections are successful in their teaching.

In the last *Review* we discussed how to demonstrate the extended tables on a regular basis and this is good preparation for this *Review*. However, it is not the accuracy of the calculation that we want students to achieve here, but the ability to use a given fact to derive a new fact.

We may want to step outside mathematics for a moment and consider logic statements in the English language:

> *Given that David is the father of Sally then we can deduce that Sally must be the daughter of David.*
>
> *If Jacob is the grandfather of Jamal then we can deduce that Jamal must be the grandson of Jacob.*

However, if my finger turns purple when I touch purple ink, I cannot deduce that if my finger is purple I must have touched purple ink. I could have dipped my finger in purple paint or coloured it with a crayon. The relationship between the substance and the colour of the finger is not one that can be reversed.

Multiplication and division are related by the laws of arithmetic. If we are given that $3 \times 4 = 12$ then we can deduce that $12 \div 3 = 4$ because division is the inverse operation of multiplication.

Starter

Display the nine-times table. Set the following questions (and more if necessary) and ask the students to write the answers down in their books, on the board or on white boards to 'show'. You need to decide whether you want to monitor all students to see what they can do, or monitor specific individuals. Much will depend on the success of the students in the previous *Review*.

$$6 \times 9 = 54$$
$$7 \times 9 = 63$$
$$3 \times 9 = 27$$

Given these facts in the nine-times table, use them to work out the answers to the following questions:

$60 \times 9 =$	$600 \times 9 =$	$6 \times 90 =$	$6 \times 9000 =$
$700 \times 900 =$	$\cdot 7 \times \cdot 9 =$	$\frac{7}{10} \times \frac{9}{10} =$	$\frac{7}{100} \times 9 =$
$\frac{3}{4} \times 9 =$	$\frac{3}{5} \times 9 =$	$\frac{3}{8} \times 9 =$	$\frac{3}{87} \times 9 =$

For less successful students, read each question as you write it on the board and emphasise the denomination. Assist students with the answers by miming them as they speak. Provide whatever assistance is necessary to allow students to be successful.

> *Sixty times nine, six **hundred** times nine, six times nine**ty**, six times nine **thousand**, seven **hundred** times nine **hundred**, seven **tenths** times nine **tenths**, and so on …*

Alternatively, for successful students, set the first two exercises to be completed as a test. Check that they can all do all the questions before moving on.

Demonstration

This lesson is not a test of students' memory of times-tables, but a demonstration of how to use a table to derive new facts. Display the nine-times table.

Select a fact such as $4 \times 9 = 36$ and invite a student to act it out using cups or bags of beads on the maths table. Explain that you are going to work in the imagination. Say and write further multiplication facts to demonstrate the links with this known fact.

Book 1 Review

> *Four times nine **hundred** is thirty-six **hundred**.*
> *Four **hundred** times nine **thousand** is thirty-six*
> ***hundred thousand**.*
> *Four **tenths** times nine **tenths** is thirty-six*
> ***tenths tenths**.*

It is important to write the questions down as you speak them to make sense of the numbers. Although students should have met this way of speaking numbers before there may be new members of the class or students may have forgotten. Study the last questions and query 'tenths tenths' with the students. Write it again as you speak it. Translate into 'hundredths'.

Essential exercises

Students who were successful with the previous *Review* should find Exercises 1 and 2 straightforward. With the less successful students do the questions altogether as a class.

Exercise 3 follows on from the first two exercises but stress the language 'if this, then this'.

Exercise 4 makes the vital link with algebra that will assist all students in moving on naturally from informal to formal methods.

Exercise 5 anticipates the use of logic with questions using negative numbers that the students may not have covered before. Introduce these gently by beginning with simple positive whole numbers.

If $3 \times 5 = 15$, then $3 \times 50 = 150$
If $^-3 \times 5 = ^-15$, then $^-3 \times 50 = ^-150$
and
If $7 \times 6 = 42$, then $42 \div 6 = 7$
If $^-7 \times 6 = ^-42$, then $^-42 \div 6 = ^-7$

Insist that students derive the new facts from the given facts rather than trying to work out the answers using different models such as the number line.

Challenging exercises

The formalisation of inverse operations in Exercise 6 is much easier for students to understand when linked with the numerical examples completed in the *Essential exercises*. You may need to assist the students in making the link between arithmetic and algebra by giving a gentle introduction.

If $3 \times 4 = 12$, then $12 \div 4 = 3$ and $12 \div 3 = 4$
If $x \times y = z$, then $z \div y = x$ and $z \div x = y$

If $3 \times 4 = 12$, then $30 \times 4 = 120$ and $3 \times 400 = 1200$
If $x \times y = z$, then $10x \times y = 10z$ and $x \times 100y = 100z$

Invite students to make up more numerical and algebraic examples like these.

Exercises 7 and 8 extend the previous work to harder examples. All students should be encouraged to complete them. All too often we keep with examples using easy numbers that can be answered intuitively. Using harder numbers encourages the students to use the connecting features because to work out each answer individually would be too time-consuming.

Problem-solving exercises

Read through each problem and get students to write down the calculation that is required. Deciding what operation to use is the most difficult part of contextualised questions. You could ask the English department to help students with comprehending questions like these.

Plenary

Summarise the work covered and check that the students understand how to derive new facts from known facts.

Discuss 'given' and 'if this, then this'. Link this with 'explicit' and 'implicit' facts and make connections with examples in geometry such as working out angles in an isosceles triangle.

Homework

Demonstrate how to make up maths stories for a given number fact. Show the students the range of calculations you might chose to use such as 80×700, $56 \div 7$, $\cdot 08 \times \cdot 007$, and so on.

Book 1 Review

 **I See Maths** Book 2

Book 1 Review

Page 12

Equivalence

Content for revision

- **Equivalence of fractions, decimals and percentages.**
- **Same value: different appearance.**
- **Ordering numbers.**
- **Solving word problems in different contexts.**

Work on fractions, decimals and percentages should have been covered extensively for all students in previous years yet it continues to be an area that needs constant revision. One of the reasons for the difficulties that students experience with this subject is that each type of representation of number is dealt with in a different way in many texts. The links and connections between the three forms of number are sadly neglected. In this *Review* we revisit the powerful idea of equivalence introduced in Book 1, pages 40–51. Further practice on this topic can be found on **Worksheet 4.**

We want students to use the phrase **'same value: different appearance'** accurately to describe numbers or algebraic expressions that are equivalent. When students see $\frac{3}{5}$, $\frac{6}{10}$, 0·6, 0·60, 60%, or 3 : 5, we want them to recognise that they are all different ways of writing the same number. They all have the same value but a different appearance.

Unity is not well understood. The idea that one whole one has the same value as 100% needs careful teaching. It is also important to teach students that, for example, the total number of people in a room can be considered as unity or 100%. Similarly, the original cost of an item may be thought of as 100%. In statistics the probability of something that is certain is also 1 or 100%. In measures we can draw a circle with a unit radius. What unit? Whatever we decide is going to be the basic measure and it could be one inch, one centimetre, one mile or one zopple! The number 1 or 100% describes whatever base unit we intend to use and this is why the number line is not always helpful.

Starter

Use this *Starter* to assess how much assistance the students need on the subject of equivalence. It is important that all the students complete this work successfully so that they do not lose their confidence. For this reason we do not recommend asking individual students questions that may force them to make mistakes.

Show the students a large cardboard cup cut into five equal parts. Hold up one fifth of the cup. *This is one fifth.* Write the number in several different ways on the board. $\frac{1}{5}$, $\frac{1}{5}$, one fifth, a fifth

Point to each piece of the cup in turn and say, *'This is a fifth.'* Hand out cards to the class each having a fifth in different forms and ask, *'Is this a fifth?'* or *'What number is this?'* Show two different forms of a fifth and ask, *'Is this the same as this?'* Get the students to say *'same value but a different appearance'.*

Pretend to cut the cup into seven equal parts. Ask the students to write the number one seventh in four different ways. Repeat with different fractions. With more successful students ask them to write the fractions in lots of different ways and monitor their answers to determine how much you need to do in the *Demonstration*.

Demonstration

Show the class a large cardboard cup.

This is a cup. This is one whole cup. I am going to cut this cup with my mathematical scissors into five equal parts. [Pretend to cut the cup with imaginary scissors. Hold up one fifth of a cup that you cut earlier.] *This is a fifth of a cup. This is a fifth of one whole one.* [Place the piece of cup on the table. Show the class the whole cup again.]

This is a whole cup. I am going to cut the cup into ten equal parts. [Pretend to cut into ten equal parts and hold up two tenths of a cup that you cut earlier.] *Is this* [Hold up one fifth of a cup.] *the same as this?* [Hold up two tenths of a cup.] *They have the same value but a different appearance.*

Repeat for hundredths of a cup and get the students to imagine each tenth cut into ten pieces so that the two tenths now has the same value as twenty hundredths.

Write the symbols for a fifth, two tenths and twenty hundredths on the board. Underneath two tenths write ·2 and 0·2 and say *'same value: different appearance'.* Underneath twenty hundredths write 0·20 and 20% and again say *'same value: different appearance'.*

Begin with three fifths and invite the students to provide equivalent fractions, decimals and a percentage. If necessary, continue this with different start fractions.

Essential exercises

Some students will be able to complete Exercise 1 by writing down the answers as they inspect the numbers in the textbook. Many will benefit from having the numbers written on cards and working in pairs to match the equivalent numbers.

Research has shown that students rarely recognise that a division is just another way of writing a fraction. Before doing Exercise 2 show how $18 \div 10$ can be written as $\frac{18}{10}$.

Exercise 3 works on common errors made by students (and adults!). The first and last statement are both true. The second statement may need some demonstration. You can imagine a cup cut into six equal parts and another into tenths and compare one sixth with six tenths. Alternatively the first number can be converted into a decimal by the division of $1 \div 6$ and compare with $0·6$. The third statement can be answered by doing a similar conversion and comparison.

Exercise 4 can be done individually if the students are confident, or by the whole class working together and individuals presenting answers at the board, with help when necessary. Get the students to explain and show their working. They may have different ways of getting to the same answer. For example, one quarter can be converted into a percentage by, (i) equivalent fractions, (ii) just knowing the answer, (iii) working out $1 \div 4$, (iv) writing a quarter as a decimal. All of the questions are straightforward and do not require any rounding.

Exercise 5 can provoke a good discussion on the best method for ordering numbers. In most cases the most efficient way of ordering numbers is to convert each one to its decimal form. However, this does require a good knowledge of place value so be prepared to revise this first.

Challenging exercises

In the *Essential exercises* students had to find equivalent forms for individual numbers. Exercise 6 requires them to work out the answer to a numerical expression before looking for equivalence. This is a lead-in to inspecting algebraic expressions that will be covered later.

The questions in Exercise 7 require some calculations because they are not immediately obvious. For example, part (a) is true but may not be seen until both fractions are reduced to a half. These are good questions to get students to present on the board. Make sure that they set out their workings correctly using the equals sign appropriately.

Exercise 8 provides a nice little investigation for students who like puzzles. It is likely to frustrate students who like to get answers quickly so do not expect everyone to do it.

Problem-solving exercises

In Exercise 9, part (c), the students need to understand that the responses to a survey on mobile phones given by ninety-six teenagers make up the total population under consideration, and is therefore 100%. Of these, 75% of the responses were positive and 25% were not. In Exercise 10 the population, or 100%, consists of all the responses about preferred food and 12·5% of the responses were in favour of chips.

Plenary

Summarise the work covered and check with a few examples how much assistance the students still need. Give the students sets of cards showing fractions, decimals and percentages, and ask them to find numbers that are equivalent. Get them to present their answers on the board making sure they explain their thinking.

Homework

Get the students to copy the grid into their books to complete for homework. Check that they understand what they have to do.

 **I See Maths** Book 2

Book 1 Review

Page 14 Proportion

Content for revision

- **Calculating fractions and percentages of quantities.**
- **Recognising that the operation 'of' has the same result as multiplying.**
- **Solving word problems in different contexts.**

All of the previous *Reviews* have dealt with numbers as objects that can be counted, added, subtracted, multiplied or divided. This *Review* looks at using a number as an operator and in particular at the operator 'of'. See Book 1, pages 44–47.

In this work we emphasise equivalence by using the words 'same value'. When students see that this is not new work but a continuation of work they already know they can see that there is less to learn.

Whole numbers

Look at $3 \times 4 = 12$. We place three cups on the maths table. We do it lots of times. We do it four times altogether. We see twelve cups on the maths table.

Look at the maths table again. We can see four lots of three cups. We can see four 'of' three cups. We can see that 4 of 3 has the same value as 12.

4 of 3 has the same value as 4×3 and has the same value as 3×4 and has the same value as 12.

Fractions

$\frac{4}{5}$ of 3 has the same value as $\frac{4}{5} \times 3$, which has the same value as $3 \times \frac{4}{5}$, which has the same value as $\frac{12}{5}$.

Decimals

·4 of 3 has the same value as $·4 \times 3$, which has the same value as $3 \times ·4$, which has the same value as 1·2.

Percentages

4% of 3 has the same value $\frac{4}{100}$ of 3, which has the same value as $\frac{4}{100} \times 3$, which has the same value as $3 \times \frac{4}{100}$, which has the same value as $\frac{12}{100}$, which has the same value as ·12.

Starter

Prepare a set of sticks that have lengths that are multiples of a unit stick. Hold up two sticks at a time and ask the students to compare the lengths. It helps if each unit is clearly marked.

Hold up a stick of three units, and then a stick of two units. Ask the students to compare. *Smaller.*
Hold up a stick of one unit, and then a stick of five units. *Bigger.*
Hold up a stick of two units, and then another stick of two units. *Same.*

Place a set of six cups on the maths table.

When I hold up the sticks like this [three units and one unit] *I want you to replace every set of three cups with one cup. You replace three cups with one cup and another three cups with one cup. You can see two cups on the maths table. One to three of six is two.* [Write '1 : 3 of 6 = 2' on the board.]
$\frac{1}{3} \times 6 = 2$

Now I am going to ask you to look at the sticks and do what they say. [Hold up three units and two units.]. *Replace every three with two. Two to three of six is four.* [Write '2 : 3 of 6 = 4' on the board.]
$\frac{2}{3} \times 6 = 4$

Now do this. [Hold up six units and one unit.] *Replace every six with one. One to six of six is one.* [Write '1 : 6 of 6 = 1' on the board.]
$\frac{1}{6} \times 6 = 1$

Now do this. [Hold up six units and six units.] *Replace every six with six. Six to six of six is six.* [Write '6 : 6 of 6 = 6' on the board.]
$\frac{6}{6} \times 6 = 6$

Now do this. [Hold up six units and twelve units.] *Replace every six with twelve. Twelve to six of six is twelve.* [Write '12 : 6 of 6 = 12' on the board.]
$\frac{12}{6} \times 6 = 12$

Now do this. [Hold up two units and nine units.] *Replace every two with nine. Nine to two of six is twenty-seven.* [Write '9 : 2 of 6 = 27' on the board.]
$\frac{9}{2} \times 6 = 27$

Demonstration

This demonstration follows on from the *Starter* but instead of looking at thirds and sixths of a number we look at hundredths of a number. You will need to make sticks so that the unit is very small. For example, one unit is 1 cm and 100 units is 1 metre.

Make a set of cards with '100' written on them and a set with '1' on them. Place six hundreds on the maths table.

[Hold up two sticks (one hundred units and two units).] *Smaller. For every one hundred on the maths table replace with two. You can see twelve on the maths table. Two to one hundred of six hundred is twelve.* [Write '2 : 100 of 600 = 12' on the board.]
$$\frac{2}{100} \times 600 = 12$$
2% of 600 = 12

Now do this. [Hold up one hundred units and one unit.] *Smaller. Replace every hundred with one. One percent of six hundred is six.*
$$\frac{1}{100} \times 600 = 6$$
1% of 600 = 6

Now do this. [Hold up one hundred units and four units.] *Smaller. Replace every one hundred with four. Four percent of six hundred is twenty-four.*
$$\frac{4}{100} \times 600 = 24$$
4% of 600 = 24

Now do this. [Hold up one hundred units and one hundred units.] *Same. Replace every one hundred with one hundred. One hundred percent of six hundred is six hundred.*
$$\frac{100}{100} \times 600 = 600$$
100% of 600 = 600

Now do this. [Hold up 100 units and 120 units.] *Bigger. Replace every one hundred with one hundred and twenty. One hundred and twenty percent of six hundred is seven hundred and twenty.*
$$\frac{120}{100} \times 600 = 720$$

Repeat for different amounts on the maths table. Repeat for one pound (one hundred pence).

Essential exercises

Draw the table in Exercise 1 on the board. Invite students to come to the board and complete boxes in the table, and get them to explain how they work out each answer. You may want them to use cards as in the *Demonstration*.

The second part of the first exercise provides an opportunity for students to look for different ways of getting the answer.

Insist that they use the table and do not let them use a calculator. For example, 19% can be worked out by doing 20% and subtracting 1%. It can also be worked out by adding 10%, 5% and $4 \times 1\%$. How many different efficient ways can they find?

Exercise 2 reinforces the different forms of writing a percentage and provides further practice. Exercises 3, 4 and 5 link fractions, percentages and proportion to enable the students to make the important connections between them.

Challenging exercises

Exercise 6 invites the students to compare quantities. For example, 90 : 360 has the same value as 1 : 4, and this has the same value as $\frac{1}{4}$.

Exercise 7 also invites comparison but the wording of the questions is different. The answers must be in the form of percentages (or hundredths). 390 : 520 has the same value as 3 : 4, which has the same value as 75 : 100, and this has the same value as 75%.

Exercise 8 formalises the work in the previous two exercises. This requires a good understanding of algebra and students should not be left on their own to struggle. Demonstrate how to work out the answer with the whole class.

Problem-solving exercises

These exercises apply the knowledge of fractions and percentages of quantities in different contexts. The students may need help with calculating the percentage of people in Exercise 10.

Plenary

Summarise the work done by getting the students to demonstrate working out percentages using sticks and number cards. Successful students and their teachers often assume that actions with sticks and cards can be discarded and replaced with memorised rules and procedures. However, it is the actions that demonstrate real understanding that will assist in developing the subject at a later date.

Homework

Demonstrate how to complete the first row of the table in the *Homework* to ensure that all students understand what to do.

Book 1 Review

Page 16 # Algebra

Content for revision

- **Using letter symbols to represent unknown numbers.**
- **Understanding that algebraic operations follow the same conventions and order as arithmetic operations.**
- **Simplifying algebraic expressions.**
- **Solving simple linear equations.**
- **Substituting into simple formulae.**
- **Drawing straight line graphs.**

Throughout Book 1 and in all the *Reviews* on number in this book, the link is regularly made between arithmetic operations and the generalisation of operations in algebra. This is done in the belief that we should not delay the introduction of algebra but should make the links between number and algebra whenever appropriate, so that students become familiar and confident in its use. This *Review* introduces algebra as a topic by revising simple arithmetical operations and then linking them to algebra.

Early introduction to the use of letters to represent unknown numbers or variables is essential to enable students to become familiar and confident in the use of symbols. The more we delay the use of symbols the harder we make it for students to accept them. This work should be completed with all students no matter what their levels of achievement. Provide sufficient assistance for the less successful students to ensure that they do not make mistakes.

Algebra as the generalisation of arithmetic can assist students in understanding the laws and conventions of arithmetic. Let us look at the example of the order of operations.

Given the expression $3 \times 4 + 7 \times 8$, students often work from left to right and get the wrong answer 152 instead of the correct answer 68. However, given $3x + 7y$ where $x = 4$ and $y = 8$, students work out each term to get $12 + 56 = 68$ and rarely make the mistake seen above.

Do not be tempted to discard the demonstration work for the more successful students. They may have memorised the procedures for algebra but they also need a deep understanding of the subject in order to make good progress.

Starter

Use this *Starter* to remind the students of the actions for the four operations, $+$, $-$, $\times$ and $\div$, using cups and cards. Invite students to work in threes at the front of the class. One student says the expression, one acts with cups or cards, and the third writes the expression on the board. Invite students to make up their own examples. Here are some to get them started.

$$2 + 4 = 6, \quad 8 - 5 = 3, \quad 2 \times 3 = 6, \quad 12 \div 3 = 4,$$
$$\tfrac{2}{5} + \tfrac{4}{5} = \tfrac{6}{5}, \quad \tfrac{8}{5} - \tfrac{5}{5} = \tfrac{3}{5}, \quad \tfrac{2}{5} \times 3 = \tfrac{6}{5}, \quad \tfrac{12}{5} \div \tfrac{3}{5} = 4,$$
$$\cdot2 + \cdot4 = \cdot6, \quad \cdot8 - \cdot5 = \cdot3, \quad \cdot2 \times 3 = \cdot6, \quad \cdot12 \div \cdot3 = 4,$$
$$^-2 + {}^-4 = {}^-6, \quad {}^-8 - {}^-5 = {}^-3, \quad {}^-2 \times 3 = {}^-6, \quad {}^-12 \div {}^-3 = 4$$

Demonstration

Make lots of cards showing x, y, xy, x^2, y^2, x^2y, and so on, and place them on the resource table. Invite students to act out the following expressions by placing cards on the maths table.

$$2x + 4x = 6x, \quad 2xy + 4xy = 6xy, \quad 2x^2 + 4x^2 = 6x^2,$$
$$8x - 5x = 3x, \quad 8xy - 5xy = 3xy, \quad 8x^2 - 5x^2 = 3x^2,$$
$$2x \times 3 = 6x, \quad 2xy \times 3 = 6xy, \quad 2x^2 \times 3 = 6x^2,$$
$$12x \div 3x = 4, \quad 12xy \div 3xy = 4, \quad 12x^2 \div 3x^2 = 4$$

Set the first two *Essential exercises* before demonstrating how to solve equations using twin maths tables to represent the left-hand side (LHS) and the right-hand side (RHS) of the equations. Two students work simultaneously at each table following your instructions, and another student writes down the solution on the board.

Explain that when 'solving' these linear equations the aim is to find the value of x that satisfies this particular case. For example, in the first question below, the general case $x + y = 15$ has an infinite number of solutions. However, when $y = 8$ there is only one solution for x.

(a) $x + 8 = 15$
Subtract 8 $x = 7$

(b) $x - 4 = 10$
Add 4 $x = 14$

(c) $5x = 20$
Divide by 5 $x = 4$

Book 1 Review

(d) $\qquad x \div 3 = 7$
Multiply by 3 $\qquad x = 21$

(e) $\qquad 3x + 6 = 18$
Subtract 6 $\qquad 3x = 12$
Divide by 3 $\qquad x = 4$

Now set *Essential exercises* 3, 4 and 5 before doing the following demonstration on substitution.

Inspect the expression $2x + 5y$. Use number cards to work out the value of the expression for different values of x and y.

If $x = 3$ and $y = 1$ then we can substitute these numbers into the expression to get
$2x + 5y = 2 \times 3 + 5 \times 1$.
Act this out on the maths table with cups or cards to get the value 11.

If $x = 2$ and $y = 2$ then we can substitute these numbers into the expression to get
$2x + 5y = 2 \times 2 + 5 \times 2 = 14$
This example demonstrates that x and y can have the same value.

Demonstrate the above for values of x and y that are large integers, fractions, decimals and negative numbers.

Essential exercises

With less successful students, work through all of these exercises together as a class. Bring students to the front and act out each question in turn, providing whatever assistance is necessary to enable them to be successful.

Worksheet 5 can be used to provide further practice with straightforward questions. **Worksheet 6** can be used to extend the more successful students.

Challenging exercises

In the *Essential exercises* we use the letters x and y to denote variables. Exercises 7, 8 and 9 show how different letters can be used. When writing an algebraic expression for a formula the letters will be relevant to the quantities involved. All the formulae should be familiar to the students.

Work through Exercise 10 with the whole class. Draw the graph of $x + y = 8$ using all four quadrants, and show how all the points on the line satisfy the equation. There is an infinite number of solutions to the equation.
Encourage the students to look for solutions other than positive whole numbers. They can check their answers by drawing a computer generated graph and placing the cursor on the respective coordinates. Students will need to

be careful because the resolution of the screen may mean that there is a margin of error in the coordinates given by the computer. However, this is an opportunity to discuss the limitations of technology.

Problem-solving exercises

All of the problem-solving exercises apply the use of algebra to geometrical examples. Explain why a formula is an economical and efficient way of setting out an expression for a general case.

Plenary

Summarise the work done by inviting students to work at the board completing examples similar to those in the exercises. Invite students to make up their own examples to set each other.

Homework

The *Homework* is straightforward revision of work done in previous years, but many students will need some reminding before they can complete it.

Draw a set of axes and label them. Ask students to come to the front and read out the coordinates of points on the x-axis. Get another student to write them down making sure that they write them correctly, for example (2, 0). Ask students what they notice, and ensure they note that the y coordinate is always zero. Write this as $y = 0$. Repeat for the y-axis to get the equation $x = 0$.

Draw any line that is parallel to the x-axis and again get a student to read off coordinates while another writes them down. Use the coordinates to work out the equations of the lines.

Book 1 Review

Angles, lines and triangles

Content for revision

- **Using the correct vocabulary, notation and labelling conventions for lines, angles and shapes.**
- **Angle properties of a triangle.**
- **Angles at a point and on a straight line.**
- **Recognising parallel lines and identifying alternate and corresponding angles.**
- **Knowing the technical terms associated with angle properties such as complementary, supplementary and vertically opposite.**

Work on angles, lines and triangles, was covered extensively in Book 1, pages 18–19, 116–127, 132–135. Successful students will be able to do this work without much revision. Insist that they use the correct technical terms and assist them in using the correct notation and conventions for labelling lines, angles and shapes.

Less successful students need careful demonstrations of the properties of angles. The best demonstrations (see *Demonstration* pages in Book 1) involve using sticks so that students can visualise an angle as a turn. An angle on a page is only a hint of a movement that has taken place. Students need to experience doing this turning themselves rather than being passive observers. There are some good dynamic geometry software packages that can be used on a computer in conjunction with these *Demonstrations* but they cannot totally replace the hands-on approach.

In order to talk about the visual image of an angle we need a technical language. The idea of 'object and image' is widely used in mathematics, with the object being the thing you start with and the image being the thing you finish with.

A drawn angle has one line as the object and one line as the image. In order to maintain a view of angle as turn, we think about these lines as being coincident initially and then one of them turning through an angle to the finishing position. Of course, in many cases we can choose which is the object and which is the image.

The measurement of angle is to be thought of as comparing a specified turn with the 'standard turn' of one degree (a denomination of one degree). Comparison is one of the 'big ideas' explained in the introduction to this book. It will be the basis for students' understanding of what they are doing when they practise the use of a protractor.

Starter

Practise number bonds to 90, 180 and 360 in preparation for calculating angles. This can be conducted as oral questions or set on the board or in books as grids like these:

x	45		19	73		82	
y		60			21		69
$x + y$	90	90	90	90	90	90	90

x	45		120		49		162
y		50		131		98	
$x + y$	180	180	180	180	180	180	180

x	45		60			320	
y		180		270	77		159
$x + y$	360	360	360	360	360	360	360

Revise the meaning of 'complementary' and 'supplementary'.

Demonstration

Angles at a point

Give all students a stick and ask them to hold it in front of them parallel to the floor. Get them to point their sticks in the same direction as you. Ensure that they are all pointing their sticks in the same direction, i.e. parallel to you, and not at the same object.

Get the students to follow your instructions and to imitate your moves.

> [Turn through a whole turn.] *I have turned through one whole turn. I have turned through 360 degrees.*

Repeat for half, quarter and three-quarter turns.

> [Turn through an acute angle.] *I have turned through 60 degrees. How much further do I need to turn through to make half a turn? I need to turn through another 120 degrees.*

Book 1 Review

Repeat this for different angles. Invite students to make turns and ask the same question of the class. These actions are crucial in getting students to visualise an angle as a turn.

Draw different angles on the board and ask students to come and write in the angle required to complete a half turn. Indicate turning with your hand.

Vertically opposite angles
Now demonstrate turning two sticks about a point along their length. Hold the sticks together and slowly rotate them about a point like this.

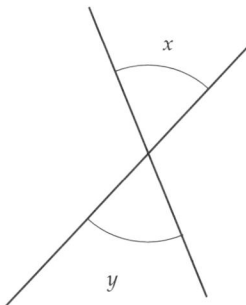

As you slowly turn the sticks, ask the students to watch the angle $x°$ as their angle.

> *The angle $y°$ is my angle. It is getting bigger. What is happening to your angle?*
> *It is also getting bigger. Look, I have stopped. My angle is 30°, how big is yours? Also 30°.*
>
> [Draw the diagram of the sticks on the board and label the equal angles.]
>
> *I am going to continue turning. My angle is now 45°, how big is yours? Also 45°.*
>
> [Draw this diagram on the board.]
>
> *And so on … .*
> *We say that vertically opposite angles are equal.*

Parallel lines
Draw a set of parallel lines on the board and use the convention of marking them with arrows to indicate parallelism. Use a stick to establish that there are an infinite number of lines parallel to these lines. Indicate one line as the object and the stick as the image. Place a stick along the line and slowly turn the stick about a point along the line so that it crosses all the lines. Draw the position of the stick.

Repeat with the stick starting on each line and turn it the same amount so that it finishes on the previously drawn line. Establish that the image you have drawn could have started from any of the parallel lines.

Inspect the diagram.

> *The **transversal** is the image of a turn from this direction* [the direction of the drawn parallel lines] *to this direction* [that of the transversal]. *I will tell you the angle turned is 73°, so this angle is 73° and this angle is 73° and …*

Establish that all corresponding angles are equal. Establish that all alternate angles are equal.

Essential exercises

Students can work through all of these exercises either individually, in pairs, or together as a whole class. If they do the work on their own make sure that you give some time to summarising, and get the students to explain how they worked out the answers.

Challenging exercises

Exercise 6 introduces Greek letters for angles. The earlier we introduce these letters the more easily they will be accepted as common practice. It is important that students become accustomed to labelling angles correctly so that they know that $A\hat{B}D$ indicates the angle at the vertex B. These two conventions are helpful in making mathematics efficient.

Exercises 7 and 8 revise the technical language associated with geometry. The meanings of words like 'similar' and 'congruent' need regular reinforcement.

Problem-solving exercises

These exercises are good practice in reading a description and visualising the diagram. Get the students to draw a rough sketch first before drawing a neat diagram. Make sure that they know the difference between a diagram (closely resembling the real thing) and an accurate drawing (with exact measurements).

Plenary

Draw a complex diagram, with some known angles, on the board and invite students to come and mark in the sizes of the other angles, and explain how they worked them out.

Homework

Students will need to have completed Exercise 7 before completing the *Homework*. Alternatively, complete the *Homework* together as a class.

Book 1 Review

 Shapes

Content for revision

- **Using a ruler and protractor to draw shapes accurately.**
- **Using a ruler and a pair of compasses to draw shapes accurately.**
- **Properties of triangles, quadrilaterals and circles.**
- **Geometrical reasoning.**

Definitions

Sketch – a rough (but tidy) drawing used as an aid to drawing more accurate pictures.

Diagram – a neat drawing, correctly labelled, that shows all the relevant information but not drawn to scale.

Construction – an accurate drawing of a shape drawn to exact measurements or to a scale.

Students are expected to be able to measure and draw angles to the nearest degree. They need to know how to use a protractor and ruler to draw accurately. Some students find this very difficult because it requires fairly fine motor skills that are not always very highly developed. However, much of the poor work we see in this topic is due to the fact that most students have never been shown how to use measuring instruments properly. Work on this topic was covered in Book 1 pages 116–119 and 124–127.

Demonstrate to students how to view a ruler or protractor from vertically above the point that you want to read. This will greatly improve the accuracy of the measurement. Insist that students use a well-sharpened pencil and undamaged ruler for all of their construction and graph work. A pair of compasses should not move once set, and students need to learn how to hold them correctly. These simple things will make such a difference to the accuracy of their work that students will experience greater success in, and satisfaction with, their work.

Drawing shapes from given information is a skill. An initial sketch helps to visualise what is required. It is an important part of the work. Notice that the word 'given' is used again here as in the earlier number work to mean explicit information. In this case the given information is used to construct shapes accurately.

Starter

Use **Worksheet 7** to revise the names of triangles and quadrilaterals, and their associated properties. You could give this to students to do for homework. Get them to work in pairs, checking their answers, and then invite them to present their answers to the class. Use this as an opportunity to get students to use geometrical language correctly, and to justify their answers.

Demonstration

This demonstration shows students how to construct a triangle using a ruler and a protractor.

Write down the lengths of two sides and the size of the included angle of a triangle ABC on the board. Inspect the 'given' information.

$\triangle$ABC: CB = 4 cm   A$\hat{C}$B = 60°   CA = 6 cm

I am going to inspect this information about triangle ABC. The side CB is four centimetres long. I will draw a rough sketch and mark CB like this:

C ———————— 4 cm ———————— B

The angle I have been given is at the vertex C, and is sixty degrees. This angle is between the line drawn and the line CA which is six centimetres long. I can sketch this:

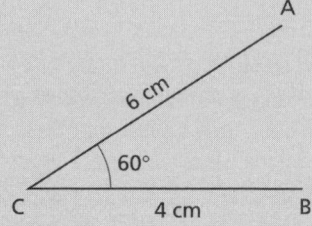

Now I can draw this accurately and complete the triangle by joining AB.

Demonstrate how to measure the two lines and the angle accurately on the board or OHP, using a ruler and protractor.

Letts I See Maths Book 2

This next demonstration shows students how to construct a triangle using a ruler and a pair of compasses. Inspect the given information.

△ABC: AB = 5 cm   BC = 4 cm   AC = 6 cm

Begin as before by drawing a sketch of the required triangle.

Although the first line of the triangle can be drawn with a ruler it is more accurate to mark off the length with a pair of compasses.

Give the instructions:

> *Draw a long line (longer than 5 cm). Place the pencil and compass point on the ruler at the exact measurement of AB (5 cm), mark off the line segment, and label it AB.*
>
> *Set the compasses to the exact length of BC (4 cm) and with centre B and radius BC, draw an arc. Set the compasses to the exact length of AC (6 cm). With centre A and radius AC, draw another arc and label the point of intersection C.*

This attention to detail will enable students to construct fairly accurate drawings.

Essential exercises

The first two exercises follow on from the *Demonstrations*. Give the students further examples if they need extra practice.

Exercise 3 is best done as paired or group work. Students should be encouraged to discuss the properties of the triangles they draw. They can produce posters of their results.

Encourage students to use the Glossary to help them answer the questions in Exercise 4. The names for quadrilaterals are used regularly, and students need to know the associated properties.

Whenever students see a circle we want them to visualise equal length radii. This property of a circle enables us to deduce many facts about shapes drawn inside a circle. Exercise 5 may best be done as a whole-class exercise.

Challenging exercises

All students should be able to complete the *Challenging exercises.* Exercise 6 can be done as paired work or with the whole class. Invite the students to inspect the sketch of the parallelogram and work like detectives. Once again we are working with given or 'explicit' information and using geometrical reasoning to deduce 'implicit' information.

You may need to make a tetrahedron and a hexagonal-based pyramid before setting Exercises 7 to 9. Some students find it helpful to take a shape apart before designing its net.

Problem-solving exercises

In the *Essential exercises* the given information described unique shapes. There is only one possible triangle to match the explicit information. In Exercise 10 the given information can be used to construct more than one possible shape. Students can visualise this better when they use sticks to make the shapes. You can use large sticks on the floor or place thin sticks on an OHP (beware of the distortion you can get with this). This exercise develops the idea of **necessary and sufficient** information required to specify a particular shape.

Once the students are convinced that they can draw more than one shape with the information given, they need to decide how to construct the shapes. The instructions can be generated through class discussion or set as a challenge. Invite students to write down the instructions like this:

(a) Draw a line and mark off a line segment AB = 6 cm. Draw arcs with compasses, radius 4 cm and centres A and B. Mark off any point on one arc and draw a line parallel to AB. The two points where this line crosses the arcs are the vertices C and D of the parallelogram. Repeat with a different point on one of the arcs to construct a second parallelogram.

Exercise 11 provides further revision of the properties of parallelograms. It reinforces the idea that rectangles and squares are also parallelograms.

Plenary

Revise the meanings of the words 'sketch', 'diagram' and 'construction'. Place a set of triangles and parallelograms in a bag. Invite students to select a shape. Ask them to name the shape and describe its properties.

Homework

Students need plenty of practice in using a pair of compasses. This exercise allows them to be creative.

Book 1 Review

 Page 22

Handling data

Content for revision

- **Representation of discrete data.**
- **Representation of continuous data.**
- **Interpreting data.**
- **Collecting data.**
- **Calculating statistics.**
- **Theoretical probability.**

Students were given a thorough introduction to Handling Data in Book 1, pages 164–211. Any student who did not complete this work may need additional teaching in order to do this *Review*.

Students are usually very confident in representing discrete data because it is something they have been doing for at least six years. However, *interpreting* discrete data may not have been practised to the same extent, and this needs revision. It is often avoided because it requires the application of number work, including fractions and percentages.

One of the purposes of calculating statistics is to enable us to compare quantities or distributions. Students need to understand that we have to calculate percentages in order to compare sets of data that are of a different size. For example, to compare test results of two schools that have student numbers of 1800 and 1200, we need to know the percentage of students gaining certain scores.

It is important to use the correct technical words on a regular basis so that students become familiar with them. Students can easily become confused between frequency tables, frequency polygons and frequency diagrams. In this *Review* they meet a frequency table and a frequency diagram. Later in the book they will be introduced to a frequency polygon.

The GCSE examination boards decided to use the term 'frequency diagram' to describe a bar chart for continuous data. It was felt that moving on to the teaching of histograms, where frequency density is plotted rather than frequency, would be too difficult a concept for most students, but there is a need to distinguish between the representation of discrete data and continuous data. Teachers must emphasise that the axis representing the variable on a frequency diagram is continuous.

Discrete data describes the sort of data that can be counted whilst continuous data is measured. However, we sometimes treat discrete data as continuous by grouping it such as, for example, test results.

Starter

Revise calculating fractions and percentages of quantities. For example:

(a) There are 400 counters in a box. 100 of them are red. Compare 100 to 400. What fraction of the counters is red? What is this as a percentage?

(b) Thirty-six students were asked what food they preferred. Eighteen of them said they preferred hamburgers and chips. Compare 18 to 36. What fraction of the students is this? What is this as a percentage?

Demonstration

Draw a frequency table on the board or OHT, using one of the contexts in the Starter. For example, use the colours of counters in a box. Provide the tally column completed. Invite students to work at the front of the class and assist them in counting and calculating the statistics. Invite other members of the class to explain how to work out the answers and write the method on the board.

> *I want someone to help me count these tallies and write the totals in the Frequency column. Good. This tells us that there are one hundred red counters, fifty blue counters, … . How many counters is that altogether? Good. Write that in the bottom row. What is the most common colour? What fraction is green? How do you know that? What percentage is blue? How do you calculate that? What …*

Show the results for two more boxes of counters, one with 40 counters and one with 3000 counters. Ask students to compare the contents of the boxes. Get them to use fractions and percentages to do the comparisons.

> *If I select a counter at random from this box (400 counters) what will be the probability of getting a red counter? And from this box (40 counters)? And from this box (3000 counters)? Which box gives the highest chance of selecting a red counter?*

Essential exercises

These exercises can be completed by working together with the whole class. Invite students to present their answers on the board. Extend the exercises by getting students to ask their own questions.

Set the *Essential exercises* before demonstrating the interpretation of continuous data.

Draw a frequency table for continuous data such as heights. You can use actual data for the class to make this more interesting for the students. Read the class intervals carefully to the students.

> *The heights of the class were measured to the nearest centimetre. In this column the height x cm is greater than or equal to 130 cm and less than 135 cm. There are five students with heights in this range. Could they all have a height of 130 cm? Yes, because the range includes this measurement. Could they all have a height of 135 cm? No, because the range does not include that measurement. In this column …*

Demonstrate how to draw the frequency diagram taking care to emphasise the labelling of the axis for the continuous data. Ask the students questions about the data. Now set the *Challenging exercises*.

Challenging exercises

Make sure that the students use the correct notation in Exercise 4, and see that they label their axes correctly. Ask students to give their own ideas for discrete and continuous data to add to the table in Exercise 5.

Problem-solving exercises

You may need to revise calculating the mean before students complete these exercises. The mean summarises a set of data with a single number but it does not tell us very much about that data. Exercise 7 is designed to show how the mean is very limited in giving adequate information. Company A has one person on a very high salary and all the rest on very low salaries whereas Company B has most of its staff on salaries within a small range.

Plenary

Discuss discrete and continuous data and ask students to give examples of each.

Show the class a bar chart and a frequency diagram and ask the students to identify the similarities and differences.

Present two sets of data such as those in Exercise 7 and ask the students to describe the data and then to summarise the data by calculating certain statistics. Discuss how good the summary statistics are in presenting a true picture of the data.

Homework

Students may need a substantial amount of guidance in deciding on what to survey and on how to conduct the survey. You may want to set the students a specific task and ask them to complete a part of it for homework, with the remainder to be completed in class during the next lesson.

Number and Algebra

Introduction

Continuity with prior learning

Book 1 made extensive use of the maths table, the resource table, cups and cards (see this book, pages 6–7). The purpose of this was to establish certain objects and actions with which mathematical operations can be visualised; not just any objects, and not a variety of objects, but a concrete reference point to consolidate continuity in the work.

For example, 'multiplication' remains the same process ('do the same thing lots of times') no matter what we are dealing with (small numbers; large numbers; vulgar fractions; decimal fractions; negative numbers; algebraic symbols). We ensure that the essence of multiplication does not get lost in a bewildering list of rules that includes counting zeros, finding common denominators, shifting numbers while the point stays still, standing on a number line and turning round before moving!). More than this, the persistent reference to cups clarifies that $3 + 4 = 7$ is radically different from $3 \times 4 = 12$.

We can see that:
3 *cups* + **4** *cups* = **7** *cups* but **3** *cups* $\times$ **4** = **12** *cups*.
It is this perception that provokes the sheer logic of
3 *fifths* + **4** *fifths* = **7** *fifths* but **3** *fifths* $\times$ **4** = **12** *fifths*.

The continuing image of the cups is very helpful for people learning maths. However, all students (especially those who are not naturally confident about maths) must be weaned off the actual use of cups (and cards). They must be enabled to develop the disposition to work with symbols; they must become disposed to accept that we can talk of $3 \times 1\frac{1}{2} = 4\frac{1}{2}$ as putting three cups on the maths table and doing the same thing $1\frac{1}{2}$ times. They must continue to recognise the difference between the 3 (being cups) and the $1\frac{1}{2}$ (being actions), but they must not fuss about the real-life problem of undertaking $1\frac{1}{2}$ actions. They must not feel any compulsion to interpret a half action as 'making a complete action but only with half the cups'. In fact, they should not feel the need to attempt any convoluted, manufactured justification. A major aim in teaching maths has to be to enable students to trust the symbols.

In this particular case, trusting the symbols means that, having established $1\frac{1}{2} \times 3 = 4\frac{1}{2}$ (because we can carry $1\frac{1}{2}$ cups a total of 3 times) then the commutative law for multiplication immediately tells us $3 \times 1\frac{1}{2} = 4\frac{1}{2}$. The purpose of all this is to ensure students develop mathematically (not only in their numeracy). To reiterate: mathematical development includes the disposition to trust the symbols,

requiring an acceptance that maths goes beyond real-life and that it operates in imaginary worlds.

Ensure that students retain the cups as a point of reference; the cups are neutral carriers of the symbols used in maths. When we use cards on the maths table, their reference point is still cups. They are one remove from the concrete objects (they are symbolic objects) but, again, they are designed as a stepping-stone to truly symbolic work (that is, symbols written on the page).

The cups and cards are like axioms in maths: they can be re-examined to test the validity of subsequent work. That is why our *Demonstration* pages persist in using cups and cards: they offer the fundamental justification for mathematical results. However, you must as often as possible refer to the cups without having them in your hands. After the initial teaching of multiplication and symbolic use of the commutative law, the result $3 \times 1\frac{1}{2} = 4\frac{1}{2}$ is referred to as *'Put 3 cups on the table.* [use an unspecific movement of a hand] *Do the same thing … one and a half times,* [use an equally unspecific movement of a hand] *and you can see* $4\frac{1}{2}$ *cups'*. However, if students do not feel confident with this, they will need you to re-trace the steps (using real cups); remember – this is meaningful because the cups will be well known to your students. The familiarity releases the students from thinking about the cups, to concentrating on thinking *with* them.

This paves the way for a truly mathematical approach to algebra. The key to *I See Maths* work in algebra is the use of symbolic objects (cards with, say, x or $3xy$ and so on, written on them); but we need to have the trained disposition to accept that we can put $3x$ on the table $2y$ times (with an unspecific movement of a hand).

 I See Maths Book 2

Number and Algebra

 Page 24 # Laws of arithmetic

Goals

The **commutative law, associative law** and **distributive law** are important frameworks in arithmetic and algebra. Students are familiar with all of these laws though not necessarily by name. The distributive law was formalised in Book 1, pages 10–11 and linked to well-known methods for mental arithmetic. Students need to know when these laws apply and when they do not apply. For example, the commutative law does not apply to subtraction or division yet many common errors are caused by students attempting to do just that.

As we begin to formalise arithmetic, and make connections with algebra, we need to reinforce the idea of a 'factor' and a 'term'. In order to clarify this we introduce the idea of a 'string of terms'. The idea of a factor was introduced in Book 1 (see pages 64–87). In this early work on factors, students identified pairs of whole numbers whose product equalled the number under consideration. In this lesson we move on to consider any number as a factor. For example, two factors of 6 are $\frac{1}{2}$ and 12. This links with the idea of a factor in algebra where x, as a factor, can be any number. Further practice on factors and multiples can be found in **Worksheets 8 and 9.**

Starter

The *Starter* should involve a great deal of practice in arithmetic together with detailed discussion. Many students will remember this work from Book 1, pages 64–67. However, with some students you may need to use the multiplication tables to find pairs of factors, and with a few students you may need to act out multiplication with cups and cards.

Think of 12. We know that $3 \times 4 = 12$ and $4 \times 3 = 12$. This is an example of the commutative law. One factor of 12 is 3 and the other factor is 4. One factor is 6 and the other is 2. One factor is 12 and the other is 1. This exhausts the whole-number factors. Consider fractions: one factor is $\frac{1}{2}$ and the other is 24 and so on.

Repeat this discussion for the second and third questions. For $6x$ ensure that the following factors (and the other factor in each case) are identified: 6; x; 3; 2; 1; $\frac{1}{2}$; $\frac{1}{2}x$ and so on. For $6xy$ use the same sort of discussion to identify the factors 3; $3x$; $3y$; 2; $2xy$; $2y$; xy; x; y; $\frac{1}{2}x$; $\frac{1}{2}xy$; ... .

Demonstration 1

Use cups to show that, for example, $2 \times 4 + 1 \times 3 = 11$. We can see that what we are doing is putting 8 cups on the table and then another 3 cups. The mathematical logic insists we deal with 2×4 and an additional 1×3. The first 'term' is 2×4 and the second 'term' is 1×3. Similarly, show $2 \times 4 - 1 \times 3 = 5$ using cups, and clarify that we are putting 8 cups on the table and then subtracting 3 cups. The expression $2 \times 4 - 1 \times 3$ is another string of two terms.

Look at *Demonstration 1.* Examine the first string of terms. There are five terms. Ask some students to read a term each. Ask other students to evaluate each term. Carefully discuss the first term $5 \times 2 \times 3$ to see that 10 cups (5 cups $\times$ 2) could be put on the table 3 times; or 5 cups could be put on the table 6 times (2×3) or 15 cups (5 cups $\times$ 3) could be put on the table 2 times (same value, but different appearance). The fact that there are three ways of evaluating $5 \times 2 \times 3$ is an illustration of the associative law for multiplication. We can treat it as if 5 and 2 were associated; or as if 2 and 3 were associated, or (if we commute 2 and 3) as if 5 and 3 were associated. The associative law is true for both $+$ and $\times$. But be clear what this means. It applies to each operation separately: not in combination.

Examine the second and third terms. These cases, $2 \times 4 = 4 \times 2 = 8$ and $1 \times 7 = 7 \times 1 = 7$ are examples of the commutative law. For example, putting 2 cups on the table four times has the same value as putting 4 cups on the table two times.

Evaluate the fourth term $3 \div 4$ as a quarter of three or $\frac{3}{4}$ or $\cdot 75$, and demonstrate that $3 \div 4$ is not the same as $4 \div 3$. Division is not commutative. Examination of the fifth term will show, once again, that multiplication is commutative.

Discuss the four operations and establish that multiplication and addition are commutative whilst division and subtraction are not.

Now evaluate the complete expression:
$30 + 8 + 30 - \cdot 75 - 1 \cdot 5 = 65 \cdot 75$

Look at the second string (the algebraic string). The first term $x \times 4 = 4 \times x$ (the commutative law) and this is abbreviated to $4x$. Similarly $y \times 7 = 7 \times y = 7y$, $b \times 3 = 3 \times b = 3b$. However, division is not commutative and so $a \div 4$ cannot be reversed, but can be abbreviated to $\frac{a}{4}$.

Number and Algebra

Demonstration 2

Although each of $3x$ and $6y$ has many factors, concentrate on the factors as shown. Point out that the string has two terms. 3 is a factor of $3x$ and 3 is a factor of $6y$; i.e. 3 is a factor of *both* $3x$ and $6y$, or put another way, *the factor 3 is common to $3x$ and $6y$*.

Show that $3(x + 2y)$ has the same value as $3x + 6y$. Do this by referring to the distributive law (See Book 1, pages 10–11). Using the 'grid' format for long multiplication. 3×62 has the same value as $3 \times (60 + 2)$ or $3(60 + 2)$. This is what is implied in:

$\times$	60		2	
3	180		6	186

and so, similarly:

$\times$	x		$2y$	
3	$3x$		$6y$	$3x + 6y$

But look at the distributive law: $3(x + 2y) = 3x + 6y$. We see that 3 is the factor that is common to both $3x$ and $6y$. The distributive law distributes 3 (spreads 3) over the x and the $2y$. It turns the product of two factors (3 and $x + 2y$) into a string of terms. Now think of the expression the other way around: $3x + 6y = 3(x + 2y)$. This starts with a string of terms and turns it into the product of two factors. The factor 3 is a factor that is common to both $3x$ and $6y$.

Use a range of examples like those below to consolidate the instructions 'Use the distributive law to express this product of factors as a string of terms' and 'Identify a common factor and express this string of terms as the product of factors'.

(1) $5(x + 4y + 2y)$ (2) $9x + 12y$
(3) $7xy - 3y$ (4) $1{\cdot}2(2x - 3y + 10y)$
(5) $5xyz + axz$ (6) $\frac{3}{4}(4x + 2y)$

Introduce the phrase 'take out a common factor' as a 'shorthand' for 'Identify a common factor and express this string of terms as the product of factors.'; and give the students practice in the use of this instruction. In the examples above, ask students to say the instruction to the class.

Worked examples

Invite students to discuss each example in detail.

In (1): *Look at $18xy$. Is it a string of terms? Is it a term? What are its factors?*
In (2): *We are told to express $3(5x - 2)$ as a string of terms. What do we call $3(5x - 2)$?*
In (3): *What do we call $9a + 3ab - 6ac$?*

Essential exercises

Before starting the exercises, you may wish to use **Worksheet 10** to practise work on the commutative law.

Lead in to Exercise 1 by selecting a few cards and evaluating the expressions. Use 'left to right' logic for the first card $2 + 5 - 4$ and think of it as 'Put 2 on the maths table; put another 5 on the maths table and now remove 4; I can see 3'. However, the commutative law applies to addition so we could reverse $2 + 5$ and write $5 + 2 - 4$. We could also think of $(5 - 4)$ as a single term and reverse $2 + (5 - 4)$ to get $(5 - 4) + 2$. (The brackets here are not necessary; they are merely used to highlight the term $5 - 4$.)

We often perform these rearrangements in our heads to make a mental calculation simpler. For example, we search for numbers that add to ten or a hundred ($23 + 19 + 77$) or perform addition before subtraction to avoid negative numbers ($4 - 9 + 8$). However, we need to ensure that we know the rules thoroughly, because we cannot rearrange just anything. For example, we cannot change that last expression to $9 - 4 + 8$ because $4 - 9$ is not the same as $9 - 4$ (subtraction is not commutative).

Now demonstrate one example from each of Exercises 2 to 5, so that all students can work through the *Essential exercises*.

Challenging exercises

Use Exercise 6 with the most confident students, with the requirement that they justify their methods by reference to the laws of arithmetic. This detailed and complex requirement makes it best that they work in pairs.

Exercises 7 and 8 are good challenges for all students. Calculators can be used to check answers in Exercise 7.

Problem-solving exercises

Exercises 9 and 10 are number investigations and puzzles involving the application of the laws of arithmetic. Students can use calculators to help them but they will need to be careful with the order of operations.

Plenary

Assist the students in writing strings of terms with and without common factors.

Homework

Work through an example of your own in front of the class and, while you do this, keep up a running commentary on your thinking. This demonstration will clarify what are the real demands of this task. If necessary, invite some pupils to undertake a similar running commentary while you assist them to construct an example.

Teacher's Notes Teacher's Notes Teacher's Notes Teacher's Notes Teacher's
Teacher's Notes Teacher's Notes Teacher's Notes
Teacher's Notes Teacher's Notes Teacher's Notes Teacher's Notes Teacher's Notes
er's Notes Notes Teacher's Notes Teacher's Notes Teacher's Not

Number and Algebra

 Order of operations

Page 28

Goals

If an expression is evaluated logically, then the laws of arithmetic are obeyed, because the language has been designed to be consistent with those laws.

There is actually no need for students to learn any tricks, mnemonics or 'make-it-easy' rules. We have looked at the laws and the logic of maths in the previous lesson; in this lesson we are consolidating much of that work and extending it to include the use of brackets to deliberately change the logic (e.g. change $2 + 3 \times 4 = 14$ to $(2 + 3) \times 4 = 20$). When the mathematical logic is being followed there is no need to insert unnecessary or redundant brackets (e.g. $2 + 3 \times 4 = 14$ should not be written as $2 + (3 \times 4) = 14$). **Worksheet 11** provides additional practice for this topic.

Starter

Invite students to act these results with cups or cards using mathematical logic. Each answer given is, of course, the only possible answer. Resist any tendency for students to assert the possibility of part (a) having the answer 27. It has never been 27; it is not 27; it never will be 27. It was, is and always will be the entirely logical, unique 11. Now insist on re-examination from the point of view of the terms in each string – and link this to the observed movement of cups. When a student acts $2 \times 4 + 1 \times 3 = 11$ we actually see 2×4 (eight) cups being put on the table; and we see a further 1×3 (three) cups put on the table.

Demonstration 1

We need all students to be able to look at a seemingly complex algebraic string and perceive its logic and simplicity. Look at the expression

$3x + (5x - 2x) \times (4 - 1) - 7x$

and enable the students to identify how many terms it has (it has three). Study the middle term in detail. They can see it is the product of two factors (they must articulate this), these being $5x - 2x$ and $4 - 1$. Each factor can be simplified, so the two factors are $3x$ and 3. Enable all the students to visualise the simplification of $5x - 2x$ (5 of those things called x; remove 2 of those things called x). It serves as a persistent, visible reminder never to make the hoary old mistake of thinking $5x - 2x$ is just 3.

Make up similar strings for evaluation. Use, for instance:
(1) $5xy - (7x - 3x) \times (2y + 3y) + (5 - 2) \times xy$
(2) $5xy - (7x - 3x)(2y + 3y) + (5 - 2)xy$
(3) $(x + 2y) \div 3 + (5x - 4y + 2x) \div 3$
(4) $(x + 2y)/3 + (5x - 4y + 2x)/6$
(5) $\dfrac{(x + 2y)}{3} + \dfrac{(5x - 4y + 2x)}{4}$

Demonstration 2

Very few people can understand the sense in the equivalence of $8 \div 2 \div 2$ and $8 \div (2 \times 2)$ unless they have been weaned on the logic of maths and practised in the related use of visual images. *Demonstration 2* uses and practises the crucially important notion of 'divided by' as 'look at it and wonder how many …' as introduced in Book 1 (see Teacher's Resource Book 1, pages 24–25).

Revise this and insist on recognising $6 \div 2$ as:

Start by putting six cups on the maths table; look at them and wonder how many piles of two cups you can see. [Stack cups in piles of two.] *Three.*

Repeat with other easy examples and move to $3 \div \frac{1}{2} = 6$ (Make students look for piles of the right size (half cups) and count the piles). Similarly, $1 \div \frac{1}{2} = 2$, $1 \div \frac{1}{4} = 4$, $3 \div \frac{1}{5} = 15$, and so on.

Now concentrate on $12 \div 2 = 6$. This is easy; but it must be made clear that we need to think of it as:

Start by putting twelve cups on the maths table; look at them and wonder how many piles of two cups you can see. Six.

Look at *Demonstration 2*.

$12 \div 2 \div 3 =$
Start by putting twelve cups on the maths table; look at them and wonder how many piles of two cups you can see. Six. [There are now six piles of two cups on the table.] *Now look at them* [the six piles of two cups] *and wonder how many piles of three of these pairs of cups you can see. Two.*
[There are now two piles of three pairs of cups on the table. There are two piles of six cups.]

Number and Algebra

Now invite students to do similar demonstrations, for instance:

(1) $12 \div 3 \div 2 = 12 \div (3 \times 2)$

(2) $15 \div 5 \div 3 = 15 \div (5 \times 3)$

(3) $12 \div \frac{1}{2} \div 3 = 12 \div (\frac{1}{2} \times 3)$

(4) $1 \div \frac{1}{2} \div 2 = 1 \div (\frac{1}{2} \times 2)$

(5) $1 \div \frac{1}{10} \div \frac{1}{10} = 1 \div (\frac{1}{10} \times \frac{1}{10})$

Extend the argument to
$a \div b \div c = a \div (b \times c)$

Worked examples

Emphasise that we use brackets only when necessary. For instance, in 1(a) it is true that $5 + (2 \times 3) = 11$ but the more elegant form is $5 + 2 \times 3 = 11$ because the mathematical logic conveys all that is needed.

Essential exercises

Exercises 1 to 4 follow on from the demonstrations and many students will be able to complete them independently. Less confident students may need assistance with identifying the terms in each expression.

Consider Exercise 1(a): $5 \times 4 + 7$. In this expression 5×4 is one term and 7 is another. We have to work out each term and add. $20 + 7 = 27$. Now look at 1(b): $4 + 6 \times 8$. In this expression 4 is one term and 6×8 is another. Add 4 and 48 to get 52. It is tempting to insert brackets around the 6×8 as a reminder that this is a term but we must resist! Brackets should only be used to change the mathematical logic.

Exercise 2 reinforces the mathematical logic. Ask students to evaluate each expression in turn by first identifying the terms and then performing the calculations.

Exercise 3 demonstrates how brackets change the mathematical logic. For example, the first expression has the value 27 as it stands. We have to insert brackets like this $(3 + 4) \times 6$ to make $3 + 4$ into a term.

Terms involving division are sometimes easier to interpret when the division is shown as a fraction. For example, Exercise 4(a) can be written as $5 + \frac{48}{8}$ and 4(c) as $\frac{10}{2} + \frac{63}{9}$. This also reinforces the connection between division and fractions.

Exercise 5 can be extended to investigate what numbers between 1 and 100 can be made with the five numbers. This provides lots of practice in using mathematical logic and brackets. There are several different ways of getting each number.

Exercise 6 replicates a well-known TV game and students love to be challenged with questions like this. Get the students to make up their own challenge questions.

The first part of Exercise 7 requires the brackets for the answer to be correct. However, parts (b) and (c) contain redundant brackets.

Challenging exercises

Exercises 8 to 10 repeat work done in the *Essential exercises* but they use letters and negative numbers to provide a challenge.

Problem-solving exercises

For Exercise 11, first evaluate the expression without inserting brackets using mathematical logic (42). Then consider what terms can be created by inserting brackets.

Exercises 12 and 13 provide practice in mathematical logic presented as puzzles. All students should be able to do these questions.

Plenary

Get the students to evaluate the first expression individually and then invite someone to present the answer on the board. Discuss the second and third expressions as a class.

Homework

Students can be set this homework task as preparation for an activity at the beginning of the next lesson.

Number and Algebra

Making connections 1

Goals

This lesson focuses on using known or given facts to deduce more facts. Given that $3 \times 4 = 12$ then we know that $300 \times 4 = 1200$; $30 \times 400 = 12000$; $\cdot3 \times \cdot4 = \cdot12$, and so on. Seeing these connections reduces the amount we have to learn by categorising knowledge into manageable packages. Students were introduced to these ideas in Book 1, pages 6–7, 14–15.

This section of the book uses the grid method for long multiplication. There are four reasons for this: (i) more students get right answers; (ii) it offers a useful image of the 'maths table'; (iii) it makes the distributive law accessible; (iv) it offers continuity with the product of two binomial factors in algebra. However, some students have still been taught this method as yet another algorithm, and although more students get right answers, in most cases they are merely carrying out the steps mechanically with no improvement in understanding. Use **Worksheet 12** with those students who need more practice in using the grid method.

In spite of the power of this method, the 'traditional' vertical algorithm is more economical. The best approach is to achieve a clear understanding with the 'grid' and then move to the more economical algorithm. This lesson sets out to do just that. Students are asked to study the two methods side by side to see how the 'traditional algorithm' works. Both methods are then employed in the long multiplication of decimals.

Starter

We need to start with a general discussion. Question (1) in the *Starter* revises the logic of the language of multiplication. The logic of 1(c): three thousand times two hundred equals six thousand hundred (written $2\,000 \times 3\,00 = 6\,000\,00$) is clear. However, in 1(a) the logic of $30 \times 60 = 1800$ needs rescuing from the vernacular 'thirty times sixty' so that it is recognised as 'three-ty times six-ty equals eighteen-ty-ty' and written $3\,0 \times 6\,0 = 18\,0\,0$.

The importance of this use of language lies to some extent in the enabling of more students getting right answers, but also, more significantly, in its continuity with 3(a) three tenths times four is twelve tenths and 3(b) three tenths times four tenths equals twelve tenths tenths. This latter is written as $\frac{12}{100}$ and known to be twelve hundredths (see Book 1).

Now we can look at each of the five questions. Use question (1) to establish accurate answers using the logic of the language as discussed above. Use these answers to make approximations in question (2).

In question (3) use the logic of the language to establish correct answers as vulgar fractions, and then establish that each of these has the same value (different appearance) as the corresponding parts of question (4). Remind students that they know that $\frac{12}{10}$ has the same value as $1\cdot2$, $\frac{12}{100}$ as $\cdot12$, and $\frac{12}{1000}$ as $\cdot012$. Then use these results to obtain approximate answers to question (5).

Demonstration 1

Work through the calculation of 62×34 using the grid. Insist that the main body of the grid is thought of as the maths table with cups on it (the outside parts of the grid are merely jottings to show how the cups got there). This is an important visual image for students – it will enable them to make sense, in due course, of algebraic multiplication and division. For this reason, emphasise that we can 'see' 2108 cups on the maths table, and that this can be calculated either as $2040 + 68$ or $1860 + 248$.

Now work through each of the 'vertical' calculations. Use the economical abbreviated language of 'multiply by thirty; put down the nought; 2 times 3 is 6; 6 times 3 is 18' etc. to complete the calculation, and ensure all students practise this. Then talk through how each step of this can be related to the 'maths table' in the grid. For instance, the 1860 in the first vertical format can be identified in the grid method as the sum of 1800 and 60, these being the separate 'piles' of cups achieved by putting 60 on the table 30 times and then 2 on the table 30 times.

Invite students to talk through the other vertical calculations and identify the connection with the grid. Refer to multiplication being commutative when looking at the several vertical forms. Repeat the demonstration for further examples.

Demonstration 2

Continue the same emphasis as in *Demonstration 1*, that is, insist on the grid being thought of as the 'maths table'. Deal with $6\cdot2 \times 3\cdot4$ and concentrate on detail:

> Look at 6·2:
> [Point to the 6] *How much is there here? Six.*

[Point to the 2] *How much is there here? Two-tenths.
Look at 3·4.*
[Point to the 3] *How much is there here? Three.*
[Point to the 4] *How much is there here? Four-tenths.*

[Write the 6 and the ·2 and the 3 and the ·4 on the grid.
Talk through the multiplications using the vocabulary of
vulgar fractions while writing decimal fractions.]
6 times 3 is 18. [write 18]
2 tenths times 3 is 6 tenths. [write ·6]
6 times 4 tenths is 24 tenths. [write 2·4]
2 tenths times 4 tenths is 8 tenths tenths. [Show this
as $\frac{8}{100}$, i.e. write 8, draw the line, write 10 and as you
say 'tenths' for the second time write the last zero:
'tenth tenths' then appears as hundredths]

Now that the figures are written in the grid, talk through
the process again as:

*We put 6 cups on the maths table 3 times: 18 cups.
We put 2 tenths cups on the maths table 3 times:
6 tenths cups. We put 6 cups on the maths table
4 tenths times: 24 tenths cups. We put 2 tenths cups
on the maths table 4 tenths times: 8 hundredths cups.*

This is extremely important in terms of mathematical
development: we are trying to develop each student's
disposition to trust the symbols and go beyond the
constraints of what is literally possible (we are trying to
make them think mathematically). The fact that we cannot
literally carry 4 cups to the table 4 tenths of a time must not
trouble the students. They must be aware that this is what is
implied, but they must be willing to accept that a wave of
the hand to indicate this movement, together with the
symbolic outcome of this (2·4), is precisely what we do in a
mathematics classroom. If students fuss about the literal
impossibility of this they demonstrate their current lack of
sophistication about maths and they need more persuasion!

Now work through the 'vertical' calculation for the same
product 6·2 × 3·4, noting that this is written differently but
we actually perform a 'numerically similar' calculation 62 ×
34 (use this phrase with the students). What this means is
that the result will be numerically similar to the correct
answer but we need to do an approximation (as practised in
the *Starter*) to determine where to place the decimal point.

In a similar way, work though the product 6·2 × ·34, again
using the vocabulary of vulgar fractions while writing decimal
fractions. Note that '*2 tenths times 4 hundredths makes 8
tenths hundredths*' and the manner in which this is written
as a vulgar fraction establishes that this is 8 thousandths.

Worked example

Given that 62 × 34 = 2108 we can also work out
·62 × ·034. Get students to find the approximate value of the
answer so that they can decide where to put the decimal
point. For example, '*Six tenths times three hundredths is
eighteen tenths hundredths (thousandths) (·018).*'

Essential exercises

Exercise 1 revises work done on extending the multiplication
tables in Book 1. It is important that the students make use
of the logic of the language and *do* not revert to tricks or
rules about adding noughts.

Use **Worksheet 13** for those students who need to revise
multiplying decimals, and **Worksheet 14** for those who
need to practise making connections. Exercises 2 to 4
provide practice in using the grid method for long
multiplication. Students who have understood this method
and moved on to the more efficient vertical method should
use these. Working out approximate answers first can help
students check their work.

Exercise 5 links number work with algebra.

Students should use whichever method of long multiplication
they are comfortable with for Exercise 6. The exercise revises
the notation for 'squaring' or 'cubing' a number.

Exercise 7 is not for the faint-hearted! Once again, do not
let the students revert to rules but use the language of
number to answer the questions. For example, 'six hundred
and nine' times 'seven hundred and twenty-seven' becomes
'six hundred and nine' hundredths times 'seven hundred
and twenty-seven' hundredths.

Challenging exercises

These exercises should only be used with the most confident
students. They apply the knowledge from the *Essential
exercises* to algebra, negative numbers and powers.

Problem-solving exercises

These exercises show how given facts can be used to solve
real-life problems.

Plenary

Before discussing questions (a) to (e) put up the grid for
62 × 34 and remind the students of the link between the
grid and the vertical algorithm.

*Look at 60 × 30. You can 'see' 60 × 3, 6 × 30, 6 × 3,
and so on. Can you 'see' ·6 × ·3?*

The grid holds so much information, yet we rarely access
this in the detailed way that is required in these questions.

Homework

Asking students to set their own questions is always
effective in getting them to understand the work they have
been doing. Reserve a time in the next lesson to let students
challenge a partner with a selection of their questions.

Number and Algebra

Equivalence

Page 36

Goals

The most important point about division is that it is the inverse of multiplication. It is knowledge of multiplication facts that enables us to write down the value of a quotient. The basic facts we know about multiplication is the explicit information that we must be able access easily; and this explicit information carries a wide range of implicit information about both other products and a wide range of quotients.

The known fact $7 \times 9 = 63$ carries the implicit information that $63 \div 7 = 9$ and this quotient can be used in two ways. It immediately gives the answer to any **equivalent** quotient like $63\,000 \div 7000 = 9$ or $\frac{63}{100} \div \frac{7}{100} = 9$ (or even $\frac{63}{179} \div \frac{7}{179} = 9$). It also enables us to calculate $\frac{63}{1000} \div 7 = \frac{9}{1000}$ or $63 \div \frac{7}{1000} = 9000$, because these are **numerically similar** to $63 \div 7 = 9$. However, we need to be able to calculate an approximate value to be sure of getting the correct result.

This lesson utilises an equivalent quotient for the calculation of the quotient of two numbers written in decimal notation. It starts by revising the use of explicit and implicit information in products and quotients.

Starter

Look at question (1). The product $2 \times 3 = 6$ provides some explicit information. Point to the six:

How much is there here? Six. [Indicate the 2×3 (all of it)] *How much is there here? Six: (same value: different appearance). Look at six* [indicate 2×3] *and wonder how many threes you can see. Two. Look at six* [indicate 2×3] *and wonder how many twos you can see. Three. So we can see $6 \div 3 = 2$ and $6 \div 2 = 3$ (this is implicit information).*

But there is much more implicit information. Look again at $2 \times 3 = 6$ and imagine that here [point to the 6 and the space after it] *you can see six hundredths; then here* [indicate 2×3] *you must be able to see six hundredths as well. What is six hundredths divided by three? Two hundredths.*

Question (2) invites a similar discussion.

Demonstration 1

This demonstration is aimed at establishing a genuine understanding of what is implied in the calculation $1{\cdot}38 \div {\cdot}01$ (and similar calculations). This begins with appreciation of the fact that $1{\cdot}38$ can be thought of as 138 hundredths or $13{\cdot}8$ tenths or 1380 thousandths, so that it is easy, from the logic of the language, to see how many hundredths or tenths or thousandths there are.

What is rarely appreciated is that $1{\cdot}38 \div {\cdot}01$ has the same value as $(1 + {\cdot}3 + {\cdot}08) \div {\cdot}01$, but it is precisely this that we prepared for in Book 1 (page 14, question (2) and its discussion in the Teacher's Resource Book). There we deliberately showed $462 \div 3$ (visualised on the maths table) as equivalent to $(400 + 60 + 2) \div 3$ or $(300 + 150 + 12) \div 3$. Revise this approach to division with the students and discuss the equivalence of $462 \div 3$ and $(400 + 60 + 2) \div 3$ and $\frac{400 + 60 + 2}{3}$. Continue this discussion with respect to $1{\cdot}38 \div {\cdot}01$ and $(1 + {\cdot}3 + {\cdot}08) \div {\cdot}01$ and $\frac{1 + {\cdot}3 + {\cdot}08}{{\cdot}01}$.

This prepares the way for looking at the representation in *Demonstration 1*.

We can see 1 and 3 tenths and 8 hundredths.

Put one on the maths table and wonder, how many piles of one-hundredths you can see. One hundred.

Put three tenths on the maths table and wonder how many piles of one-hundredths you can see. Thirty.

Put 8 hundredths on the maths table and wonder how many piles of one-hundredths can you see. Eight.

That is one hundred and thirty-eight one-hundredths altogether.

Now repeat a similar discussion with $13{\cdot}8 \div {\cdot}1 = 138$ and $138 \div 1 = 138$.

These are equivalent calculations. In each case we have made the two numbers bigger by the same scale factor (10 : 1). When we are faced with a quotient we can always use an equivalent calculation (same value: different appearance). When dividing, an equivalent calculation can always be written down by using the same scale factor on the two numbers.

Illustrate this by acting out, say, $6 \div 2$ with cups: [Put 6 cups on the maths table.] *Look at the cups and wonder how many piles of two cups you can see.*

Increase both 6 and 2 by a scale factor of 4 : 1 and calculate 24 ÷ 8 (with cups); then increase both 6 and 2 by a scale factor of 10 : 1 and do the calculation 60 ÷ 20. Consolidate the point by making each number smaller by a scale factor 1 : 2 (hence 3 ÷ 1) and then by a scale factor 1 : 4 (hence $1\frac{1}{2} \div \frac{1}{2}$).

Demonstration 2

Demonstration 2 confirms the use of a 'whole number' quotient as equivalent to one that looks more complicated: *46·2 ÷ ·3 has the same value as 462 ÷ 3*. Confirm that we are dealing with an equivalent quotient by examining the scale factor that has been used for each number (10 : 1). Work through the division, referring to cups on the maths table as usual.

In some cases, students will have an uncertain view of division lingering on from previous experience: having 'moved the decimal point' they will be determined to 'move it back again' following the calculation, that is, they will not easily recognise that 46·2 ÷ ·3 is *really* equal to 154 (they will toy with numbers like 15·4). This is the purpose of referring heavily to the fact of the calculations being equivalent. Do not let previous misunderstandings interfere with the clarity afforded by insisting on recognising the equivalence.

Worked example

This example is used to show that division and factors are closely linked. If a number is divisible by three, then three is a factor of that number.

When we partition a number we are really expressing that number as a string of terms. It is unfortunate that recent practice has been to call this 'chunking' the number. When we find a common factor of all the numbers in the string we can use the distributive law to express the number as a product of two factors.

Essential exercises

The first exercise requires knowledge of multiplication tables. For less confident students put up posters of the tables around the room.

The remainder of the exercises are not tests of memorised facts. It is important that students are given results and that they then look for ways of using these results to work out the answers to the questions.

All the questions in Exercise 2 have the same answer. Say the questions together with the class to emphasise that the same question is being asked each time.

*(a) Fifty-six-**ty** divided by seven-**ty***
*(b) Fifty-six **hundred** divided by seven **hundred***
*(c) Fifty-six **thousand** divided by seven **thousand**, etc.*

Similarly with Exercise 3:

*(b) Three hundred and forty-five **tenths** divided by twenty-three **tenths**.*

Exercises 4 and 5 have the same answers. Students should use partitioning to work out the answers to Exercise 4 and recognise the equivalence of the questions in Exercise 5.

In Exercise 6 students use their knowledge to make decisions about which operation to perform. Normally we would try to make the divisor a whole number. However, the students may select other equivalent expressions but they should justify their choice.

Challenging exercises

Exercises 7 and 8 are just extensions of the *Essential exercises* using algebra. Exercise 9 reinforces the idea that division can be written as a fraction.

Problem-solving exercises

Calculating the mean value is an application of division. These exercises are straightforward examples revising division and means.

Plenary

These four examples check that students have understood how to create equivalent expressions for the purpose of simplifying division.

Homework

Asking students to write their own questions is a good test of whether they have understood the work. Get students to pose their questions to the class at the beginning of the next lesson.

Making connections 2

Page 40

Goals

In the previous lesson we looked at expressions that gave exactly the same result (24 ÷ 3 has the same result as 2·4 ÷ ·3). In this lesson we consolidate this and also look at using a given result to calculate an expression containing the same numbers of different order (given that 24 ÷ 3 = 8 then we can see that 24 ÷ ·03 = 800). In these cases approximation is used to determine the order of the required result.

Relatively few people benefit from literal memory (a sort of photographic memory), and even when they do, it is prone to erroneous application. But almost everyone benefits from development of semantic memory, that is, that their efforts to memorise techniques are the more successful for having a clear understanding of what they are 'really' doing.

One of the most potent elements of semantic memory is the practised use of accurate language: it is the logic of mathematical language that enables students to make sense of maths. It is this approach that is seen here. We emphasise the distinction between undertaking **equivalent calculations** and **numerically similar calculations.** When we can identify an easily executed equivalent calculation we do so. In some cases we can use a numerically similar calculation that is preferable to the intended one, and then, employing an approximation, write down the required answer.

It is these two approaches that are usually used in calculations of the quotients of any two decimal numbers. For instance, 4·24 ÷ ·2 is equivalent to 42·4 ÷ 2 = 21·2 (same value: different appearance) and it is numerically similar to 424 ÷ 2 = 212. When we use an equivalent calculation we obtain the required answer immediately; when we use the numerically similar calculation we use an approximate answer (4 divided by 2 tenths is 20) to establish where to place the decimal point.

Starter

The *Starter* confirms how the use of multiplication tables (in this case the three-times table) enables a wide range of products to be calculated. It is very important to use the logic of the language in this exercise, not the abbreviations or tricks typically employed. For instance, emphasising the words in bold type:

1(a) three **tenths** times two equals six **tenths**
1(c) three **hundredths** times two equals six **hundredths**
1(e) three **tenths** times two **tenths** equals six **tenths tenths**, equals six **hundredths.**

You will see 1(a) and 1(g) are precisely the same (as are 1(c) and 1(i), 1(e) and 1(k), and so on). The purpose of this is to emphasise that the same calculation can appear in different forms, and to use the language of vulgar fractions when faced with written decimal fractions. This means that 1(k) can be said as:

> three **tenths** *times two* **tenths** *equals six* **tenths tenths**, *equals six* **hundredths**, *equals point nought six.*

Work through the questions in the *Starter* one by one, each time asking a student to read the question and another student to write the answer on the board. Then go through them again with every student writing answers on paper.

Demonstration 1

Examine the quotient 12 ÷ 3 = 4 from the perspective of each of the related results in the diagram. For each result, discuss the scale factor involved. For example:

> Look at 1200 ÷ 30 = 40.
> Compare 1200 to 12 (bigger) 100 : 1. Compare 30 to 3 (bigger) 10 : 1. The scale factors are different. It is not an equivalent quotient, that is why the answer is not 4. It is a numerically similar quotient.
> Look at 1·2 ÷ ·3 = 4.
> Compare 1·2 to 12 (smaller) 1 : 10. Compare ·3 to 3 (smaller) 1 : 10. The scale factors are the same. It is an equivalent quotient. That is why the answer is 4.

Demonstration 2

The calculation in this demonstration is one that would normally be done using a calculator. It is worked here as a long division problem in a manner that is designed to clarify the nature of long division. It is accompanied by language that specifically refers to 'factors' so that it establishes ideas that are continuous with, and important in, algebraic long division. Of course, when the process is undertaken in algebra, it is much easier. We do not expect students to replicate this division algorithm but to follow it in order to gain a better understanding of the process.

> *Look at 5·72 ÷ 2·3.*
> *It is equivalent to 57·2 ÷ 23 and 572 ÷ 230 (and many more). It is easier to divide by a whole number rather than one containing a decimal fraction. Both 23 and 230 are whole numbers; but it is easier to divide by 23 than by 230.*
>
> *We will use the equivalent calculation 57·2 ÷ 23 . First find an approximation: 57·2 ÷ 23 is approximately 57 ÷ 25, which is approximately 2. This enables us to decide where to put the decimal point [look at the diagram]. We know the answer will begin 2 point something, and this in turn shows us that, in order to work to three decimal places, we need to deal with the number 57·200.*

Now redraw the grid (the maths table) as shown, and deal with a numerically similar calculation that has a divisor of 23 and 57 200 in the grid.

> *Working with 'same value: different appearance', each time we are selecting numbers that have a factor of 23.*
>
> *Use the 23-times table on the page. Each time, find the largest number that can be expressed as a product of two factors, one of which is 23.*

Work through each of the steps of the calculation in turn. This will make it possible to see that, with 23 as one factor, 57 200 has another factor of 2486 (approximately!). When we place these figures into the grid that has correctly placed the decimal point, we can write in the approximate answer to the original problem, correct to two decimal places.

Essential exercises

The first exercise is designed to get students to see the relationship between the given result and the set questions.

Exercise 2 demonstrates the relationship between the divisor and the dividend. Given that $6 ÷ 3 = 2$ then $6 ÷ 2 = 3$. Both of these statements come originally from the fact that $2 × 3 = 6$. This important relationship will be looked at in Book 3 in the form:

If $\frac{6}{3} = 2$, then $\frac{6}{2} = 3$, and if $\frac{a}{b} = c$, then $\frac{a}{c} = b$.

Exercise 3 revises equivalent expressions and Exercises 4 and 6 revise the ways in which we can use multiplication facts and relate them to division facts. Exercise 5 gets students to decide what calculation to perform to make the division question easier to do.

Challenging exercises

Exercise 7 formalises the ideas using algebra and Exercise 8 reinforces the idea of inverse operations. These exercises should only be completed by very confident students or by the teacher working through them with the whole class.

Problem-solving exercises

Exercise 9 shows how the ideas from the lesson can be applied to real-life problems.

For Exercise 10 get students to decide what calculation they will perform to work out the number of wooden poles. They could, for example, choose to do $2340 ÷ 15$ or $468 ÷ 3$, and so on.

Plenary

Use the question in the Plenary to check that students know how to work out the answer using the result in *Demonstration 2*.

If necessary, set further questions, such as $572 ÷ ·23$.

Homework

Make sure that all students either know the six-times table or have access to a written table. This exercise is not a test of memory but a check that students can use a set of known facts to work out further facts.

Number and Algebra

Page 44 Powers and roots

Goals

In this lesson students will be introduced to the economical notation for powers and roots so that they will feel comfortable in using it in Book 3. Links and connections are made with ideas that students already know well, such as factors and prime numbers. Practice is provided in identifying factors of a number, listing all the integer factors, recognising 'proper' factors, picking out common factors and the highest common factor, and expressing a large number as the product of prime factors. All this provides the background to becoming comfortable with powers and roots (the latter being based on the idea of repeated factors).

Research has shown that students invariably want to give a single numerical answer to any question. When asked to 'simplify $2 \times 2 \times 2 \times 2 \times 2$' they prefer to evaluate the expression as 32 rather than simplify it as 2^5. However, they are far less likely to be tempted to do this when faced with the request to simplify $89 \times 89 \times 89$ (*Essential exercise 1*) since the evaluation involves difficult multiplication, or reading a six-figure number on a calculator.

Similarly, students are often uncomfortable giving an answer using letters. When asked to simplify $x \times x \times x$ they would much rather assume a value for x and evaluate the expression. They need practice in giving answers using letters and notation, and we recommend that you use **Worksheet 15** for students who need more time to get used to this idea.

Starter

Use question (1) to revise the idea of a factor, and alert students to the assumption that in such a question we are looking for whole-number factors. Clarify that 'all the factors' includes unity and the number itself.

The numbers under consideration in question (2) are the same as in question (1). This, of course, is deliberate, being an effective way of clarifying what are the 'proper factors' (excluding unity and the number itself).

Question (3) requires that students be able to identify factors that are common to both terms.

Demonstration 1

Inspect the number 2520. Work through the method of identifying the prime factors of 2520 systematically, as shown in the demonstration. Begin by searching for the smallest possible prime factor (2), then look for the next prime (3), and so on. Use the vocabulary: *I can see that 2 is a factor of 2520 (it is even); I can find the other factor by dividing by the factor 2. The other factor is 1260. Any factor of 1260 is also a factor of 2520. I can see that 2 is a factor of 1260 (it is even) …*

The prime factors of 2520 are 2, 3, 5 and 7. We can write the number 2520 as a product of its prime factors like this:
$2 \times 2 \times 2 \times 3 \times 3 \times 5 \times 7$
This product can be simplified using index notation
$2^3 \times 3^2 \times 5^1 \times 7^1$

Now inspect 2700 and identify its prime factors. Write the number as a product of its prime factors.
$2700 = 2 \times 2 \times 3 \times 3 \times 3 \times 5 \times 5 = 2^2 \times 3^3 \times 5^2$

We have expressed 2520 and 2700 as products of their prime factors. Inspect $2^3 \times 3^2 \times 5 \times 7$ and $2^2 \times 3^3 \times 5^2$, and look for common factors. We can see 2^2 in both numbers, and we can see 3^2 and 5 in both numbers. The highest common factor is therefore $2^2 \times 3^2 \times 5$.

Demonstration 2

The demonstration shows various ways of expressing 36 as the product of two proper factors. One of the expressions is especially interesting because the two factors are the same (it has a repeated factor). The interesting expression is $36 = 6 \times 6$ and this can be written $36 = 6^2$.
We say *'thirty-six equals six to the power of two'* (6 is the base; 2 is the index); we also say *'thirty-six equals six squared'*.

When we know 'thirty-six equals six to the power of two' we can change the subject of the sentence and say: *'six equals the square root of thirty-six'* and write:
$6 = \sqrt{36}$
Look at the graph in *Demonstration 2*.
Read the title of the graph: $y = \sqrt{x}$ or $y = x^{\frac{1}{2}}$.
Look at the point (4, 2). The graph is a hint that $\sqrt{4} = 2$. It is also a hint that $2^2 = 4$. Look at the point (2, 1·41). This is a hint that $\sqrt{2} = 1·41$; it is also a hint that $1·41^2 = 2$.

The graph enables us to change the subject of the sentence. Use the graph for a variety of examples of changing the subject of the sentence. Enable students to use a calculator to check the evidence from the graph.

Number and Algebra

Number and Algebra: **Powers and roots**

Worked examples

Discuss the instructions 'evaluate', 'calculate' and 'calculate the value of' as expecting a numerical answer that is the result of a calculation. The instruction 'estimate' expects the student to use any available information to work out a value of an expression that is the best possible with the given information. Compare these with the instruction 'simplify' as a requirement to use mathematical symbols or notation to write the expression in its simplest possible form.

You can see how difficult this is for students to understand when you see the range of actions you may take as a response to the instruction 'Simplify'. 'Simplify a fraction' means 'reduce the size of the numbers in a fraction by dividing the numerator and denominator by their common factors'. 'Simplify an algebraic expression' means 'collect together any like terms'. 'Simplify the product of a set of numbers' means 'use index notation to reduce the number of items in the list'.

Essential exercises

The first exercise provides practice in using index notation to simplify a product where all the numbers are identical. The second exercise moves on to considering index notation to simplify expressions where the factors are of more than one value. In both exercises stress the use of the instruction 'simplify'.

Exercise 3 instructs students to work out the numbers by recognising that the index notation requires multiplication. A single value is wanted for each number in the sequence. Extend the exercise by asking students to give the next three terms in each sequence and then to work out the nth term for each sequence. The first is straightforward 2^n, but the second sequence provides a challenge. The nth term in this case is 5^{6-n}.

Using index notation for the decimal system provides a good introduction to writing numbers in standard index form, and to the use of the negative index. Exercise 4 is relatively easy because students can complete the headings using prior knowledge and number patterns. The importance of the exercise is to make the link between the accepted headings for decimal numbers and the index form of the heading.

The decimal system is so familiar to us that we often accept it without question. Studying a different system, such as the binary system, is one way of making the ideas more explicit. Exercises 5 and 6 give some practice in moving between the two systems.

Exercises 7 and 8 introduce the different notations for roots. We want students to become familiar with both the root sign and the fractional index form. Although the latter is often not introduced at this stage, it is more consistent with the whole number index form that students use regularly.

Challenging exercises

The *Essential exercises* asked students to simplify expressions involving products of numbers. Exercise 9 introduces the idea of simplifying an expression that already contains numbers written in index form. You will need to demonstrate these ideas to students before setting this exercise. Write out in longhand the expression $3^2 \times 3^5 = 3 \times 3 \times 3 \times 3 \times 3 \times 3 \times 3 = 3^7$ to establish that: $x^a \times x^b = x^{a+b}$.

Exercise 10 introduces students to the idea of writing numbers in standard index form. This will be covered extensively in Book 3 but it is useful to introduce it here so that students understand how to interpret large and small numbers in their calculator display.

Graph plotters enable students to study topics that were previously inaccessible at this stage of their learning. We often hear people discussing 'exponential growth' and Exercise 11 provides the opportunity for students to explore the meaning of this statement. Use graphical calculators or a computer graphics software package to generate and investigate these graphs.

Problem-solving exercises

Exercise 12 is an application of powers. Exercise 13 is a well-known investigation called 'The Towers of Hanoi'. Let students use discs to try out the least number of moves needed, and get them to record their results in diagrams and tables.

Plenary

Work with the whole class to identify the full set of prime factors of 1251 and get the students to write the number as a product of these prime factors in its simplest form.

Consider $(\sqrt{x})^2$ and $\sqrt{x^2}$. The first expression must give a positive result since the number has to be squared. In the second expression the square root can result in a positive or a negative number. However, some mathematicians use the convention that unless stated otherwise the positive square root is always considered.

Homework

Set the *Homework* as a 'finding out' exercise and get students to report back at the beginning of the next lesson. Make sure that all students record the correct answers to keep as a reference.

Number and Algebra

Conventions for answers

Page 48

Goals

This lesson deals with a variety of conventions for writing answers enshrined in well-known instructions such as 'Give your answer to 2 d.p.' or 'Give your answer to 3 sig. figs.', or 'Write your answer in standard index form'.

Instructions like 'Give your answer to 2 d.p.' or 'Give your answer to 3 sig. figs.' require, of course, an approximation culled from a more precise answer. The instruction 'Write your answer in standard index form' does not in itself require an approximation: it requires that an equivalent form must be supplied for an answer that has been calculated to an already decided level of accuracy.

Worksheet 16 provides further practice with straightforward examples for those students who need more assistance with this topic.

Starter

Look at the decimal number. It is written to 9 decimal places, or, in this case, 10 significant figures. Ask:

> *How many decimal places are shown in red?*
> *If the number is truncated after the last red digit, how many decimal places could you round the number to?*
> *How many significant figures are there if the number is truncated after the last red digit?*
> *What number is in the third decimal place and what is its value?*
> *What is the most significant figure?*
> *What are the two most significant figures?*
> *etc.*

Demonstration 1

The first two statements are provided simply to illustrate the inappropriateness of using measurements with a large number of decimal places for everyday things; and the equally inappropriate use of 'about 5 cm' for a vital component in a complex piece of engineering. This can be further illustrated by citing the not untypical student response to a maths 'problem', 'I want to cut a 5 metre plank into seven pieces to make it easy to store the wood for my fire. How long will each piece of wood be? Answer: 0·7142857 metres (by using a calculator).

The diagram is a way of making clear what we are doing when we are dealing with decimal places and significant figures.

On the board, sketch a neutral window (it simply has an arbitrary number of empty frames) and then insert a 'decimal point' to allow for a specified number of decimal places. Then, with a frame that allows one decimal place (as in the first window in the demonstration) fit in the supplied number 4·571283069 and show it omits many figures. Our job is to write the number that would appear in the window, but it needs to give as good an idea as possible of the actual known value of the number. This requires looking beyond the edge of the frame and reading as a vulgar fraction what is 'beyond' the window. We can see $\frac{57}{100}$ which is closer to $\frac{60}{100}$ than it is to $\frac{50}{100}$ which means it is closer to $\frac{6}{10}$ than it is to $\frac{5}{10}$. So, the answer we give using this window is 4·6 (to 1 d.p.) Make it clear that the abbreviation d.p. is routinely used for 'decimal place' or 'decimal places'.

Invite individual students to draw on the board as you speak:

> *Draw a neutral window* [cultivate the confidence to draw any number of frames: it can always be adjusted later!].
> *Modify your window to show 3 d.p.* [the student marks a decimal point].

Write on the board a number such as 346·5537 for the student to write in and beyond the window; and then determine the approximation to 3 d.p. Ask about different numbers of significant figures.

Use the same number for a window prepared for 1 d.p. (first neutral, then modified) and then for a window for 2 d.p. Use a number with 4 d.p. and a window prepared for 3 d.p. and ask for an approximation to 2 d.p. (the fourth d.p. is not considered at all). Ask about different numbers of significant figures.

Discuss the convention for approximating numbers that are exactly halfway between two points on the scale. For example, 3·25 is written as 3·3 to 1 d.p.

Demonstration 2

When students use calculators to perform calculations, the answers in the display may be given in standard index form. The way in which this is shown varies between different makes of calculator. First, students need to know

 **I See Maths** Book 2

Number and Algebra

Number and Algebra: Conventions for answers

what is meant by standard index form, and then they need to know how to interpret the calculator display. This topic is often left until a later stage, but the delay can cause difficulties for students using calculators for very large or very small numbers. They may also encounter numbers written in standard index form in other curriculum areas.

Write on the board a range of numerically similar numbers:
·049362   ·49362   4·9362   49·362   493·62   4936·2

> *I want to examine these values of x to find which one has a value greater than or equal to one, and less than ten.* [Identify:]
> ·049362   ·49362   (4·9362)   49·362   493·62   4936·2

Compare the other numbers in the list with 4·9362.
$·049362 = 4·9362 \div 100$ $·49362 = 4·9362 \div 10$
$49·362 = 4·9362 \times 10$ $493·62 = 4·9362 \times 100$
$4936·2 = 4·9362 \times 1000$

We can write these numbers using powers of 10.
$·049362 = 4·9362 \times 10^{-2}$ $·49362 = 4·9362 \times 10^{-1}$
$49·362 = 4·9362 \times 10^{1}$ $493·62 = 4·9362 \times 10^{2}$
$4936·2 = 4·9362 \times 10^{3}$

We say: '$4·9362 \times 10^{3}$ is in standard index form.'

The definition of a number x in standard index form is:
$a \times 10^{n}$ **where $1 \le a < 10$ and n is an integer.**

Look at the number 217·918.
It has the same value as $2·17918 \times 100$,
and this has the same value as $2·17918 \times 10^{2}$. This is standard index form.

Worked examples

Invite students to explain each of the worked examples and get them to copy them into their books. Check that all students can do these examples before starting the exercises.

Essential exercises

Exercises 1 to 3 provide practice in rounding numbers using words such as 'to the nearest ten' and 'to the nearest centimetre'. Students have done work like this on rounding in Book 1, pages 92–95.

Exercises 4 to 6 give practice in writing numbers to a specific number of decimal places. First they are given numbers to write to one decimal place, and then two decimal places, and then they have to do calculations before writing an approximate answer. Remind the students that they should not round numbers before performing calculations. This is a common mistake that students make. However, this leaves them with a dilemma in Exercise 6, part (h). What approximation should they use for π? Since they are told to use a calculator they should use the value for π that is stored in the calculator (discuss the fact that

this is actually an approximation to a set number of decimal places). If they do not have a scientific calculator they will have to decide how many decimal places to enter. This question can be used to revise what is meant by π and what approximations are commonly used.

Exercise 7 asks students to work out approximate answers to calculations. Invite students to explain how they do these questions on the board.

Challenging exercises

Link this work on standard index form with the previous lesson on powers. Provide lots of practice in writing numbers like this: $567·432 = 5·67432 \times 100 = 5·67432 \times 10^{2}$.

When students use a calculator to do the questions in Exercise 8 they may get the answer displayed in standard index form. However, different makes of calculator display this in different ways and you may need to spend some time discussing this.

Students looked at the result of multiplying $2^{3} \times 2^{7} \times 2^{5}$ in the previous lesson. Exercise 9 is an extension of this work. Write 9(a) on the board like this:
$1·32 \times 10^{2} \times 2·46 \times 10^{3} = 1·32 \times 2·46 \times 10^{2} \times 10^{3}$
$= 3·2472 \times 10^{5}$
And 9(b):
$3·47 \times 10^{3} \times 8·74 \times 10^{5} = 3·47 \times 8·74 \times 10^{3} \times 10^{5}$
$= 30·3278 \times 10^{8}$
$= 3·03278 \times 10^{9}$

Students can easily become confused between writing numbers to a certain number of decimal places and to a certain number of significant figures. They may also have difficulty deciding whether a zero is significant. Exercise 10 can be omitted here because the work will be covered again in Book 3.

Problem-solving exercises

Exercises 11 to 14 provide practical examples where approximation is used in maths. They are good for revision of other topics.

Plenary

Check the students' understanding of this lesson by getting them to answer the questions in the *Goals*. Select appropriate points for discussion.

Homework

This activity provides practice in converting fractions to decimals and giving an answer to a required degree of accuracy. You may need to demonstrate a similar example before setting the *Homework*.

Teacher's Notes Teacher's Notes Teacher's Notes Teacher's Notes
Teacher's Notes Teacher's Notes Teacher's Notes
Teacher's Notes Teacher's Notes Teacher's Notes
er's Notes Notes Teacher's Notes Teacher's Not

Number and Algebra

 Page 52 # Decimal fractions

Goals

Calculating the number halfway between two given numbers is relatively straightforward but very often not appreciated as one example of calculating a given ratio of an interval (that can then be added to the smaller quantity). The problem is, as so often in maths teaching, that easy examples are taught with a specific algorithm that does not generalise to more complex examples.

In dealing with 'halfway between' examples, *I See Maths* concedes to some extent to the established tendency to make $\frac{1}{2}$ most importantly 'half-way' rather than a 1 : 2 ratio. However, it is necessary to bear in mind those examples in statistics where it is necessary to estimate the value of the median when given a cumulative frequency based on grouped data – implicating the use of ratio.

Starter

The continuing concern with decimal fractions should be to ensure that students appreciate the value of each digit, and combinations of digits, in terms of vulgar fractions. Do not point to a digit and ask what is its place value. Instead ask 'How much is there here?' This requires a reply of the form 'three tenths' or 'seven hundredths' or, taken together, 'thirty-seven hundredths' – and notice this last, important form is not possible when emphasis is put on 'place value' because, while each digit has a 'place value', there is not a similar question available for a combination of digits.

One element of teaching 'place value' in *I See Maths* concerns the Arabic convention (different from the Roman development) of capitalising on the position in which digits are placed. The most important aspect in this regard is to see 462 and to know that there is 400 and there is 60 and there is 2; the actual writing of 462 is an abbreviation of $400 + 60 + 2$ in which the zeros are concealed. Similarly, 4·62 is comprised of 4 and 6 tenths and 2 hundredths, that is, 4·62 has the same value as $4 + \frac{6}{10} + \frac{2}{100}$ (having the same value as $4 + ·6 + ·02$).

Demonstration 1

Indicate each of the digits in part (a) and consolidate:

> There is seventy here; there is two here; there is eight tenths here; there is two hundredths here; there is seven thousandths here.
> There is seventy here; there is two here; there is eight tenths here; there is three hundredths here.

Also indicate combinations of digits, so:

> There is 728 tenths here; there is 27 thousandths here; there is 82 hundredths here; there is 72 827 thousandths here; and so on.

Calculation of a number that is halfway between two given numbers is deliberately represented in part (b) as the smaller number plus half the difference between the two numbers. Do not emphasise 'counting on' because this is un-mathematical as it does not lead readily to similar problems in algebra. Equally, it is preferable not to calculate the mean of the two numbers because, although this is mathematically valid and applicable to algebraic quantities, it does not lend itself to the other extension of, for instance, finding the number that is one fifth of the way from the smaller number to the larger number.

Ideally, calculation of $\frac{1}{2}$ of 1·06 would be recognised as the ratio 1 : 2 so that for every two we can see we replace with 1. This, then, would be consistent with the way we will in due course view, say, $\frac{2}{5}$ of 1·06.

Demonstration 2

Establish that $3 ÷ 4$ has the same value as $\frac{3}{4}$ by using cups.

> $3 ÷ 4$ means put 3 cups on the maths table; how many piles of 4 cups can we see? None – but there is something there. Compare this pile of three cups with a pile of four cups; it is smaller; it is a bit of a pile; it is a fraction of a pile; it is $\frac{3}{4}$ of a pile.

Now use calculators to calculate $3 ÷ 4$ to establish the decimal 0·75 has the same value as $\frac{3}{4}$. Next, use calculators to calculate the decimals in the demonstration, taking the opportunity to revise '2 d.p.'; '3d.p.' and so on.

Emphasise that 'point 6 recurring' is an accurate value for $\frac{2}{3}$ but ·666 666 666 666 666 666 666 666 666 666 666 7 is only approximate. Demonstrate how we write this as ·$\dot{6}$. You can find additional examples on recurring decimals in **Worksheet 17**.

Teacher's Notes Teacher's Notes Teacher's Notes Teacher's Notes Teach
Teacher's Notes Teacher's Not
Teacher's Notes Teacher's N

Number and Algebra: **Decimal fractions**

Worked examples

Demonstrate how to write the decimal for $1 \div 11$ as $\cdot 0\dot{9}$, indicating two repeating digits, and as $\cdot 091$ to three decimal places.

Essential exercises

When we consider the size or magnitude of a number we are talking about the 'cardinality' of a number. When we place numbers in order using a number line or scale we are considering 'ordinality'. When we order numbers on a number line we say that if a number x is to the left of a number y then x is 'less than' y, and we write '$x < y$'. This distinction between cardinality and ordinality is important when we consider negative numbers. Negative six is bigger than negative two (when we consider their magnitudes), whereas it is less than negative two ($^-6 < {}^-2$) when the numbers are placed on a number line.

All of the *Essential exercises* are about considering numbers that are placed in order. You may need to produce a number line indicating positive and negative numbers to assist the students. They may need some assistance for Exercise 1, part (e). $^-2\cdot 9$ is to the left of $^-2\cdot 4$ and so $^-2\cdot 9 < {}^-2\cdot 4$.

Students may be able to work out that $44\cdot 5$ is halfway between 42 and 47 intuitively. However, insist that they write down the full workings with this example so that they can do the harder examples.

$47 - 42 = 5$

$5 \div 2 = 2\cdot 5$

$42 + 2\cdot 5 = 44\cdot 5$

Exercise 3 follows on from Exercise 2, provided the students have been following the steps above.

There are an infinite number of answers to Exercise 4. Discuss the different ways of working out the two limits. Students could select the difference between $0\cdot 35$ and each limit and use a calculator to work them out. They will quickly begin to generate negative numbers for the left-hand limit.

At first glance some students may think that there are no numbers between $3\cdot 23$ and $3\cdot 24$. Mark two points on a number line and consider zooming in and looking at different points. Discuss several possibilities with the class before getting them to do the question.

Ask students to complete Exercise 6 mentally first, and then to check their answers using a calculator.

Discuss finite and recurring decimals before setting Exercise 7.

Challenging exercises

Invite students to explain their methods for Exercise 8. Discuss whether converting the fractions to decimals is quicker than using equivalent fractions.

Although students are not tested on their understanding of rational and irrational numbers these days, it is a fascinating subject for discussion. They have already met the number π and they will meet the roots of two and three when they encounter Pythagoras' theorem, so these numbers cannot be avoided. Use a computer to generate more decimal places of these numbers.

Writing recurring decimals as fractions requires a simple operation. Consider the number of recurring digits. Look at Exercise 10, part (b).
Let the number be x. This number has two recurring digits so multiply the number by one hundred to get $100x$.

$$100x = 45\cdot \dot{4}\dot{5} \quad \text{so} \quad 100x - x = 45\cdot \dot{4}\dot{5} - \cdot \dot{4}\dot{5}$$
$$= 45$$
$$\text{or} \qquad 99x = 45$$
$$\text{hence} \qquad x = \tfrac{45}{99} = \tfrac{5}{11}$$

Encourage students to write the answer to Exercise 11 as $26\cdot 5 \leq 27 < 27\cdot 5$ to indicate up to but not including $27\cdot 5$ km.

Problem-solving exercises

Exercise 12 is an investigation. Students will need scientific calculators or a computer in order to obtain sufficient decimal places to see the patterns. Exercises 13 and 14 apply what students have learnt to real-life problems.

Plenary

Revisit the *Goals* to check understanding, and use the points for discussion in the *Plenary* to challenge the students' thinking.

Homework

The *Homework* is a continuation of the investigation in Exercise 12.

Letts I See Maths Book 2

Number and Algebra

Reasoning with negative numbers

Page 56

Goals

Two very important results are represented in the demonstrations in this lesson: the product of a negative number and a positive number; and the quotient of two negative numbers. This work assumes that students have completed the work in Book 1 on negative numbers, (pages 52–63) and can confidently do the *Review* of negative numbers in the first part of Book 2. If not, then you will have to begin with that work before attempting this lesson. Additional examples are provided on **Worksheets 18, 19** and **20**.

The meaning of, for instance $2 \times 3 = 6$, is very specifically defined in *I See Maths* as 'we start by putting two cups on the maths table; do the same thing lots of times; do it 3 times; we see 6 cups on the maths table'. Furthermore, the lessons establish that, knowing both $2 \times 3 = 6$ and that multiplication is commutative, we can immediately and confidently assert $3 \times 2 = 6$ (without doing any additional work).

The use of the cups to generate $2 \times 3 = 6$ must be thought of as reasoning. The application of the commutative law is also reasoning. Now look how powerful this reasoning can be. We can reason that $\frac{1}{2} \times 3 = 1\frac{1}{2}$ (put a half-cup on the maths table; do the same thing lots of times; do it 3 times; we see $1\frac{1}{2}$ cups). But the commutative law immediately tells us that $3 \times \frac{1}{2} = 1\frac{1}{2}$ which involves putting 3 cups on the maths table $\frac{1}{2}$ a time. And the beauty of maths is that we know that just a half an action was made (it really was!) but we do not have to fuss about what half an action looks like. One of the purposes of teaching maths is to create in students the disposition to accept this without fussing. It is a key aim of teaching maths to prevent students resorting to the literal and to learn to trust the symbols.

The same reasoning applies to $^-2 \times 3 = {}^-6$. (Put negative two on the table; do the same thing three times; we see negative six.) Further, our trusty ally the commutative law then allows us confidently and accurately to assert that $3 \times {}^-2 = {}^-6$. And we do not turn a hair at the thought of walking to the maths table $^-2$ times!

We have a similar opportunity for reasoning with $^-6 \div {}^-2 = 3$. We put $^-6$ on the maths table; look at it and wonder how many piles of $^-2$ we can see; whereupon we count 3 of those piles. Of course, $^-6 \div {}^-2 = 3$ carries implicit information: that $^-6 \div 3 = {}^-2$ (with all its marvellous symbolic implications).

The disposition to trust the symbols will lead us in Book 3 to discuss the result $^-1 \times {}^-1 = 1$ and to use this startling result as an introduction to formal proof.

Starter

Our determined approach to reasoning begins by revising such examples as $0 - 1 = {}^-1$, $0 - {}^-1 = 1$, and $3 - {}^-2 = 5$, because this practises recourse to a well established result and reasoning from it. The result $^-1 + 1 = 0$ can be seen immediately from the idea of $^-1$ being a hole in the ground and 1 being a lump of earth: together they have the same value as zero. This is, of course, analogous to mathematical axioms that assert that there is an inverse of 1 (such that under the operation of addition, 1 and its inverse yield the identity for addition).

Rather than defining the inverse of unity totally theoretically, *I See Maths* provides students with an enduringly useful metaphoric picture of the nature of this inverse (the 'garden story' introduced in Book 1). Beware of misinterpretation here. The 'garden story' is not provided as a real-life context, nor is it an analogy for negative numbers like temperature or lifts in blocks of flats or credits and debits in bank accounts.

Look at question (1) in the *Starter.* Use cards with 1 and $^-1$ written on them.

> $^-1$ *How much is there here? Negative one.*
> 1   *How much is there here? One.*
> $^-1 + 1$ *How much is there here? Zero.*

1(a) *Look at zero.* [See this as one and negative one, or any equal number of ones and negative ones.] *Take away one. We get negative one.* $0 - 1 = {}^-1$
1(b) *Look at zero. Take away negative one. We get one.* $0 - {}^-1 = 1$

1(c)–(f) *It follows from $^-1 + 1 = 0$ that, for instance, $^-3 + 3 = 0$ and $^-1\cdot72 + 1\cdot72 = 0$.*

2(a) *Put three on the maths table; remove ... ah! We need to remove negative two.* [Find two zeros and remove two negative ones leaving two ones.] *We get five.*

Number and Algebra: **Reasoning with negative numbers**

Demonstration 1

Before demonstrating the commutative law for negative numbers you may need to establish its truth with positive numbers. Demonstrate that $2 \times 4 = 4 \times 2 = 8$. Tell students that this is the commutative law and that all multiplication of numbers obeys this law.

There is no physical way in which we can demonstrate multiplying by a negative number. The beauty of maths is that it goes beyond real life into an imaginary world. Some mathematical facts are the result of logical thinking. Since all other real numbers obey the commutative law then we assume that negative numbers also obey the commutative law.

Use negative-one cards to demonstrate the actions for $^-2 \times 4 = ^-8$. Pick up two negative one cards from the resource table and place them on the maths table. Do it four times altogether. You can see negative eight.

> Is $^-2 \times 4$ the same as $4 \times ^-2$? It has the same value but a different appearance. This is the commutative law.

Once this law has been established we can deduce further facts.

> $^-2 \times 4 = 4 \times ^-2 = ^-8$
> How much is there here ($^-2 \times 4$)? Negative eight.
> Look at negative eight and wonder how many negative twos you can see. Four.
> Look at negative eight and wonder how many fours you can see. Negative two.

Any multiplication fact generates two division facts.

Demonstration 2

The result $^-8 \div ^-2 = 4$ has been derived in *Demonstration 1* from the product $^-2 \times 4 = ^-8$. In this demonstration the same result is perceived directly from our definition of division.

Throughout *I See Maths* division is always visualised as 'look and wonder how many'. Students have looked at eight cups and wondered how many piles of two cups they can see. $8 \div 2 = 4$. They have looked at eight fifth cards and wondered how many piles of two fifth cards they can see. $\frac{8}{5} \div \frac{2}{5} = 4$. In this demonstration they look at eight negative-one cards and wonder how many piles of two negative-one cards (i.e. piles of negative two) they can see. (Four) $^-8 \div ^-2 = 4$. It is this continuity with the visualisation of division that assists the students with this work.

Repeat similar demonstrations as many times as necessary to assist students. Invite students to help with the demonstrations so that they can perform the actions as well as participate in the visualisation.

Worked examples

These two examples remind students that division is the inverse operation of multiplication. Practise with some easy number examples before showing students the algebraic example.

Essential exercises

Students will need to be familiar with the 'garden story' as told in Book 1 (pages 52–63) to do Exercise 1. Lumps of earth and holes in the ground are used as metaphors for one and negative one to demonstrate that their sum is zero.

Exercises 2 and 3 give practice in the addition of positive and negative numbers.

Exercise 4 reinforces the commutative law for multiplication whilst Exercise 5 reinforces division as the inverse operation of multiplication. Exercise 6 provides practice in dividing negative numbers.

Challenging exercises

Exercises 7 and 8 extend the ideas into algebra. You may wish to leave these exercises until the students have completed some of the algebra lessons.

Exercise 9 introduces the idea of multiplying a negative number by a negative number. Once again, this is not an operation that can be demonstrated with physical actions. We have to use the distributive law to find an equivalent expression. There are many different ways of doing this. For example:
$^-3 \times ^-5 = ^-3 \times (0 - 5)$ or $^-3 \times (1 - 6)$ or $^-3 \times (5 - 10)$

Problem-solving exercises

These exercises use very simple maths but require a good comprehension of the English language. Help the students read the questions and unpack what is being asked.

Plenary

Go through all the questions in the *Goals*. Ask the students to write the answers on the board and explain their working. Act with cards to reinforce the answers.

Homework

Once again the students must have completed the work in Book 1 before attempting to do this activity. They can make up some questions of their own to illustrate.

Number and Algebra

Page 60 # Reasoning with fractions 1

Goals

In *I See Maths* there is a very clear and deliberate use of fractions in two guises. In dealing with sums like $\frac{3}{5} + \frac{1}{5}$, differences like $\frac{3}{5} - \frac{1}{5}$, products like $\frac{2}{5} \times 3$, or quotients like $\frac{6}{5} \div \frac{2}{5}$, each fraction is thought of as an object (as a noun): it is a small part of a cup. When a fraction is placed in the context of $\frac{3}{5}$ of 20, then $\frac{3}{5}$ is treated as part of the instruction 'replace with a smaller number of cups' – it is implicated in an imperative verb. It is the context that gives the clue as to whether, say, $\frac{3}{5}$ is a noun or an imperative verb. We are used to this ambiguity in normal speech. The word 'run' can be either a noun or an imperative verb; it depends on the context in which it is used (e.g. 'I went for a run,' and 'I run every day.').

There are other aspects of reasoning with fractions that are often ignored, being most often taught as rules, algorithms or tricks. One fairly innocent example is in dealing with equivalent fractions (when some effort is usually made to enable students to make sense of the process). Multiplying or simplifying fractions by using cancelling (dividing by any common factors in the numerators and denominators), can be taught without any noticeable effort to give it a meaning. But the method is pregnant with possibilities in terms of ensuring students practise mathematical reasoning. This lesson treats equivalent fractions, multiplication of fractions and cancelling as potent sites for developing reasoning skills.

Before starting this topic you may like to revise addition and subtraction of fractions, using **Worksheet 21**, and some straightforward multiplication using **Worksheet 22**.

Starter

Revise the meaning and calculation of equivalent fractions. The comparison represented by the two sticks shown in question 1 is 'smaller'. In the form shown, we call the comparison 2 to 3; or 2 : 3; or $\frac{2}{3}$. The justification for calling it 'two to three', in its various forms, is that we are measuring the two sticks with a small stick that we take to be 1 (unity). However, if we now choose to call that same stick 2 the comparison becomes 'four to six' (4 to 6; 4 : 6; $\frac{4}{6}$). The same two sticks were used for the comparison so $\frac{2}{3}$ and $\frac{4}{6}$ have the same value (different appearance). Re-naming the stick that was initially known as 1 yields the fractions that are equivalent to $\frac{2}{3}$.

Faced with question 2(a), $\frac{2}{3} = \frac{}{21}$, we reason: *The stick was called 3, but we now want to call it 21 – so we are replacing every unit with seven units. This means that the other stick (which we previously called 2) is now called 14. The comparison becomes 14 : 21 or $\frac{14}{21}$.*

Demonstration 1

Demonstration 1 introduces a visual meaning for cancelling (division by common factors) based on reasoning from earlier axioms. The illustration shows the successive calculation: $\frac{1}{2}$ of $\frac{2}{3}$ of 6. It is an axiom of *I See Maths* that $\frac{2}{3}$ of 6 means 'for every three you can see replace with two'. This is shown with cups in the diagram. At this stage we can see that the value of $\frac{2}{3}$ of 6 is 4; but continue seeing it as 2 and 2 on the maths table. If we now carry out the next instruction $-\frac{1}{2}$ of $-$ we can actually see that the 2 and the 2 that must be replaced by 1 and 1. So the outcome of these successive operations is 1 and 1, or 2. We see that $\frac{1}{2}$ of $\frac{2}{3}$ of 6 = 2.

Point out that the six cups with which we started were partitioned as 3 and 3. Each 3 was initially replaced with 2; and each 2 was then replaced with 1. So where we started out with 3s on the maths table we finished with 1s. The overall effect of our successive operations was to replace each 3 with 1. (Note that this 'straight through' effect is only possible because the 'replacing number' of the first instruction is equal to the 'starting number' of the second instruction – **2** : 3 followed by 1 : **2**. Finding $\frac{1}{5}$ of $\frac{2}{3}$ of 15 would require a little more rearrangement of the cups.)

Mathematically, the double instruction $\frac{1}{2}$ of $\frac{2}{3}$ of 6 has the same value as the single instruction $\frac{1}{3}$ of 6.

Suppose now we did not find $\frac{1}{2}$ of $\frac{2}{3}$ with six cups, but we did it with an unspecified number of cups. Illustrate this by using a hand movement to indicate an imaginary spreading of cups on an imaginary maths table. Then when we partition all those cups into 3s (no matter how many!) what we do is replace each 3 with 2 (no matter how many!) and we then replace every 2 with 1 (no matter how many!) So, in effect, we have arranged lots of 3s on the maths table and, in due course, replaced them with the same number of 1s. Of course, that is what is achieved by finding $\frac{1}{3}$ of that unspecified number of cups.

We can see that '$\frac{1}{2}$ of $\frac{2}{3}$' of has the same effect as '$\frac{1}{3}$ of' (no matter how many cups we start with!).

Number and Algebra

This whole process is typical of advanced mathematical reasoning. It is an example of a core disposition in being mathematical: *trusting the symbols and talking in general terms* (i.e. 'no matter how many'). Persevere with enabling students to engage in this reasoning.

You may decide to invite individual students to demonstrate a range of specific examples ($\frac{1}{2}$ of $\frac{2}{3}$ of 12; $\frac{1}{2}$ of $\frac{2}{3}$ of 3; $\frac{1}{2}$ of $\frac{2}{3}$ of 18) but in each case make them articulate the generality of what they are doing. And beware! Our aim is to enable them to reason with the generality of an unspecified number of cups; we want to avoid any encouragement to think that because it works with several examples, it means it works with all examples. Using specific examples beyond the introductory one does carry dangers (one of which was outlined above). The only purpose of this demonstration is to practise the act of replacement (introduced and consolidated in Book 1 pages 40–51).

Now write a number of combined operations on the board:
$\frac{5}{7}$ of $\frac{7}{39}$ of ... $\frac{8}{17}$ of $\frac{17}{11}$ of ... $\frac{56}{13}$ of $\frac{13}{671}$ of ...
(note the repetition of numbers again).

Enable invited students to reason that, for instance:

> *When we see $\frac{5}{7}$ of $\frac{7}{39}$ of ... it means we put some cups on the maths table. We group them into 39s. Each time we see 39 we replace it with 7. Then, each time we see 7 we replace it with 5, so everywhere we started with 39 we have eventually replaced it with 5. We can see $\frac{5}{7}$ of $\frac{7}{39} = \frac{5}{39}$.*

Of course, students will rapidly spot the pattern and there is no harm in that; but it is even more reason for insisting they articulate its meaning. The aim is to teach reasoning and understanding as a long-term contribution to making sense of algorithms.

Demonstration 2

In *Demonstration 1* we concentrated on products of fractions where the numerator of the second fraction was identical to the denominator of the first fraction. *Demonstration 2* extends this by dealing with any fractions; and it implicates the need to deal with equivalent fractions (which is why this is rehearsed in the Starter).

Write $\frac{3}{5}$ on the board. Think sticks. Smaller. Every time you see 5 cups replace with 3 cups.

Suppose we have 5 5 5, we replace it with 3 3 3.

Now look at the 3 3 3 and consider $\frac{5}{3}$.
We replace 3 3 3 with 5 5 5.
Which is what we started with.

Doing a $\frac{5}{3}$ job undoes what a $\frac{3}{5}$ job does.

$\frac{5}{3}$ is the multiplicative inverse of $\frac{3}{5}$.

$\frac{3}{5}$ is the multiplicative inverse of $\frac{5}{3}$.

Practise some multiplicative inverses:
$\frac{7}{11}$ and ... are multiplicative inverses.
$\frac{17}{9}$ and ... are multiplicative inverses.
$\frac{37}{5 \cdot 911}$ and ... are multiplicative inverses.
93 : 100 and ... are multiplicative inverses.

Use a calculator to find:
$\frac{3}{4} \times \frac{4}{3}$ $\frac{5}{8} \times \frac{8}{5}$ $\frac{5}{100} \times \frac{100}{5}$ $\frac{93}{100} \times \frac{100}{93}$

Worked example

These examples follow directly from the demonstrations.

Essential exercises

Exercises 1 to 3 replicate the demonstrations. By the time the students have completed Exercise 3 they will probably have noticed that $\frac{3}{8} \times \frac{7}{11} = \frac{3 \times 7}{8 \times 11}$. Discuss this result and check the truth with some further examples. Students can now use either method for working out the answers to Exercise 4.

Work through some of the questions in Exercise 5 and demonstrate the need to convert the fractions to vulgar fractions before performing the multiplication.

Exercise 6 demonstrates multiplicative inverses.

Challenging exercises

Exercises 7 and 8 extend the previous work into algebra and harder examples.

Problem-solving exercises

Exercises 9 and 10 provide applications of this work on fractions.

Plenary

Check that students can do the questions in the *Goals*. Discuss the generalisation $\frac{a}{b} \times \frac{c}{d} = \frac{ac}{bd}$.

Homework

Multiplication is often seen by students to be an operation that 'makes numbers bigger'. Get students to explain their answer and illustrate it with some examples.

Teacher's Notes Teacher's Notes Teacher's Notes Teacher's Notes Teacher's Notes Teacher's
Teacher's Notes Teacher's Notes Teacher's Notes Teacher's Notes Teacher's Notes
Teacher's Notes Teacher's Notes Teacher's Notes Teacher's Notes Teacher's Notes

Number and Algebra

Reasoning with fractions 2

Page 64

Goals

Division of a vulgar fraction by a vulgar faction is famously mysterious. Generations of students have either responded in resigned fashion to the requirement to 'change divide to multiply and invert the divisor'; or given up. In fact, division of vulgar fractions is rather straightforward when $6 \div 2 = 3$ is interpreted as, *'Six cups on the table; look at it and wonder how many piles of two can you see. Three.'*

This visualisation of division was well established in Book 1 and leads to $8 \div 3 = 2\frac{2}{3}$, where the remaining pile of two cups is recognised, by comparing it with three cups, as 'smaller: 2 : 3' (see *Starter*, below). This approach was extended in Book 1 to establish that, say, $\frac{8}{10} \div \frac{2}{10} = 4$ (see Book 1, page 37). The importance of this work was in emphasising that the essence of division (look at it and wonder how many ….) can be applied to fractions in the same way as to whole numbers.

At that stage we were concerned solely with this essence and deliberately focused on fractions with the same **denomination**. Notice that we refer to the denomination (sevenths) because it is this, not the **denominator** (seven), which carries the important idea. This approach is revised in *Demonstration 1* and extended in *Demonstration 2* so that quotients of fractions with different denominations can be calculated by using an equivalent calculation.

Starter

Recall our introduction to ratio using sticks (see Book 1, page 40) and the practice of this idea with cups (Book 1, page 44, *Demonstration 1*). Use cups to act the quotient $8 \div 3 = 2\frac{2}{3}$ by putting eight cups on the maths table; looking and wondering how many piles of three cups we can see. Carefully establish that we are making piles of 3 cups:

This is a pile of 3 cups; this is a pile of 3 cups; this is a pile of … ? This is not a pile of three cups. Look at this pile; compare it to a proper size pile; it is smaller; this [2 cups] is not a proper size pile; it is a bit of a pile; it is a fraction of a pile; the comparison is 2 : 3; it is two thirds of a pile. We have 2 piles and we have $\frac{2}{3}$ of a pile. We have $2\frac{2}{3}$.

Practise with other examples, for instance:
(a) $8 \div 5 =$ (b) $5 \div 8 =$ (c) $101 \div 99 =$ (d) $93 \div 87 =$

Demonstration 1

Use cards to demonstrate $\frac{6}{7} \div \frac{2}{7} = 3$ and then do a variety of examples (merely referring to cards rather than using them). For example:

(a) $\frac{6}{7} \div \frac{3}{7} =$, (b) $\frac{6}{13} \div \frac{2}{13} =$, (c) $\frac{12}{87} \div \frac{4}{87} =$,
(d) $1 \div \frac{2}{5} =$, (e) $4 \div \frac{2}{3} =$

Invite students to invent and calculate similar quotients. Examine attempts like $\frac{8}{7} \div \frac{3}{7}$ and put them on one side for the moment because they are not of the same type as those discussed so far (having an integer as the value). Then deliberately introduce $\frac{8}{5} \div \frac{3}{5}$ and establish its value as $2\frac{2}{3}$ by actually using the cards. This involves comparing $\frac{2}{5}$ to $\frac{3}{5}$ and noting that the comparison is 2 : 3.

Demonstration 2

The four calculations in this demonstration each illustrate a quotient involving two vulgar fractions of different denominations. It must be impressed upon students that it is not possible to calculate the value of the given quotients; but it is possible to select an equivalent calculation. The first quotient will require one fraction re-written to give an integral value. The second, also, will need one fraction re-written, but this time the quotient is not an integer. The third requires both fractions to be re-written for the equivalent calculation to be calculable; and so will the fourth, but to begin with it needs the mixed numbers to be re-written as improper fractions. The layout of the demonstration is designed to emphasise the similarity of the four calculations.

We need to look carefully at writing fractions with a specified denomination. Book 1 (page 30) contained exercises that were to be done by thinking of the fraction as a bit of a cup (as a noun). Later lessons in Book 1 introduced the related idea of a vulgar fraction as a comparison by 'thinking of sticks' (Book 1, page 40). This meant that the fraction $\frac{2}{3}$ could now be thought of as a comparison represented by two sticks, one of length 2 and the other of length 3. But the length of each stick is known only in relation to a standard stick that is said to be of length 1. If instead, we let the standard stick be 4 then the comparison of the same two sticks (initially 2 to 3) is now seen to be 8 : 12 (same value : different appearance). This is a method of generating equivalent fractions.

Number and Algebra

Look at $\frac{3}{7} \div \frac{3}{14}$. The two fractions have different denominations. Look at $\frac{3}{7}$ and 'think sticks'. If we measure each stick with the standard stick re-named as 2, the comparison 3 : 7 becomes 6 : 14. So $\frac{3}{7} \div \frac{3}{14}$ has the same value as $\frac{6}{14} \div \frac{3}{14}$, which equals 2.

Use this approach with each of the four calculations.

Discuss the process of writing down equivalent fractions. Show that $\frac{3}{7}$ has the same value as

$$\frac{3 \times 2}{7 \times 2} = \frac{6}{14}$$

and use a number of examples as in:

Which of these has the same value as $\frac{3}{11}$?

$$\frac{3 \times 2}{11 \times 2} \qquad \frac{3 \times 2}{11 \times 5} \qquad \frac{3 \times 3 \cdot 9}{11 \times 3 \cdot 9} \qquad \frac{3 \times a}{11 \times a}$$

$$\frac{3 \times a}{11 \times b} \qquad \frac{3a}{11a} \qquad \frac{3b}{11a} \qquad \frac{3e}{11e}$$

Worked examples

Work through the examples with the whole class. You may wish to leave the algebraic examples until the students have completed all the *Essential exercises.*

Essential exercises

Students may need the assistance of using cards to complete Exercise 1. The cards may be imaginary (such as those for eighty-ninths) but they can still visualise the operations. Algebra is used in parts (g) and (h) to emphasise that no matter what the denomination, provided each fraction has the same denomination, $\frac{8}{x} \div \frac{2}{x} = 4$.

Get the students to write equivalent operations for Exercise 2. For example, $\frac{8}{5} \div \frac{3}{5}$ has the same value as $8 \div 3$, which equals $2\frac{2}{3}$. Algebra is used again in parts (e) and (f) to formalise the idea. $\frac{8}{x} \div \frac{3}{x}$ has the same value as $8 \div 3$.

Exercise 3 extends the idea of approximations with fractions. This should help students judge whether their accurate answers are about right.

Exercises 4 and 5 introduce the idea that multiplying by the multiplicative inverse of a number gives the same result as dividing by that number. This is the result that most of us remember as: 'to divide by a fraction turn it upside down and multiply'. However, we rarely knew why it worked. In these exercises the students follow the mathematical logic and gain a better understanding of the result.

Challenging exercises

Exercise 6 consolidates the idea that multiplying by the multiplicative inverse has the same result as dividing. It extends the idea to algebra.

Exercise 7 extends the idea of 'multiplicative inverse' to that of finding the reciprocal of a number. Demonstrate that $n \times \frac{1}{n} = 1$.

Problem-solving exercise

Enlargement and reduction are good examples of division being the inverse operation of multiplication. Exercise 8 provides practice in this.

Plenary

Check that students can answer all the questions in the *Goals.* Discuss division having the same result as multiplying by the multiplicative inverse.

Homework

Students need to complete Exercise 8 before doing the *Homework.*

Number and Algebra

Page 68 Percentages 1

Goals

Percentages were introduced in Book 1 in a way that clearly underlines their relationship with vulgar fractions: they are quite simply one and the same thing (for example, $\frac{5}{100}$ and 5% have the same value but a different appearance). Book 1 also clarified in the same matter of fact way that decimal fractions and vulgar fractions can be inter-changed at will (they are quite simply one and the same thing). **Worksheets 23** and **24** provide additional practice in this work.

Now we need to show how knowledge of equivalent fractions (as used in the previous lesson) enables some vulgar fractions to be converted into percentage form. Other vulgar fractions require use of a calculator.

This lesson emphasises the fact that the term 'equivalent fractions' can be applied as accurately to 93% and $\frac{93}{100}$ as it can to $\frac{5}{6}$ and $\frac{10}{12}$.

Demonstration 1 makes this point in context: it reminds students that $\frac{93}{100}$ of 200 = 186 and 93% of 200 = 186 are equivalent calculations carried out with the two equivalent fractions $\frac{93}{100}$ and 93%. It also makes the point that the conversion of $\frac{3}{4}$ to a percentage implicates the equivalent fraction $\frac{75}{100}$. Confirm the equivalence of the fractions by referring to 'sticks'.

The really important thing about seeing $\frac{75}{100}$ and converting it to a percentage is that there is not much to do apart from re-writing it in its abbreviated form as 75%. It does not involve *'dividing 75 by 100 and calling it 'percent"!* This little speech gives the wrong idea.

Similarly, converting 75% into a vulgar fraction does not involve anything other than speaking the language '75%; 75 compared to 100; $\frac{75}{100}$'.

Starter

The vulgar fractions used here are not easy to convert to the form 'something compared to 100'. Use a calculator. Use it to determine the scale factor of the enlargement that will be applied to the numerator and the denominator. Demonstrate the thinking that goes something like:

What do I multiply 8 by to get 100?

Well, $100 \div 8 = 12 \cdot 5$ so I would multiply 8 by $12 \cdot 5$. The scale factor is $12 \cdot 5$, and if I find $5 \times 12 \cdot 5$, I get $62 \cdot 5$. We can write $\frac{5}{8}$ as $62 \cdot 5\%$.

Alternatively, recognise that $\frac{5}{8}$ has the same value as $5 \div 8 = 0 \cdot 625$ (using a calculator) and recognise that this has the same value as $\frac{625}{1000}$ or $\frac{625}{100}$ or $62 \cdot 5\%$.

Discuss both methods and get students to work out each number both ways.

Demonstration 1

Use this demonstration to consolidate the equivalence of the two calculations. That is, each of 93% and $\frac{93}{100}$ represent a comparison (they each provoke the thought 'smaller').

Use calculators to calculate both $\frac{93}{100}$ of 200 and 93% of 200. Use the calculation $\frac{93}{100}$ to look at what happens with $93 \div 100 \times 200$ and $93 \div 200 \times 100$ and $93 \times 200 \div 100$ because this involves testing out the calculator to see how it must be tamed to do what is required (not to assume that the calculator will know what to do).

Demonstration 2

Demonstration 2 looks at calculations of the type 5% of $x = 19$, and requires the use of the multiplicative inverse.

The twin maths tables were introduced in Book 1 (pages 76–85). Use the twin maths table to solve the equation 5% of $x = 19$, using a calculator for the arithmetic work.

Use this opportunity to stress what is happening on the twin maths tables:

How much is on this table? 5% of x. How much on this table? 19. They are the same value (different appearance). How do we know that? Because that is what the 'equals' sign tells us. Look at what happens if we use the multiplicative inverse $\frac{100}{5}$ on the left-hand table: we get x. So when we do the same operation on the right-hand table we get $19 \times \frac{100}{5}$. [Use a calculator to establish $x = 380$.]

Number and Algebra: **Percentages 1**

Worked examples

In Example 2, stress the use of '**Let** the quantity be x'. Once this is established we can write an equation to be solved. When we multiply both sides of the equation by the multiplicative inverse of $\frac{113}{100}$ we have the value of x.

Essential exercises

Exercises 1 and 2 are revision of work covered in Book 1 (pages 40–43 and 48–51). Most students will be able to answer these questions orally. Further practice on questions of this type can be found in **Worksheet 25**.

The questions in Exercise 3 can all be worked out by simple mental methods. However, this is an opportunity to formalise the written method. For example:

(a) Let the number be x.

20% of $x = 6$ $\frac{20}{100}x = 6$ $\frac{1}{5}x = 6$ $x = \frac{5}{1} \times 6 = 30$

Exercises 4 and 5 require a clear understanding that 100% has the same value as $\frac{100}{100}$, which has the same value as 1. Any quantity that we start with, such as the original price in a shop or the original mass of an object, is thought of as 100%. Any increase or decrease of this original quantity is added to or subtracted from 100%. Thus an increase of 6% means that 6% has to be added to the original 100% to give 106%. A decrease of 6% means that 6% has to be subtracted from the original 100% to give 94%.

Challenging exercises

Exercise 6 develops the idea of successive increases or decreases. The most common error that students make is to consider an increase of, say, 15% followed by a further increase of 15% to be equal to a total increase of 30%. They need to practise calculating successive increases and decreases to see that this is not the case. (It is, of course, a 32·25% increase.) Students should use their calculators for this exercise.

Ask students to suggest the correct answer to Exercise 7 before doing any calculations. Get them to justify their answer. For example: *When I increase my savings by 7% I have more money. When I calculate 7% of this new quantity it will be more than 7% of the original so a decrease of 7% will give me less than I started with.*

Problem-solving exercises

Exercise 8 provides practice in converting scores to percentages. Students can use a calculator for this work.

Exercise 9 is more difficult. Get the students to read the

questions and ask them to formulate each question as an equation to be solved. For example:

(a) If you increase a quantity by 250% you now have 350% (100% + 250%) of the original.
Multiply the original amount by $\frac{350}{100}$ or 3·50 (or 3·5)

$1·2 \times 3·5 = 4·2$ Answer: 4·2 million pounds

(b) Increase in test score = 3   Original score = 12
Percentage increase $= \frac{3}{12} = \frac{25}{100} = 25\%$

Plenary

Check the students' understanding by setting the questions in the *Goals* as a test. Get the students to check their answers in pairs, and then ask them for the answers.

Homework

This exercise provides further practice in converting numbers to different forms.

Page 72 # Percentages 2

Goals

Lessons in Book 1 developed students' understanding of percentage in relation to expressions of the form '5% of 200', where the principal is an integral multiple of 100. This was then extended to expressions of the kind '5% of 273' where, by replacing each 100 with 5, we were able to 'see' 5 on the maths table lots of times (2·73 times). We calculate $5 \times 2{\cdot}73$ to find the value.

Demonstration 2 in the previous lesson applied the idea of multiplicative inverse to equations like 5% of $x = 19$, and now in *Demonstration 2* of this lesson we move to calculating percentage increase and compound percentages. *Demonstration 1* emphasises a key result (that 100% of 498 = 498), so that it is fully appreciated that 498 has the same value as 100% of 498 (different appearance). This means they are interchangeable: every time we see 498 we can, without fuss or embarrassment, write 100% of 498. This is the key to dealing mathematically with percentage increase and percentage decrease.

Aim to avoid a 5% increase being thought of as the original amount plus 5% of it. Instead, cultivate from the start, the understanding that a five percent increase is calculated as 105% of the original, and a 5% decrease is calculated as 95% of the original. This is done in anticipation of algebraic manipulation.

Starter

The *Starter* revises and consolidates the idea of and use of multiplicative inverse. Insist that students use the words 'multiplicative inverse' as they state its value. Ensure that students invited to the board actually articulate what happens when they find the product of the fraction and its inverse on the left-hand side, and what they do with it on the right-hand side. Also insist they clarify what they use the calculator for: which calculation they have selected to do, and why it is valid.

Invite several students in turn to create similar equations and go through the entire articulated process with their own equation.

Demonstration 1

This demonstration reinforces the ideas that were met in the previous lesson. You may not need to do this demonstration with students who are already confident with this work.

Use the equation in the demonstration to underline the crucial point that the number 498 can always be replaced by 100% of 498 if you choose to do so. In fact, if you chose to do so, you could count by saying:
100% of 1
100% of 2
100% of 3
100% of 4
100% of 5
It is not strange! It is not wrong! It is perfectly valid!

> *Think of the number 100% of 498.*
> *The number that is 5% more than 100% of 498 is 105% of 498 (it is 100% and another 5%).*
> *What about the number 5% less than 100% of 498?*
> *It is 95% of 498.*

Practise this with a number of examples (there is no need to calculate the answer: just write down the expression).

Once these ideas have been established, remind students of the work they did in Exercises 4 and 5 of the previous lesson. To increase a number by 5% we want 105% of that number ($105\% = \frac{105}{100} = 1{\cdot}05$) so multiply the number by 1·05

Demonstration 2

Part (a) of this demonstration revises the type of calculation studied in the previous lesson. Assist invited students to articulate accurately what this involves with the multiplicative inverse.

Ensure that students appreciate that x is what we started with (we do not know the value of what we started with). We know that after the object x (whatever that is) has been enlarged by 5% (relate this to the 105% shown) the image was 3·72. Use calculators to check the object is 3·54. Insist on examining the object and the image to be confident that the object was enlarged (Yes! $3{\cdot}72 > 3{\cdot}54$).

Part (b) considers an object of 98 and an image of 107.

> *Compare the image to the object: bigger. The comparison is 107 : 98.*
> *But wait! What is the actual increase? It is 9.*

Number and Algebra

> *What if we now compare the actual increase of 9 to the original value (the object) of 98. The comparison is 'smaller'. It is 9 : 98. Compare increase to object: smaller; $\frac{9}{98}$.*
>
> *Convert the vulgar fraction $\frac{9}{98}$ to a percentage. We must first find a vulgar fraction (with a denominator 100) that has the same value as $\frac{9}{98}$ (using a calculator). What do we need to multiply 98 by to get a hundred?*
> *Well, if we divide 98 by 98 we get 1, and if we multiply 1 by 100 we get 100, so $98 \div 98 \times 100$.*
> *If we do the same thing to the 9 we get*
> $9 \div 98 \times 100 = 9.1836...$.
> *So $\frac{9}{98} = \frac{9.18}{100} = 9.18\%$ and we can say the percentage increase is 9·18% (to 2 d.p.).*

It is of course the practised use of language that will consolidate what the 'percentage increase' actually means. Go though this process many times, while students study the data in *Demonstration 2* (b):

> *What is the increase?* 9
>
> *Compare the increase to the object: smaller; 9 to 98. What is the comparison as a vulgar fraction?* $\frac{9}{98}$
>
> *What is the equivalent vulgar fraction shown?* $\frac{9.18...}{100}$
> *What is the comparison as a percentage?* 9·18%

Look at part (c). Discuss the calculation of this, using a calculator.

Worked examples

Work through both of the examples, showing students how to set out their work. The students should use calculators for this work.

Essential exercises

Exercises 1 to 3 provide practice in calculating a percentage increase. Although students may be able to do the first exercise mentally by calculating 5% and adding it to the original quantity, we want them to formalise the method of multiplying (in this case by 1·05) using a calculator. Real-life problems are rarely this simple and we need to give the students the skills to solve any problem. They can check that both methods give the same result. Exercise 4 provides practice in reducing prices. Again, get the students to work out the answers by multiplying (in this case by 0·9) using a calculator. Insist that they write down the calculations they are doing.

The questions in Exercise 5 need reading through and interpreting. You may need to do this with the whole class. Get the students to decide what it is they are wanting to

work out and let the unknown be x. Set up the equation with the students and then let them solve it.

Exercise 6 is another exercise in comprehension. As with all real-life problems the maths is often hidden in the story. Discuss why you cannot merely look at the actual increase.

Exercise 7 is a test in understanding. All of these statements need logical thinking. Ask the students to explain their answers.

Challenging exercises

Exercise 8 is a good question for discussion. To reduce by 5%, multiply by 0·95. To make a further reduction of 5%, multiply again by 0·95. So a reduction of 5% followed by another reduction of 5% has the same result as multiplying by 0.95^2. To reduce a price on five successive days multiply by 0.95^5.

However, the method above may not necessarily comply with rules about sale prices. Suppose you had to round down the price each day in favour of the customer. Would the result be different if you worked out the reduction on each day's actual sale price? Try it!

Exercise 9 also looks at successive increases. Discuss inflation and compare the 3% increase to the present day inflation rate. Look at inflation rates around the world.

Exercise 10 is not easy! $(100 + x)^2 = \frac{96.8}{80}$. Why? Now solve the equation.

Problem-solving exercises

Exercise 11(a) is a classic question. In fact it does not matter which way round the calculation is performed because multiplication is commutative. Exercise 12 is similar to Exercise 7 in the previous lesson.

Plenary

Set the questions in the *Goals* to check understanding. Pose the question in the *Plenary* and discuss why the answer will always be the same (because multiplication obeys the commutative law). Discuss also, why this is different from finding 11% of x, followed by finding 28% of the result.

Homework

Explaining why an answer is wrong is often a good way of unpacking common errors and misconceptions. Ask students to explain their answers in the next lesson.

Number and Algebra

Page 76 ## Sequences

Goals

This lesson continues the work started in Book 1 (pages 96–99) where we emphasised that a sequence of numbers is a list of numbers that has a specified rule to calculate further terms. The rule can be presented either in 'term-to-term' form or in 'position-to-term' form. These sequences were dealt with informally (so that a term-to-term rule might be specified as 'add 4') and then more formally (so that a position-to-term rule might be specified as 'nth term $= 4n - 1$'). In this lesson we work more formally, concentrating on one type of sequence where the difference between consecutive terms is constant. We introduce the **arithmetic sequence**. The demonstrations examine the form of the terms and, informally, find the sum of an arithmetic sequence.

Starter

The *Starter* recalls work that students practised in Book 1. Although the questions ask for the third and fifth terms, the students will have to work out each term because they have been given the term-to-term rule. Assist them in working out the second term.

> *Zero subtract one is negative one. Negative one times two is negative two.*

And the third term:

> *Negative two subtract one is negative three. Negative three times two is negative six.*

You may want to select an easier example to start this lesson for less confident students. For example,

> *The first term of a sequence is 1. The term-to-term rule is 'add two and multiply by three'.*

Demonstration 1

This demonstration deals with arithmetic sequences. This is, of course, typical of many sequences that students have already dealt with informally. The major purpose of this demonstration is to formalise that earlier work, and to very deliberately teach certain vocabulary and its meaning and use, together with conventional symbols. The language

includes 'first term', 'constant difference', and 'nth term'. The conventions include the information implicit in saying: *An arithmetic sequence has $a = 3$, $d = 4$, $n = 40$.*

The sequence is very familiar, informally; but the conventional language needs very detailed teaching. The following gives the flavour of this teaching.

> [Write on the board: 3   7   11   15]
> *This is a **list** of numbers. What is the next number? We do not know: we are told it is a list, so the next number could be anything.*
> [Again, write on the board: 3   7   11   15]
> *This is a **sequence** of numbers. What is the next number? We do not know. We suspect it is 19 because we can see a pattern of 'add 4' but we do not actually know.*
> [Again, write on the board: 3   7   11   15]
> *This is a **sequence** of numbers. The term-to-term rule is 'add 4'. What is the next number? We know it is 19.*
>
> *Look at this sequence again. We know the term-to-term rule is 'add 4'. Look at a pair of consecutive terms, say, 7 and 11. The difference is 4. Look at another pair, say, 3 and 7. The difference is 4.*

Establish that the difference between any pair of consecutive terms in the sequence is 4 and then say: *This sequence has a **constant difference** of 4.*

Invite students to write on the board in response to your instructions:

> (a) *I want you to write a sequence of numbers. The first term is 5; the constant difference is 4; … carry on.*
> (b) *I want you to write a sequence of numbers. The first term is 1.4; the constant difference is 3; … carry on.*

Use several examples of this type.

Explain that any sequence that has a constant difference between terms is called an **arithmetic sequence**. So if we say: *Look at this arithmetic sequence: 3, 7, 11, 15,* then we know that the next term must be 19 because the words 'arithmetic sequence' tell us that the pattern of constant differences we can see must be repeated.

In maths, we use even more shorthand. We refer to the first term of a sequence as the letter 'a' and in an arithmetic sequence we call the constant difference 'd', and when we want to tell someone that there are forty terms we say '$n = 40$'.

Invite students to write on the board as you give instructions of this type:

> *I want you to write an arithmetic sequence* [Emphasise here that you cannot yet write anything but you do know that you will soon hear what it starts with and what the pattern is],
> *with $a = 23$,* [The student immediately writes 23]
> *$d = 10$,* [Ensure the student writes 33]
> *and $n = 5$.* [Ensure the student continues writing to complete 23   33   43   53   63, and very visibly count the terms so all students appreciate the implication of $n = 5$.]

Invite other students to complete similar sequences, for example:
(a) Arithmetic sequence: $a = 2$, $d = 9$, $n = 7$
(b) Arithmetic sequence: $a = 2$, $d = 9$, $n = 3$
(c) Arithmetic sequence: $a = 2·4$, $d = 3$, $n = 6$
(d) Arithmetic sequence: $a = 19$, $d = ^-2$, $n = 5$
(e) Arithmetic sequence: $a = ^-5$, $d = ^-2$, $n = 6$

Examine the demonstration again. Ensure that students appreciate the implicit information in the words 'arithmetic sequence'. Ask them: *For the sequence in Demonstration 1, what is the value of a? What is the value of d? What is the value of n?*

Continue to analyse the sequence:

> *Look at the second term. We add one lot of the difference to the first term. Look at the third term. We add two lots of the difference to the first term. What about the fourth term? Add three lots of the difference to the first term. What about the tenth term? Yes, add nine lots of the difference to the first term.* [$3 + 9 \times 4 = 39$] *What about the twenty-fifth term? Add twenty-four lots of the difference to the first term.* [$3 + 24 \times 4 = 99$] *What about the nth term? Add $n - 1$ lots of the difference to the first term.* [Establish that the nth term is $a + (n - 1)d$.]

Demonstration 2

This demonstration can be omitted for less confident students. It is not essential for the exercises but it is a delightful little proof of how to sum n terms of an arithmetic sequence. Karl Gauss (1777–1855) worked out this formula for himself at the age of 8 years!

The proof depends upon recognising that when we write down the forty terms of the arithmetic sequence in

ascending order and then repeat beneath it the forty terms in descending order, the sum of the matched pairs of terms will always be the same. In this case the sum of the pairs of terms is always 162. Twice the sum can be found by adding all these terms together. The sum of the series is then half this amount.

Worked example

Use this example to check the students' understanding.

Essential exercises

Exercises 1 and 2 are revision of work done in Book 1. Exercise 3 focuses on arithmetic sequences that follow on from *Demonstration 1*.

Exercise 4 is set as an investigation to establish that with nth terms that are linear the difference between consecutive terms is constant. There is also a relationship between the coefficient of n and the common difference (it is the same).

Challenging exercises

Using the result of Exercise 4, students can work out the nth terms because they are told that the sequence is linear. Exercises 6 and 7 move them on to consider the first, second and third differences of quadratic and cubic sequences.

Problem-solving exercise

Exercise 8 links the work on sequences to an investigation involving a pattern. The justification for the result has to be in the geometrical properties of the consecutive shapes produced.

Plenary

Use the questions in the *Goals* to check the students' understanding. For those students who have seen *Demonstration 2*, discuss the sum of twenty-four terms of the sequence of numbers. Assist the students in presenting this formally.

Homework

This activity is another investigation where the justification for the sequence of numbers is given by referring to the geometrical properties of subsequent shapes.

 **Letts** I See Maths Book 2

Number and Algebra

Page 80 Algebraic expressions

Goals

The first lesson in this section of Book 2 (pages 24–27) studied the laws of arithmetic and formally defined the idea of a 'term', 'a string of terms' and utilised the vocabulary of 'factor', 'common factor', 'commutative law', and 'distributive law'. All this was utilised further in the second lesson and has informed much of the later work. Those early lessons incorporated algebraic notation into the discussion, capitalising on and extending the algebra in Book 1 (pages 76–87).

The coherence of this earlier work has been designed to make further extension of algebra accessible to all students. They will become confident in identifying common factors and highest common factors in a string of algebraic terms, and will appreciate how the collection of 'like terms' implicates the identification of common factors. This develops further their understanding of algebraic manipulation in Book 1.

Recall how algebraic notation was formally introduced as cards with symbols written on them – so that, for instance, $3x$ is thought of as 'three of those things called x' and $6y$ as '6 of those things called y'. One bonus from this is that $3x + 6y$ does not tempt students make any of the typically bizarre (and infuriating) mistakes of writing $9xy$ or whatever! They can see the things called x and the things called y are quite distinct. Note, however, that it is simply wrong to say to students: *You cannot add 3x and 6y.* You certainly can. Watch us do it: $3x + 6y$! What should be asserted in the early stages is that you cannot **simplify** $3x + 6y$, in the way that you can simplify $3x + 6x$. This lesson shows that there are things you can do with $3x + 6y$, but you need to use the distributive law in reverse – and call it 'taking out a common factor'. You also need to know that normally you 'take out' the highest common factor.

Starter

Use the *Starter* to revise the work covered in the first lesson in this book (pages 24–27). Note that in 1(a) the three terms are $5x$, $7x$ and $2x$. If a student asserts that the three terms are $5x$, $7x$ and ^-2x then it looks as if some worthwhile thinking is going on, but the assertion is still wrong. Discuss it – pointing out that the correct assertion is *'If we re-write the string as 5x + 7x + ⁻2x (same value : different appearance) then the three terms are 5x, 7x and ⁻2x'*. But, as shown in the *Starter*, the three terms are $5x$, $7x$ and $2x$.

Demonstration 1

Revise the idea of a factor of a term being visualised as 'the thing written on a card'. So, looking at the term $5mx$ we can say:

> x could be on a card; x is a factor; the other factor is $5m$.
> m could be on a card; m is a factor; the other factor is $5x$.
> 5 could be on a card; 5 is a factor; the other factor is mx.
> $5x$ could be on a card; $5x$ is a factor; the other factor is m.
> $5m$ could be on a card; $5m$ is a factor; the other factor is x.
> mx could be on a card; mx is a factor; the other factor is 5.

The importance of this is to use the vocabulary in relation to an established visual image, and to emphasise that identification of factors is a kind of wide-ranging idea (so we promote flexible thinking).

A similar analysis of each of the terms, including students writing the factors and the 'other factors' allows us to identify a factor that is *common to all terms* – and speak it in this form before using the abbreviated form of 'common factor'. Notice that 5 is a common factor and x is a common factor and $5x$ is a common factor, and explain that mathematicians usually choose the highest of those common factors to write the original string as the product of two factors (in this case one factor is $5x$ and the other factor is $m + 3y − 2z$).

When this process is applied to $3x + 5x − 2x$, one factor is x and the other factor is $3 + 5 − 2$ (value = 6) so we have x six times, i.e. $6x$; and this is a reassertion of our ability to simplify $3x + 5x − 2x$ by thinking of cards with x on them (see *Goals,* above). In this case, when each of our terms has a number followed by the same 'card', we call the process 'collecting like terms'.

Demonstration 2

Demonstration 2 emphasises the point that there is not some kind of law that all the terms in a string must be included in the process of identifying a common factor. With the string shown, we could choose to identify a

Number and Algebra

common factor xyz in two of the terms (and, in this case, collect like terms). Or we might identify a common factor xy across all three terms, write the string as a product of two factors (the other factor is $6z - 11 + 3z$), and then collect like terms. The students need to practise different ways of writing a given string with a different appearance (but ensuring they have the same value).

Worked examples

Work through these examples with the class.

Essential exercises

Exercise 1 provides practice in collecting together like terms. Make sure that the students know what is meant by a 'like term'. Use cards for students who are less confident.

Exercises 2 and 3 provide practice in multiplying out brackets. The questions get progressively more difficult so use **Worksheet 26** for students who need more practice with straightforward examples.

Exercise 4 should be used to get students to inspect each term carefully to see which terms are 'like terms'. Students often find these more complex terms easier to work with because they do not make assumptions about what they see.

Exercises 5 to 9 build up the students' knowledge of factors from simple whole number factors of numbers to common factors and on to factors of algebraic terms. They are designed to link prior knowledge with new knowledge.

Although set notation is not normally introduced at this stage, curly brackets are used here to group together a set of terms for students to find common factors. The notation helps to clarify that we are looking for factors that are common to all the terms inside the brackets.

Exercise 7 asks for all the factors of the expressions. We are, of course, limiting the factors of the numbers to those that are whole numbers. Otherwise the factors of $5x$ would include $\frac{1}{2}$, $\frac{1}{4}$, and so on. You may wish to discuss this with the students, but at this stage they are not expected to give anything other than whole number factors.

The instruction 'factorise' needs explaining in Exercise 9. We normally look for the highest common factors of the terms and take these outside a bracket.

Challenging exercises

Exercises 10 to 12 are particularly challenging. Omit these for the less confident students.

Exercise 10 will probably need to be worked through with the class. Look at part (a):

> *How many terms are there? Two. The first term is $2(3x + 4)$ and the second term is $3(x − 3)$. The terms are connected with a minus sign. First of all, work out each term.*
> *First term: $6x + 8$*
> *Second term: $3x − 9$*
> *Putting them together we have $(6x + 8) − (3x − 9)$*

This is the first time that students have encountered two subtraction signs like this. Discuss how you will deal with this operation. One way is to consider that the second bracket has the same value as $3x + {}^-9$ so that the instruction is to 'take away $3x$ and take away negative nine'. This has the same value as 'take away $3x$ and add negative nine'. Check this result by giving x a value such as 4.

Exercise 11 is further practice on factorising. It is not expected that students should multiply out the brackets in Exercise 12. They are merely confirming the identity by substituting values for x and y on each side of the identity sign.

Problem-solving exercises

Formulae are often quoted in different forms with or without factorising. Exercises 13 and 14 provide examples of factorising formulae.

Plenary

Use the questions in the *Goals* to summarise the work in this lesson. Discuss the examples in the *Plenary* and invite students to complete them on the board.

Homework

An example is given to help students with the *Homework*. Ask students to try the questions for homework and go over them at the beginning of the next lesson.

Number and Algebra

Formulae

Goals

A formula is a short way of remembering how to do a calculation. In a sense, there is nothing much to be done about formulae: all the work has been done for you. Of course, you have to be able to do the arithmetic, but that is nothing unique to formulae – and if you understand the logic of the language of arithmetic and algebra, then what else is to be said? Well, there are a number of things. The ability to manipulate formulae leads to a reduction in the number of formulae that have to be learnt, and promotes a deeper understanding of the units used in measurement.

There is a need to be comfortable with the purpose of formulae, and that requires some practice. There is a need to memorise some formulae, and that is best done in relation to understanding them. There is a need, on meeting a new formula, to cull from it a range of implicit information. And since formulae are, by their very nature, some summary of a real-life situation implicating measurement, then formulae do have something to do with basic units and derived units. And this is really the point: the very nature of derived units is intimately related to associated formulae.

If you know that speed is measured in miles per hour, you can immediately deduce that calculation of speed involves dividing distance by time; and, having deduced that, you can choose if you like to measure speed in nautical miles per second, or any other exotic derived unit. We need to give students some flavour of all this.

Starter

Calculations with formulae inevitably involve using one or more of the basic arithmetical operations but sometimes they appear in a slightly unusual form; and very often they can be quickly evaluated by using the laws of arithmetic. The *Starter* practises looking at some simple calculations and appreciating their implications.

Use 1(a) to address again the fact that 3 cups put on the maths table 24 times has the same value as putting 12 cups (i.e. 3 cups times 4 equals twelve cups) on the table 6 times. This is an important idea when we unpack calculations with associated units in a formula.

1(b) suggests the use of the commutative law to allow us to calculate the equivalent calculation 10×7.

1(c) Look at the commutative law for 10 and 8·7
1(d) Clearly $72 \div 2 = 36$
1(e) $12 \times 3 = 36$
1(f) Make 72 smaller: every time you see 2 replace with 1. You get 36.
Discuss the connections.

Demonstration 1

Discuss how each mathematical formula expresses the same thing as the word expression (it simply has a different appearance) – and how economical the mathematical formula is!

Look at the written expressions. Perimeter of a rectangle is the subject of the sentence. Hence P is the subject of the formula.

Area of a rectangle is the subject of the sentence. Hence A is the subject of the formula. [If the students' knowledge of written English is good, they will appreciate that in the first sentence 'Area of a rectangle' is the subject and 'is twice the length plus twice the width' is the predicate. In the second sentence, the area is predicated on (that is, it is based on, is dependent upon) 'is twice the length plus twice the width'. And that is exactly the case in the associated mathematical formulae. Discuss this with your English Department!

Look at $P = 2l + 2w$
Suppose we want to calculate the value of P. The formula carries the implicit information that you need to know l and w.

Enable students to select the units (their own choice) for l and w. If they assert l as metres and w as miles then they cannot easily add those things called metres and those things called miles. *I See Maths* specifically attenuates understanding by talking of, say, 3 cups add 2 cups is 5 cups; we need to capitalise on this straightforward logic and substitute the word 'cups' consistently, hence: l metres add w metres equals P metres. (Similarly if we consistently use 'miles'.) Insist on considering other units.

Look at $A = lw$ and recall earlier work where the logic of the language of multiplication was practiced, for example we have learnt to say '3 hundred times 4 thousand equals 12 hundred thousand'. The logic says l metres times w metres gives A metres metres, and our work on powers enables us to see that we are dealing with m².

Number and Algebra: **Formulae**

More particularly 3 m × 4 m = 12 m m = 12 m². And here we encounter the sheer beauty of maths. We have deliberately practised calculation of area (Book 1, pages 88–90 and 140–143) as, say, 3 m² × 4 = 12 m² to emphasise we are measuring area with those things called m². We can see we have 3 m² four times (the four has no units), giving 12 m².

Working with formulae, and applying the logic of the language, we see that the units for area are generated, algebraically, from the combination of the units for length. Use this kind of discussion for the remaining formulae.

Demonstration 2

This demonstration reiterates much of *Demonstration 1* to clarify that in a formula we have some aspects that are pure numbers and some that are quantities with units. It is the careful, logical combination of these that yields the units of the subject of the formula.

The third formula in this demonstration involves density, mass and volume. Mass divided by volume clearly gives grams per cm³. There is a very logical reason for writing g/cm³ as g cm⁻³, but for the moment simply state this and practise writing it accurately. More of this later.

Worked example

Show students how to set out this example on the board.

Essential exercises

Students should know all the formulae in Exercise 1 by heart. Encourage them to use logic to work out the pairings for any they have forgotten.

Exercise 2 is straightforward practice in substituting values into formulae. Students have done this before in Book 1 and should be confident doing these examples.

Pythagoras' theorem has not been derived as yet. This is deliberate. Students can see that they do not need to know the context to be able to substitute values into a formula or rule. In fact, when doing maths we should not be concerned with the context but should keep at a distance from it lest we are persuaded to take account of our own opinions.

Students are being asked to calculate the value of the hypotenuse, so the calculations are straightforward practice of square roots. The formula does not need to be rearranged in these questions.

Challenging exercises

Exercises 4 and 5 provide two different formulae on which to practise substitution. Part (b) of Exercise 4 requires students to work out the height of a trapezium given the formula for the area. This is in preparation for rearranging formulae to change the subject that will be covered in Book 3.

Problem-solving exercises

Exercises 6 and 7 are showing once again that students do not need to know the context in detail to be able to do the calculations. They may not know the formulae that have been presented but they can still do the maths.

Exercise 6, part (a) is straightforward substitution into the formula. Part (b) requires the value of R given V and I and this needs a little rearrangement of the formula. Work through this example with the whole class so that they can attempt Exercise 7, part (b), which requires a similar rearrangement.

Plenary

Check that students know the formulae (a) to (f) in the *Goals*. Invite students to give answers to the last two questions in the *Goals* and get them to explain their answers.

Discuss different formulae and ask students to give the units for the measurements involved.

Homework

This conversion formula for temperature is probably well known by the students. Weather forecasters continue to give both Celsius and Fahrenheit temperatures, so get students to estimate the temperature in Fahrenheit before working out the approximate measurement using the formula.

Teacher's Notes Teacher's Notes Teacher's Notes Teacher's Notes Teacher's Notes
Teacher's Notes Teacher's Notes Teacher's Notes Teacher's Notes Teacher's Notes
Teacher's Notes Teacher's Notes Teacher's Notes Teacher's Notes Teacher's Notes

Number and Algebra

 Page 88 # Solving equations 1

Goals

Our work in number and arithmetic has relentlessly pursued the idea of the transparent logic of symbolisation. We have sought to be economical (a distinctive mathematical virtue) by, for instance, not inserting unnecessary brackets in such remarkable and beautiful simplicities as $2 \times 4 + 1 \times 3 = 11$. There are two reasons for this: firstly, it is mathematically correct; secondly, the gratuitous insertion of brackets, assumed to make life easier for students, ultimately makes things more difficult.

We want now to bring to life expressions such as $5x + 2$ and $5(x + 2)$ so that their distinctive difference can be understood by all students. On the basis of this clarity, we will examine the solution of equations such as
$$5x + 2 = 19 \qquad \text{and} \qquad 5(x + 2) = 19$$

The manner in which we do this will be immediately applicable to other equations, for instance:
$$5 \cdot 2x + 2 \cdot 3 = 19 \cdot 7 \qquad \text{and} \qquad 5 \cdot 2(x + 2 \cdot 3) = 19 \cdot 7$$

The key to this is the use, and later visualisation, of successive operations using a function diagram. You will see that the construction of this is linked to logical interpretation of algebraic symbolisation. The solution of equations rests on our practised use of the fundamental idea of 'same value : different appearance' (in this case, related to each of the 'sides' of an equation).

Starter

The *Starter* employs the organising idea of object and image; and the same notation (an arrow) is used to symbolise an operation as is used throughout *I See Maths* (for example in geometry and in fractions).

> *If x is the object,* [write x on the board] *and $x + 7$ is the image,* [draw an arrow to symbolise the act of the doing of an operation] *the operation we did was to add ... how much? ... 7 .* [Write $+ 7$ along the arrow].
>
> $$x \xrightarrow{\ +7\ } x + 7$$

Invite students to create similar diagrams on the board for each of the examples in the *Starter.* Insist they articulate

which is the object, which the image, and the nature of the operation, as they write. While your initial invitation to students asks them to draw 'a similar diagram', introduce quite naturally the instruction 'draw a function diagram for part (d)' so that the diagram becomes formally named quite naturally.

Notice, of course, that these function diagrams require just a single operation.

Leave the function diagrams on the board and beneath each one draw an arrow from right to left so that, for 1(a), we assert that $x + 7$ is the object and x is the image. Which operation is now needed for the object to image transformation? (Subtract 7). Insert this on the function diagram. The two operations shown are **inverse operations**. Each 'undoes' the other.

$$x \xrightarrow{\ +7\ } x + 7$$

$$x \xleftarrow{\ -7\ } x + 7$$

Invite students to complete each function diagram in a similar way.

Demonstration 1

Before starting this demonstration, you may wish to use **Worksheets 27** and **28** to practise solving equations, as covered in Book 1.

Examine the first equation in the demonstration.

Think of x as the object and $3 \cdot 1x + 2 \cdot 7$ as the image. We can identify two operations (multiply by $3 \cdot 1$; and add $2 \cdot 7$). The very act of reading it, responding to the way it is written, supplies the implicit information that the $3 \cdot 1$ is 'closer' to x than $2 \cdot 7$: it tells us the operation 'multiply by $3 \cdot 1$' has been done first; followed by 'add $2 \cdot 7$'. This enables us to draw the function diagram accurately, as shown in the demonstration.

Look at the image $3 \cdot 1x + 2 \cdot 7$.
The initial equation tells us that this has the same value as $18 \cdot 6$; this means that in the part of the function diagram that deals with inverse functions we can write $18 \cdot 6$ and operate on this with the inverse operations. This leads us to see that the value of x is $5 \cdot 1$ (to 1 d.p.).

Number and Algebra: **Solving equations 1**

This is the same work that was done in Book 1 with the twin maths tables. Talk through the several stages in the use of the two maths tables, linking it with the images in the demonstration.

Now work through the formal solution, linking this to the twin maths tables and the function diagram. Discuss the use of the multiplicative inverse, having the same value as dividing by $3 \cdot 1$.

Construct similar equations for students to draw the function diagram (carefully writing the operations in both directions) and using the diagram to construct a formal solution. Use examples like:

(a) $3 \cdot 1x + 2 \cdot 7 = 43 \cdot 2$ (b) $3 \cdot 1x + 2 \cdot 7 = 1 \cdot 3$
(c) $4x + 2 \cdot 1 = 6 \cdot 4$ (d) $4x - 2 \cdot 1 = 6 \cdot 4$
(e) $\frac{x}{23} + 5 \cdot 3 = 16 \cdot 7$

Demonstration 2

Discussion of this function diagram follows the same purpose and pattern as in *Demonstration 1*. The important difference, of course, is that the expression $3 \cdot 1(x + 2 \cdot 7)$ is a single term (unlike the previous demonstration where we dealt with two terms). This term consists of two factors, $3 \cdot 1$ and $x + 2 \cdot 7$, and the use of the bracket is a clear sign that $x + 2 \cdot 7$ was formed first – implying that $2 \cdot 7$ is 'closer' to x than the $3 \cdot 1$, so the 'add $2 \cdot 7$' was done first.

The function diagram now shows the object x being operated on first by $+ 2 \cdot 7$ and then $\times 3 \cdot 1$. The inverse function diagram shows the image $18 \cdot 6$ being operated on in the reverse order by the inverse operations $\div 3 \cdot 1$ followed by $- 2 \cdot 7$.

Demonstrate some further examples such as:
$4 \cdot 5(x + 3) = 22 \cdot 5$ and $6 \cdot 2(x - 2 \cdot 4) = 43 \cdot 4$

Worked example

These two equation are imitations of the demonstrations. Show the students how to set the questions out. They can use function diagrams as in the demonstrations, or they can write the instructions in a list to one side of the rows of working.

Essential exercises

Students have done questions like those in Exercises 1 to 3 in Book 1, so treat these as revision. Use twin maths tables for students who are less confident in their work. For questions in Exercise 3 students may need to draw function diagrams to remind themselves which operations to do first. The phrase 'work out the value of x' is used in all of these exercises so that students become familiar with what is required. Eventually they need to relate this phrase with the instruction 'solve'.

Get students to solve the equations in Exercise 4 in two ways. First they can draw function diagrams as in *Demonstration 2* and then they can multiply out the brackets before solving them as in *Demonstration 1*.

The equations in Exercise 5 all need simplifying before they can be solved. Help the students with this first step before getting them to solve the equations.

The table is an extension of the tables that students completed in Book 1. When students work out the values to enter into the table they are not always aware of the fact that they are solving equations.

Challenging exercises

Exercise 7 extends the work to solving simple quadratic equations. Work through the examples with the class, drawing function diagrams. For example:
(e)

$$x \xrightarrow{\;+2\;} (x+2) \xrightarrow{\text{square}} (x+2)^2 \xrightarrow{\;+5\;} (x+2)^2 + 5$$

$$5 \xleftarrow[\;-2\;]{} 7 \xleftarrow[\text{square root}]{} 49 \xleftarrow[\;-5\;]{} 54$$

Exercises 8 and 9 are used to show students that when we have two variables, the value of one depends upon the value of the other. Finding solutions does not always mean a single solution as these questions show.

Exercise 10 provides a visual image of the solution of a simple linear equation. This is good preparation for work on simultaneous equations in Book 3. Get students to suggest the graphs they would draw to solve the equations in Exercises 1 to 3.

Problem-solving exercises

Exercise 11 is a typical question seen in national tests. It is an application of the work on equations in this lesson. Students will probably need some help in interpreting the question.

Plenary

Use the questions in the *Goals* to check students' understanding of the work. The points for discussion in the *Plenary* are all challenging. Assist the students with their responses.

Homework

It is not easy writing real-life stories for maths stories. Give some examples such as 'I bought seven CDs and I now have twenty CDs. How many CDs did I have to start with?'

Number and Algebra

 Linear graphs

Page 92

Goals

This lesson continues the work started in Book 1 (pages 104–111) where students were enabled to look at a linear equation, imagine its graph and sketch it. This required examining coefficients, identifying gradients and routinely recognising the relationship between linear graphs with the same coefficient of x. They were assisted in all this by using graphical calculators and computer software, and by the requirement that every time they drew a pair of axes they labelled them with two names:

x-axis $y = 0$ on the horizontal axis
y-axis $x = 0$ on the vertical axis.

Although this must be done routinely, students must also understand the relationship between the names of the axes and their linear equations. They must be able also to routinely draw $y = x$ and $y = {}^-x$, and appreciate the significance of the linear equations and their relationship with the linear equations of lines parallel to them.

It is especially important that students understand the relationship between, say, $y = x$ and $y = x + 3$, $y = x - 2$, and so on (as a linear transformation visualised as a translation and described by referring to an object and image).

The earlier we introduce the correct mathematical language related to graphs the more likely students are to accept it and use it confidently. Regularly refer to (0, 0) as the origin and always label the axes as shown. Use 'coefficient of x' to describe the constant a and 'intercept' to describe the constant b in the equation $y = ax + b$. Exercise 9 introduces the notion of 'gradient' as measured using a right-angled triangle and then relating it to the coefficient of x. Some caution is advised here because the relationship between the coefficient of x and the gradient of the graph depends upon the form of the equation being $y = ax + b$, i.e. the coefficient of y has to be unity before the link can be made.

Starter

I See Maths places considerable emphasis on students interpreting inequalities; the *Starter* begins by practising this in the typical context of an instruction to draw a pair of axes. Examine the inequalities carefully, demonstrate how to respond to them, and ensure every student can do this accurately.

Ensure that students can articulate the reasons in questions 2 and 3, by referring to the coordinates of points on the axes.

Demonstration 1

All the graphs illustrated in the demonstrations were studied extensively in Book 1 (pages 102–111). This lesson revises that work and reinforces the language of graphs.

Draw the three graphs in the first illustration on the board. Although you could generate these with computer software the resulting graph may lack some of the detail we wish to emphasise here. Many software packages do not show axes or graphs correctly labelled, and the scale may not be clear. We also have to be careful with graphical calculators because the screen is not 'square' unless we deliberately make it so and linear graphs can be distorted.

Inspect the three graphs and invite students to respond to questions. Note the significance of the arrows on the graphs indicating that the lines continue beyond the boundaries of the drawn axes.

What can you tell me about the graph $y = x$? [It passes through the origin. The graph is at 45° to the x- and y-axes. Points on the line are (1, 1), (2, 2) … $(\frac{1}{2}, \frac{1}{2})$, ($^-1$, $^-1$) etc. The coefficient of x is one. The gradient of the graph is 1. The graph is a linear graph.]

What can you tell me about the graph $y = x + 3$? [It is parallel to $y = x$. It has the same 'steepness', 'gradient', or 'slope'. It cuts the y-axis at (0, 3) – the intercept on the y-axis is 3. It cuts the x-axis at ($^-3$, 0). Points on the line are (0, 3), (1, 4) etc. The coefficient of x is one – the gradient is one. The graph is a linear graph.]

Repeat for the graph of $y = x - 2$, and then for other graphs that are parallel to $y = x$. Invite students to give the equations of graphs parallel to $y = x$.

Repeat the exercise for the second illustration. Note that the equations are written as $y = 0 + 3$ to be continuous with the previous set of graphs. This can be abbreviated to $y = 3$ once the students have understood the significance of the zero.

What can you tell me about the graph of $y = 0$? [It is coincident with the x-axis. Points on the line are ($^-2$, 0), (0, 0), $(\frac{1}{2}, 0)$, (1, 0), (2, 0), (3, 0) etc.]

What can you tell me about the graph of $y = 0 + 3$?
[It is parallel to the x-axis – it is parallel to the graph of $y = 0$. It cuts the y-axis at $(0, 3)$. Points on the line are $(1, 3)$, $(2, 3)$ etc.]

Discuss the three lines in each diagram in terms of object and image. Use hand movements to show that if $y = x$ is the object then $y = x + 3$ is an image, and motion in an upward direction. Similarly with $y = x$ and $y = x - 2$ motion in a downward direction.

Demonstration 2

The first set of graphs illustrates the effect of changing the value of the coefficient of x. In this case we begin with the graph of $y = x$ and note the change of gradient with the change of coefficient. Note that all the graphs pass through the origin.

The second illustration moves on to look at graphs that are parallel to the graph $y = 2x$. Invite students to give further examples of graphs belonging to this set of graphs.

Now invite students to imagine the graph of $y = 3x$ and ask them to sketch the graph of $y = 3x + 2$. Ask them to explain what they know about this graph. Repeat this with further examples until you are sure that all the students can visualise any linear graph.

Use hand movements to indicate the connections between:

(a) object $y = x$; image $y = x - 3$
(b) object $y = x$; image $y = 2x$
(c) object $y = 2x$; image $y = 2x + 3$

Worked example

The *Worked example* brings together the knowledge the students have of the equation of a straight line. For one line to be parallel to another their gradients must be equal, i.e. the coefficient of x must be the same. For the intercept on the y-axis to be $y = 5$ the constant value must be 5. Hence the required equation of the line is $y = 2x + 5$.

Essential exercises

The first exercise is designed to check students' understanding before moving on to examples that are more difficult. It also ensures that the correct language is used.

In Exercise 4 students are told to sketch and then draw accurately. Sketching does not involve laborious plotting of points – students must be taught to exploit their visualisation from the symbols and sketch the appropriate line.

Challenging exercises

In Exercise 6 students should specify some points on each line and note the relationship between the x and y values. The intercept on the y-axis can be used to confirm that the equation is correct.

In Exercise 7(a) students should use the words, 'linear equation' and confirm that the only powers in the variables are unity.

Problem-solving exercises

Answering these questions confirms and consolidates important ideas encountered in this lesson, and develops a method for calculating the gradient of a straight line.

Plenary

First check the students' understanding with the questions in the *Goals*.

Confirm that $y = {}^-x$ is a linear equation and invite a student to sketch it on the board, assisted by your questions to other students (e.g. *If $x = 3$, what is y?*). Look again at $y = {}^-x$ and discuss the coefficient of x; and the intercept on the y-axis. Then invite a student to sketch the graph. Use hand movements to discuss and connect the drawn object with its images. Establish, using hand movements, how the object and the image are related by translations.

Confirm that $y = x^2$ is not a linear equation. Sketch it, accompanied by a running commentary and questions to students. Using $y = x^2$ as the object show how $x^2 + 3$ and $x^2 - 2$ are related as before, by translations.

Homework

Before setting the *Homework*, consolidate the meaning of 'gradient' and 'intercept' and their relationship with the linear equation $y = ax + b$.

Number and Algebra

Page 96 Solving equations 2

Goals

The work in this lesson capitalises on the work done in Book 1 and in previous lessons. It moves students on from solving simple linear equations to solving more complex linear equations. Examples with x on both sides of the equals sign, or brackets that need expanding are explored, and seen as straightforward extensions of previous work.

Students need to see the two methods for solving linear equations, using twin tables and using graphs, alongside each other. We begin by demonstrating the two solutions with simple linear equations and then move on to more complex linear equations.

The instruction 'solve' has different meanings in different contexts. Suppose we ask you to 'solve' the equation $x + y = 10$. You would say that there is an infinite number of solutions. You could limit the solutions to pairs of positive whole numbers: (1, 9), (2, 8) etc. You might say that you cannot possibly list all the answers but you could represent the solution by drawing the graph on rectangular axes. The value of y depends upon the value of x (or the value of x depends on the value of y). Their sum must always be ten.

The instruction to solve $x^2 + 5x + 6 = 0$ has a different meaning. In this case we want to find two values of x that satisfy the equation, and we call these values 'roots' of the equation. We can draw the graph of $y = x^2 + 5x + 6$ and look for the intersection of this graph with the x-axis ($y = 0$). This will tell us the roots, and we will be able to solve the quation.

In this lesson we are asking for one specific value of x that satisfies a linear equation such as $x + 5 = 13$. However, the equations are presented in more complex forms and need simplifying before a solution can be found. Students need to know that they should expand brackets and collect together like terms before considering a solution.

Starter

Set out twin maths tables and invite students to work in pairs solving the equations using cards on the tables. Get another student to give the instructions and write out the solution on the board using symbols.

(1) $x + 3 = 5$
   Take away 3 $x = 2$

(2) $2x + 3 = 7$
   Take away 3 $2x = 4$
   Divide by 2 $x = 2$

Now solve each equation using function diagrams. For example:

$$x \xrightarrow{\; +3 \;} x + 3$$

$$2 \xleftarrow[\; -3 \;]{} 5$$

Demonstration 1

Study the graphs in *Demonstration 1*. Inspect the graph of $y = x + 3$. Invite students to give the coordinates of points on this line. All of these points are solutions of the equation $y = x + 3$. How many solutions are there? An infinite number.

Now look at the graph of $y = 5$. Invite students to give coordinates of points on this line. All of these points are solutions of the equation $y = 5$. The two lines, $y = x + 3$ and $y = 5$ intersect at the point (2, 5). The values, $x = 2$ and $y = 5$ is a solution to both the equations. It is the solution to $y = x + 3$ and at the same time it is the solution to $y = 5$. We say that it is simultaneously the solution to both equations.

When the y value is the same for both equations $x + 3$ is then equal to 5 (i.e. $x + 3 = 5$) and the graphs show us that this is when $x = 2$.

Now inspect the two graphs $y = x + 3$ and $y = 2$ and follow the same process to eventually solve $x + 3 = 2$.

Demonstration 2

Study the sets of graphs in *Demonstration 2*. Consider the graphs $y = 2x + 3$ and $y = 7$. These two graphs intersect at the point (2, 7). The simultaneous solution of the two equations is $x = 2$ and $y = 7$.

Using the mathematical logic: if $a = b$ and $a = c$ then $b = c$, we can see that $y = 2x + 3$ and $y = 7$, so we can write $2x + 3 = 7$. From the graphs we can see that the solution to this equation is therefore $x = 2$.

Number and Algebra

We can set the equation out using twin tables.

$$2x + 3 = 7$$

Take away 3	$2x = 4$
Divide by 2	$x = 2$

Now study the graphs $y = 2x + 3$ and $y = x + 2$. Using the same logical argument we can see from the graphs that the solution of $2x + 3 = x + 2$ is $x = {}^-1$

Using twin tables we have:

$$2x + 3 = x + 2$$

Take away x	$x + 3 = 2$
Take away 3	$x = {}^-1$

Essential exercises

First get the students to use twin tables to solve the equations in Exercise 1. Then discuss what graphs to draw and ask the students to solve each equation graphically. They should then check that their answers agree with those found by using the maths of the twin tables.

Exercise 2 checks that students understand the process of drawing graphs to solve the equations.

Work through Exercise 3 with the class. Discuss what needs to be done first. Expand the brackets and simplify each side of the equations. This can be thought of as tidying up each table before working on it. These questions are designed to show students the logical steps they have to take when solving equations.
1. Expand brackets.
2. Simplify each side of the equation.
3. Use twin tables and/or graphs to solve the equation.

Exercise 4 begins with the graphs and works back to the equation that can be solved.

Challenging exercises

The questions in Exercise 5 are similar in nature to those in Exercise 3 but they involve more complex calculations at the outset.

Consider the right-hand side (RHS) of the equation in 5(a). $45 - 3(4 - a)$. This expression has two terms connected with a subtraction sign. The first term is 45. The second term is $3(4 - a)$. Expanded that is $12 - 3a$ or $12 + {}^-3a$.

It is time to establish that $- - 3a$ has the same value as $- {}^-3a$, which has the same value as $+3a$. Do this by considering the expression below.

$$\begin{aligned} 45 - 3(4 - a) &= 45 - (12 - 3a) \\ &= 45 - (12 + {}^-3a) \\ &= 45 - 12 - {}^-3a \\ &= 45 - 12 + 3a \\ &= 33 + 3a \end{aligned}$$

There are other ways of reaching the same result, and students may wish to offer alternatives.

Discuss 5(c) and consider the first step. Consider multiplying both sides of the equation (both maths tables) by 6 to give
$$3(2b - 5) = 2(6b - 11)$$
$$6b - 15 = 12b - 22.$$

5(d) is the same sort of question written in a different form. Discuss these different ways of presenting the same information.

Exercise 6 extends the work to consider inequalities. Discuss how to present the answers to these questions. For example, 6(a) has the answer $x \leq 4$ and this can be shown using a number line like this.

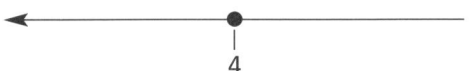

Had the solution been $x < 4$ the circle would be empty like this.

Problem-solving exercises

Exercises 7 and 8 put these ideas into contexts. Get the students to begin each question with 'Let x be …'.

Plenary

Check that students can solve the equations in the *Goals*, and discuss the example in the *Plenary*.

Homework

Ask the students to complete the instructions in the *Homework*, and get them to make up some more examples for themselves.

Page 100 **Proportion**

Goals

The concept of direct proportionality is rather complex. The idea is encapsulated in its distinctive expression $y \propto x$, and its consequent equation $y = kx$ (a linear equation passing through the origin). Students need to use these two closely associated expressions to appreciate their relationship with linear graphs. The introduction to linear graphs in previous lessons has, among other things, anticipated this work on proportionality.

It must be borne in mind that the equation $y = kx$ does express the particular qualities of direct proportionality; but $y = kx + c$ does not. Although both imply 'equal steps in x being associated with equal steps in y', this does not capture the full meaning: it has to be 'equal steps from zero' which, of course, is captured in $y = kx$ but not in $y = kx + c$. But, of course, it is the idea of 'equal steps' that tends to be used as an introduction to proportionality.

If we rewrite the equation $y = kx$ as $\frac{y}{x} = k$, we can see that $\frac{y}{x}$ is a ratio, that is, y compared to x is a constant. It is this fundamental idea that we want students to appreciate in this lesson. Of course, students have met this kind of relationship in several mathematical topics and possibly in other areas of the curriculum. For example, the circumference of a circle is proportional to its radius ($C = \pi d$); distance travelled is proportional to the time when an object is not accelerating ($d = st$), and amount in pounds sterling = current exchange rate × amount in American dollars.

Book 3 explores $y \propto x^2$, $y \propto x^3$, $y \propto \frac{1}{x}$ and so on. In this book however, study is restricted to y being directly proportional to x.

Starter

The first activity in the *Starter* revises work already done on arithmetic sequences. All such sequences generate terms that are linear in nature. However, not all linear relationships generate linear graphs that pass through the origin.

The second activity reminds students of linear graphs, all of which pass through the origin, in preparation for the work on proportion.

Demonstration 1

Inspect each graph in turn and discuss the relationship. The first set of graphs all show relationships where y is *not* directly proportional to x. (Why?) Inspect each graph or sets of coordinates. What are we looking for? Ask questions.

Inspect graph (i). Does the graph pass through the origin? No. Is the graph a straight line? No. Is y directly proportional to x? No.

Repeat for graphs (ii) and (iii).

Now look at the set of points in (iv). What is the relationship between x and y? Each value of y is one less than three times the value of x. ($3x - 1$) The relationship is $y = 3x - 1$. Will the graph of this relationship pass through the origin? No. Is y directly proportional to x? No.

Look at part (v). What is the relationship between x and y. Each value of y is the square of the x value. $y = x^2$. y is proportional to x^2 but is not proportional to x.

Look at the second set of graphs and coordinates. Inspect the first graph. It passes through the origin. The relationship is $y = x$. We can see that y is directly proportional to x. The ratio of y to x is one. In the second graph the ratio of y to x is a third and in the third graph the ratio of y to x is five. What about the fourth graph? The line has a downward slope, rather than an upward slope (it has a negative gradient). The ratio of y to x is negative one-third.

Demonstration 2

This demonstration clarifies the language of proportionality and introduces the symbol '$\propto$'. We want students to be able to interpret a situation, write a statement using the proportional symbol, and convert this into an equation that can be solved. The letter 'k' is used to denote some constant term.

Dr Rahman invites some students to tea. There are two variables. The number of students can vary (x) and the number of pancakes they eat can vary (y). By recording each variable over a number of visits, we can see that there is a relationship between the number of students and the number of pancakes.

We can see that the number of pancakes is always five times the number of students. That is: $y = 5x$. Now Dr Rahman can work out how many pancakes she needs to buy when she has a hundred students to visit her. (500)

Dr Muir has rooms he wants painted. There are two variables, the number of rooms to be painted (y) and the number of painters needed (x). He knows that there is a relationship between the number of rooms painted and the number of painters. He knows that the number of rooms painted is directly proportional to the number of painters. He knows that five painters completed seven rooms in a day. He can work out the constant k. The ratio y to x is 7 to 5. He can write $y = \frac{7}{5}x$. He decides to get twenty-one rooms painted (he has a very large house!) and he wants it all done in a day. He works out that he needs fifteen painters.

Worked example

Show the students how to set out questions on proportionality. In this example the variables are given but explain that when this is not the case they will have to begin with 'Let x be …'.

Essential exercises

The questions in Exercise 1 can be answered intuitively but use this as an opportunity to formalise the method. It is easy to see that in part (a) wheel A makes four times as many turns as in the opening statement, and so wheel B must also make four times as many turns (32). Let the number of turns for wheel A be x and the number of turns for wheel B be y. Compare x to y.

(a) $x : y$ is 3 : 8 so $\frac{y}{x} = \frac{8}{3}$. When $x = 12$, $y = \frac{8}{3}$ of 12 = 32.

(b) When $x = 225$, $y = \frac{8}{3} \times 225 = 8 \times 75 = 600$.

A conversion graph can be used to estimate the cost but unless the scale is very large it cannot be used to calculate accurate answers. Discuss how accurate the answers can be in Exercise 2.

For added interest, you could substitute values in Exercise 3 using up-to-date exchange rates for different currencies.

In Exercise 4 the car is travelling at a constant speed and so the distance is directly proportional to the time. See if the students can work out the speed in km per hour.

Challenging exercises

Exercise 5 tests whether students can see the simple logic that if $a = b$ and $a = c$ then $b = c$. The logic tells us that \$1·48 = €1·56, so \$1 = €$\frac{156}{148}$.

Get students to check that each pair of numbers in Exercise 6 is connected with the same relationship and then get them to draw the graph.

Problem-solving exercises

Exercise 7 is a common question asked in tests. Students frequently make the mistake of adding on amounts instead of recognising the need for multiplication. Insist that they set out their work beginning with 'Let the number of litres of blue paint be x and the number of litres of yellow paint be y. The ratio of x to y is 7 to 5. Therefore $x = \frac{7}{5}y$ and $y = \frac{5}{7}x$.

Exercise 8 shows a graph that someone might use in a fruit farm. Discuss whether it is best to try to estimate the values from the graph or to work out the relationship and calculate exact values.

Plenary

Discuss the graph in the *Goals* and get the students to work out the equation of the line. Discuss the graphs of the equations in the *Plenary* and ask students which ones represent direct proportion.

Homework

Students need to know where to find recent exchange rates and how to use them. This could be linked to a project in another area of the curriculum.

Number and Algebra

Interpreting graphs

Page 104

Goals

Throughout these books we teach students to inspect graphs in certain ways. They are taught to read the titles, examine the axes, work out the scales, study the shape of the graph, ask questions about points on the graph, and discuss the orientation of the graph. We want students to do all of this before they worry about the questions being asked. Students often need persuading that all of this work is necessary, particularly when they know that at some time they will be presented with questions in tests with very limited time for such luxuries. The demonstrations in this lesson are designed to show them why this scrutiny is necessary as they study what at first appear to be eight identical graphs.

The graphs being studied in this lesson are all representing real-life situations. We know that students find real-life contexts very distracting. They see the words 'velocity' or 'acceleration' and for some students such words induce anxiety and fear. We want to assist students in becoming detached from the context so that they focus on the maths story.

Initially students study the explicit information on a graph. What does the title tell us? What are the labels on the axes? What are the units of measure? What is the range on the scale on the axes? Are both scales the same? What is the shape of the graph?

This paves the way for interrogation of the implicit information. Is the graph linear? Is the relationship directly proportional? Does x increase at the same rate as y? And for more detail we can start looking at points on the graph for hints of the real-life story. As students become more familiar with different graphs, so the implicit information will become so obvious that it can be considered as explicit information.

Remember that the graph represents a maths story and that any point on the graph must be regarded as a hint about the real-life story. Students are able to ascertain certain facts about the real-life story from the graph. They can use these facts to build an imaginary story. Encourage students to be creative but remind them to retain the correct factual information.

Starter

Read each equation (or formula) in turn. They are all about distance, speed and time. The ratio of distance (d) to time

(t) is constant (s) when there is no acceleration. In other words the speed is constant.

What are the units of measure for the first one? Distance is measured in miles and time in hours. $\frac{d}{t}$ = miles/hours so the speed is given in miles per hour. In the second example speed is measured in metres per second ($\frac{m}{s}$ or ms^{-1}).

The last two examples give the formula in a different form. Distance is directly proportional to time. $d \propto t$ or $d = st$. Ask students to give the units of measure in each case.

Demonstration 1

All four graphs in the demonstration have the same shape but they do not represent the same story. Each graph is a hint of a real-life story. Let us interrogate each one.

The first graph is a story about John's journey, showing the distance from his house. The time is measured in hours and the distance is measured in kilometres. The graph shows us three parts of John's journey. Each part is a straight line so he must have been travelling at a constant speed in each part.

Look at point A. John begins his journey 20 km from home. He travels to a point B that is 50 km from his home in 3 hours. He is travelling at a constant speed of $\frac{50}{3}$ km per hour. That is nearly 17 km per hour so he cannot have been walking. For the next three hours he does not get any further from home. We do not know what he was doing but we could speculate and make up a fictional story about it. After three more hours (point C) John makes his way home at a constant speed of $\frac{50}{2} = 25$ km per hour (point D).

The second graph is a story about the volume of water in a bath. The volume is measured in litres and the time is measured in minutes. At the beginning of the story (point A) the bath has 20 litres of water in it. That is not very much water. The volume of water increases at a constant rate for three minutes until there are 50 litres of water in the bath (point B). That is still not very much water. My kettle holds two litres of water so the volume of water is about 25 kettles of water. Maybe it is not a very big bath or maybe it is a bath for a baby. The water is left in the bath for only three minutes (point C). That isn't long. Then the water is let out of the bath at a constant rate for two minutes until it is empty (point D). That is 25 litres a minute.

Get the students to tell stories for the last two graphs. They are both about the volume of a balloon. What is different about the two graphs? The only difference is in the measure for time. What sort of balloon is this? Consider the volume of the balloon. Consider the time taken to put gas into the balloon.

Demonstration 2

Here there are four more graphs that look just like those in the first demonstration. What is different about these? They are all about journeys but some are about journeys with constant speed and some are about journeys with constant acceleration.

Assist the students in telling the stories. Make a distinction between fact and fiction. The maths story provides the facts and the imagination provides the fiction.

Essential exercises

Read the text in Exercise 1 and inspect the graphs. The y-axis shows the distance from Colebrook in miles. Sam begins her journey at Colebrook so the red line graph must represent Sam's journey. Andrew sets of from Hamerton (the blue line graph) and this is 20 miles from Colebrook.

Assist the students in answering the questions in Exercise 1. Inspect the scales on the axes. Each small square on the x-axis represents one-fifth of an hour. That is twelve minutes. Each small square on the y-axis represents half a mile. Look at the red line graph after one hour. Sam has travelled four miles. Get pairs of students to discuss the questions and then go through each question in turn as a class.

Before setting Exercise 2, get the students to talk through each situation. As water pours at a steady rate into beaker (a) what happens to the depth of the water? It increases at a constant rate. How do we show that on a graph? For each step along the x-axis the depth increases in equal steps on the y-axis. This is a straight-line graph.

Look at beaker (d). The depth of water increases at a faster rate as time increases. Show how to build up the picture in a graph by plotting a series of points at equal steps along the x-axis with increasing additional height along the y-axis until you get a nice smooth curve.

Challenging exercise

The four situations in Exercise 3 need to be discussed before students draw the graphs. They must consider what

it is they are plotting. When they have matched the graphs to the statements they could consider how the graphs would look if the y-axis represented speed instead of displacement (distance).

Problem-solving exercise

Exercise 4 provides a practical situation for study. This question should not present any difficulties for the students.

Plenary

Check that students can interpret the graphs in the demonstrations. Invite students to use the same shape graphs and create their own axes to match a story.

Discuss why the graph in the *Plenary* is a curve. Talk through different parts of the graph and discuss the significance of the steepness of the curve.

Homework

Prepare students for the *Homework* by asking a student to tell his or her own short story involving a journey. Note the key points of the story on the board. Invite a student to use a graph to describe the journey.

Number and Algebra

Page 108 Investigating graphs

Goals

This lesson prepares students for work to come in Book 3. Much time has been spent studying linear graphs and the solution of linear equations. This is important work and students need to have a good understanding of such work before moving on to more complex graph work.

Now that we have access to so much technology we can make use of it to introduce students to work that in the past was just too laborious to tackle. We can generate graphs using computer software or graphical calculators with such speed that we can consider a very different approach to teaching graphs. Students do not need to be able to substitute values into complex expressions to draw graphs. Instead, they can delight in the visual images of graphs at the press of a button.

No student should be denied access to the aesthetic wonders of trigonometric graphs and polynomial graphs. All school students can get pleasure from creating visual images on a computer screen and for many this work can be an inducement to study the subject further.

For some reason, topics such as trigonometry have been delayed until quite late in the mathematics curriculum. It is a subject that is often omitted for the less confident students. Yet there is nothing particularly difficult about the subject when it is introduced first as a function. The hardest work in trigonometry is in applying it to right-angled triangles and using a ratio to calculate lengths. This work is covered in Book 3 when students have been taught the skills required. This lesson sets out to stimulate the students' curiosity with the study of trigonometric functions.

We have already introduced the idea of simultaneous solutions for simple linear and then more complex linear graphs. Some examples of other types of simultaneous solutions are included here to enable the students make important connections.

Starter

The first two questions here review the work done in the previous lesson. Question 3 is a simple introduction to the existence of the sine and cosine functions.

Demonstration 1

Use computer graph software or a graphical calculator to generate the graph of $y = x^2$. On the same axes generate the graph of $y = 2x + 3$. Compare the images with the illustration in *Demonstration 1*.

Inspect the linear graph $y = 2x + 3$. Ask questions:

> *What are the solutions to this equation? There are lots and lots of solutions. Some of them are written in the table. Can you give me some more? What about when $x = \frac{1}{2}$? What about when $x = 0.2$? Give me some more. All the points on the line are solutions of this equation.*

Inspect the curve $y = x^2$:

> *What are the solutions of this equation? Again there are lots and lots. There are some in the table. Can you give me some more? What about when $x = \frac{1}{2}$? What about ...*
>
> [Inspect the two points where the line and curve intersect.] *What are the simultaneous solutions of these two equations? $x = 3$, $y = 9$ and $x = {}^-1$, $y = 1$.*

Repeat the demonstration for the pairs of equations:
$y = x^2 + 2$ and $y = x + 4$
$y = x^2 - 1$ and $y = x + 1$

Demonstration 2

Use computer graph software or a graphics calculator to generate the curves $y = \sin x$ and $y = \cos x$. The Greek letter θ is used in the illustration because this is the standard letter used in trigonometry. However, many software packages only respond to the letters x and y. You will need to check this before the lesson.

Draw the curves on the same axes. Note the similarities and differences. The curves have the same shape. Cos x has been displaced by 90°. It is a translation in the x-direction. The curves repeat themselves again and again. Discuss the maximum and minimum values of sin x and cos x. Inspect specific points such as sin 90° and cos 90°. Estimate the value of sin 45° and cos 45°. Students will discover more about these graphs when they do the *Problem-solving exercise*.

Number and Algebra

Discuss the names of the curves. Explain that the full titles are 'sine x' and 'cosine x'. The word sine is a derivation of 'sinus'. Get the students to look this up in a dictionary or on the Internet.

Essential exercises

Exercise 1 revises all the work on linear graphs. This exercise can be completed orally with confident students using a single computer and projector to generate the graphs. Make sure that all the students understand this work and use the correct mathematical language. Revise the words 'coefficient', 'gradient', 'intercept', 'origin', 'parallel', 'variable', 'constant', 'linear', and 'translation'.

You will find it more efficient to use a projected image of the graphs to discuss Exercise 2 with the whole class. Invite students to come to the computer and take in turns generating different quadratic curves.

Discuss what happens to the graphs as you change the value of the constants. Note that varying the value of c translates the original curve of $y = x^2$ in the y-direction. Note that the curve is squashed or stretched in the x-direction when the value of a is varied.

All students will be able to see and describe the movement of the curves in 2(c)(i). With more confident students you can suggest that they factorise equations such as $y = x^2 + x$ to get $y = x(x + 1)$. Compare this with the graph and they will notice that the curve crosses the x-axis at $(0, 0)$ and $(\tilde{}1, 0)$. The curve has been translated in both the x and y directions.

You can extend this work for very confident students and investigate cubic and quartic graphs. You will need to select appropriate graphs so that their visual images can easily be displayed on the screen.

Challenging exercise

Exercise 3 introduces the idea of solving quadratic equations graphically. This is good preparation for work that will be introduced in Book 3. It should follow on quite naturally from the work done in solving linear equations. Although this can all be done using computer software you do have to be aware that some software packages to not provide sufficient detail to identify specific points on the graphs. You may have to estimate the solutions and get students to substitute the values into the equations to check them. This is a good exercise for confident students to undertake.

Problem-solving exercise

It is surprising how few people know that the trigonometric functions originate from points on a unit circle. The first

thing that needs explaining in Exercise 4 is this idea of a 'unit circle'. The unit (as with any measuring unit or scale) can have any physical length we choose. However, once we have chosen our 'unit' we have to measure everything else against it. In the illustration we use five small squares to represent a unit. This is an appropriate choice because we can divide this up to show 0·2, 0·4 etc very clearly.

Mark any point P on the circle and demonstrate how to measure the distances OQ and PQ as shown in the diagram. Explain that we call the horizontal distance the cosine of the angle θ and the vertical distance the sine of the angle θ. These are words the students met in the second demonstration and they should begin to make the links between this work and the graphical work.

Ask the students to draw radii of the circle every 10° and get them to measure the vertical and horizontal distances as shown. Invite them to think how many measurements they need to take. What is the minimum number of measurements required? This encourages them to look at the symmetry of the circle and appreciate the repetitive nature of the measurements.

Get the students to draw the graphs themselves and then ask them to compare these with the graphs they generated in the demonstration.

Plenary

Discuss the questions in the *Goals* and ask students to describe the graphs of the equations given.

Ask the students to conduct the discussions in the *Plenary* in pairs and then get some students to present a summary of their discussions.

Homework

Use the *Homework* to prepare a discussion at the beginning of the next lesson.

Shape and Space

Introduction

Geometry and geometrical reasoning

Properly taught, geometry nurtures the disposition not only to perceive, say, a simple shape, but also to inspect it for clues, piece together those clues and generate some information that goes beyond perception.

In geometry we study what information is given (or is explicit) and use it to deduce or infer new (or implicit) information. Such deliberation is a characteristic of each of the subjects in the curriculum (each having its own perspective), and each makes its contribution to developing students' ability to think. Geometry makes the particular contribution of developing disciplined formal reasoning with, most often, visual images.

An example of geometrical reasoning
Inspect the lines below.

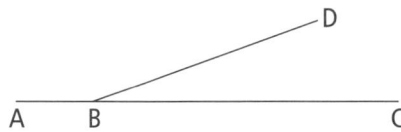

What can you see?
A straight line ABC and another straight line BD meeting ABC at the point B.
What do you know?
One full turn equals 360° and one half turn equals 180°.
What does this tell you about the diagram?
The sum of angles ABD and DBC is 180°.
If you are given that angle ABD equals 160°, what is the size of angle DBC?
180° − 160° = 20°

The language of geometry
Geometrical reasoning will remain difficult for students unless they routinely use correct technical language. This must be practised so that its use does not take up valuable cognitive space: attention can be then be focused on reasoning.

Difficulties arise for students when technical words (with very specific meanings) are already known with everyday (less specific) meanings. For example, in geometry, shapes are 'similar' when corresponding angles are equal and corresponding lengths are in the same ratio. In the vernacular, things are 'similar' when one is suggestive of the other. Teaching geometry cannot concede to the vernacular.

There is another important example. You will see that these lessons maintain the geometrical convention that distinguishes between a line (having infinite length) and a line segment (of finite length). This is not mere pedantry. Practising the use of these terms clarifies earlier work and builds a bonus for the future.

Developing understanding and skills

In this book we revisit work on angles and parallel lines that was started in Book 1. Although Book 1 introduces a dynamic approach to geometry, students still need similar demonstrations using sticks (bamboo, dowel or similar). This physical, visual dynamic geometry provides an essential foundation for simulations with graphical packages on a computer. It provides a 'feel' for the subject.

Sticks are used to develop the skill of visualising lines and line segments. Lines, of course, are always visual images because they have no width; and points have no magnitude. That is why they have to be visualised. This level of detail develops an important disposition in geometry.

Angles are visualised as a 'turn'. This means that they are visualised dynamically as movement, a rotation, from one position to another. Emphasising this, the 'arms' of a drawn angle are recognised as two lines, an object and its image, that, originally coincident, have been subjected to an operation. The object is the starting position and the image is the finishing position.

Skilled, accurate construction needs careful teaching; and it must be distinguished from the related skills of 'sketching' and 'drawing diagrams'.

A **sketch** is a drawing that uses given information to build a picture of a shape. It can be drawn freehand but should indicate measurements.
A **diagram** is a neat drawing indicating all known information. It should be drawn with a straight edge where appropriate.
A **construction** is an accurate drawing of a shape using exact or scaled measurements. Geometrical instruments such as a ruler, a set-square, a pair of compasses and a protractor should be used where appropriate.

Shape and Space

Shape and Space

Measures and scales

Goals

One of the 'big ideas' in maths is comparison. Basic measures of, for instance, length and mass are comparisons with a standard measure. Measures such as speed are derived from these basic measures by logical use of language and symbols.

The metric system uses standard prefixes to enable us to gain an immediate impression of the size of the unit in use. The equivalent measures in the Imperial System are not so obvious and students are generally unfamiliar with these units. However, for as long as they continue to be used in some contexts they need to be known.

Encourage students to look up the origins of the nautical mile on the Internet. There are several good 'history-of-maths' sites that provide this information.

Starter

All measurement is given within limits determined by the measuring instrument and the skill of the person reading the scale. The *Starter* anticipates the need to recognise these limits by considering the value of x within a given range.

In the first example the value of x can be as small as 7 and as large as 11 because the inequality signs are 'greater than *or equal to*'.

In the second example we cannot answer the question. We do know that x is greater than 7 but it could be 7·1 or 7·01 or 7·001 and so on. All these answers are acceptable. Similarly the largest value could be 10·9 or 10·99 or 10·999 and so on. The third example, where the degree of accuracy required is specified, allows us to give the answers 7·1 and 10·9.

Demonstration 1

The unitary method is one that we use in many different topics in maths. We find 1% in order to calculate 15%, we work out the cost of 1 kg in order to calculate the cost of 5 kg, and so on. Emphasise this idea of working out the value of one, or a unit, of something in order to calculate the value of many. Explain that the abbreviation for pound is lb or lbs and has been derived from the Latin 'libra'.

> We know the value of 2·2 lb is approximately 1 kg. We want to know what 1 lb is equal to. Divide 2·2 by 2·2 (1) and divide 1 by 2·2 ($\frac{1}{22}$). We want to know the value of 5 lbs. Multiply 1 by 5 (5) and multiply $\frac{1}{22}$ by 5 ($\frac{5}{22}$). Answer: 2·3 kg (to 1 d.p.).

Repeat the process for different values of pounds. Consider the metric equivalents for given masses (including some historical measurements) such as: a newborn baby of mass 7·5 lb; an adult with mass 10·5 stone (1 stone = 14 lb); a sack of potatoes with mass 1 cwt (one hundredweight = 112 lbs). Consider how the authorities dealt with some standard packaging at the time of metrication, such as: a 2 lb bag of sugar, a $\frac{1}{2}$ lb pack of butter, and so on.

Demonstrate how to read the conversion graph. Draw a graph on the board or OHT and invite students to come to the front and find conversions by reading from the graph. Get them to use a ruler to draw vertical and horizontal lines on the graph to get as accurate values as possible. Compare their results with those of the unitary method. Discuss the merits of each method such as the superior accuracy of the unitary method versus the speed and ease of reading from a graph.

Demonstration 2

The convention in most geometrical topics is to rotate or turn in an anticlockwise direction starting from the horizontal position (or positive x-direction when using rectangular axes). When measuring a bearing, however, this convention is not followed and can therefore cause some confusion unless it is demonstrated clearly at the outset.

The instructions for drawing the diagram in the demonstration are in the last *Goal*. Get the students to draw an accurate diagram in their books.

Worked example

Remind the students that:

$$1 \text{ km} = 1 \times 1000 \text{ m}$$

So $\qquad 4{·}3 \text{ km} = 4{·}3 \times 1000 \text{ m} = 4300 \text{ m}$

and $\qquad 1 \text{ cm} = 1 \times 10^{-2} \text{ m} \qquad (\frac{1}{100}\text{m})$

So $\qquad 13 \text{ cm} = 13 \times 10^{-2} \text{ m} = {·}13 \text{ m}$

Shape and Space

Letts **I See Maths** Book 2

Essential exercises

In Exercise 1 remind the students that they need to work out the area in metres squared first, and then convert to hectares.

Area of land = 16×17 m^2 = 272 m^2
$$= 272 \div 10\,000 \text{ ha}$$
$$= 0.0272 \text{ ha}$$

Discuss the degree of accuracy required in Exercise 2. If we give the answers as fractions there isn't a problem. For example, part (b): $22 \div 3 = 7\frac{1}{3}$ so there are $7\frac{1}{3}$ yards and therefore approximately $7\frac{1}{3}$ metres. However, if we give the answer as a decimal, we have to decide whether to give our answer to one, two or more decimal places. Unless the degree of accuracy is specified then it is best to leave the answer as a recurring decimal and decide on the number of decimal places when we know the context within which we are working.

Demonstrate how to read the axes in the graph in Exercise 3. Indicate different points on the graph and ask students to say how far Paula is away from home, and how long she has been travelling for. Make sure that students realise that the graph indicates distance away from home and not up and down hills. The average speed is calculated by dividing the total distance covered by the total time taken.

Get the students to sketch a drawing of the positions of A and B in Exercise 4 part (a). Explain that you always begin with the position of the place the bearing is 'from' and in this case that is the point A. Mark the point A and draw a vertical line (the object) through A to denote the direction north. Turn *clockwise* through an angle of 73° and draw the image. The point B is somewhere along this line (the distance is not relevant to this question). Mark a point B and draw a vertical line (the object) through it to denote north. Turn *clockwise* until you arrive at the line BA (the image). You have turned through an angle of 73° + 180° (the bearing is 253°).

Emphasise the importance of drawing a sketch in Exercise 4 part (b) before embarking on making an accurate scale drawing.

Students need to know the convention for rounding numbers in order to complete Exercise 5. The greatest distance would be 674 m and the least distance would be 665 m.

Challenging exercises

Discuss these with the class. The correct way of answering questions in Exercise 6(a) is:

We can specify the minimum measurement because the convention for rounding numbers is to include the value 73.5. However, we cannot specify the maximum value without knowing the degree of accuracy required. The maximum value could be 74.49, 74.499 and so on. When we know the context

we can make a decision on the number of decimal places to give.
So we can say: $73.5 \leq x < 74.5$.

Similarly, the area of the plot of land should be given within bounds. $(18.5 \times 21.5) \leq x < (19.5 \times 22.5)$.

Discuss the units of measure for each of the examples in Exercise 8. In part (a) the distance travelled could be measured in miles, kilometres, metres or other units (leagues for example!) and time in hours, minutes, seconds, weeks etc. Speed can therefore be specified in miles per hour (m/h), km per hour (km/h), metres per second (m/s), miles per week etc. Discuss when each of such units might be used, and show students the different ways of writing them such as metres per second, ms^{-1} or m/s, and stress that 'per' means 'divided by'.

Most students will need help with Exercise 8 (d). It is not easy to see that 'metres per second per second' translates into ms^{-2} or m/s^2. Consider the meaning of 'per' as 'divided by' and think of 'one divided by two divided by two'.

Problem-solving exercises

To assist the students with Exercise 9, provide them with approximate metric and imperial equivalents, or get them to look them up.

Plenary

Get the students to write all of the standard prefixes for metric units in their books. Ask them to find out the distance round the equator, and if it is given in miles or kilometres to convert this to nautical miles.

Read the instructions for the journey and ask students to draw a sketch in their books. Invite a student to draw the sketch on the board. Discuss what is meant by 'the finishing position relative to the starting position'.

Homework

Liaise with the Geography Department and try to plan this work to coincide with work on maps.

Further homework is available in the worksheets. **Worksheet 29** provides substantial practice in the use of both basic and derived units (including speed and density). The worksheet can usefully be used with all students.

Worksheet 30 provides some information about electrical units, with questions that will be most suitable for the most confident students. Discussion with the Science Department may persuade you to use this sheet with all students.

Shape and Space

Shape and Space

 Page 120 **Angles and parallel lines**

Goals

The work in this lesson assumes that students have covered the work on angles and parallel lines in *I See Maths* Book 1. If that is not the case, you may have to do some preparatory work covering some of the ideas and vocabulary from that book.

When we say that two parallel lines are three centimetres apart, what do we mean? Clarify that we mean the perpendicular distance between the lines. We must construct the line that is perpendicular to both lines, and it is this that measures 3 cm. It is this definition that gives us a clue about how to construct two lines that are parallel and three centimetres apart. Two methods for this construction are given in the first demonstration.

A line crossing a series of parallel lines (a **transversal**) is thought of as an image of a line that was initially lying in the same direction as the parallel lines. The angle of turn is from the object direction to the image direction. The values of corresponding, vertically opposite, alternate, complementary and supplementary angles can be visualised from this.

Students need to differentiate between a diagram and a scale drawing in geometry. We use conventions in diagrams to imply given properties, such as arrows to indicate parallelism, dashes to indicate equal line lengths and single or double arcs to indicate equal angles.

Geometrical reasoning is used to deduce new facts from given facts. We look at a triangle and see the angles given. We know properties of triangles such as the sums of the interior and exterior angles. We use what is given and the known properties to work out the sizes of further angles.

Starter

The activities in the *Starter* remind students of the very precise language in geometry. A line has infinite length but a line segment AB is defined by the points A and B on the line. When we draw a line on a page it can have any length because what is drawn is only a hint of the line that can be produced (continued) in either direction. Invite students to draw a line and a line segment on the board.

For questions 2(a) and 2(b) invite students to go to the board and carry out spoken instructions.

Draw three parallel lines. Show they are parallel [draw arrows on the lines]. Label the lines l_1, l_2, l_3. Draw a transversal and label it. Look at this angle [indicate one of the angles made by the transversal crossing the parallel lines and mark it with an arc] and show all the angles that are equal in size to this angle.

As the students mark the equal angles assist them in giving reasons such as 'this angle is alternate to the given angle' and 'this angle is vertically opposite the given angle' and 'this angle is corresponding to the given angle'.

Question 2(c) revises the dynamic visualisation of an angle as an object that turns through a number of degrees to the position of the image.

This is the object; this is the image. The image turns through an angle of 62°.

Demonstration 1

Place a straight edge on the board. Place a set-square along the line of the straight edge as shown in *Demonstration 1*. Draw a line along the set-square. Slide the set-square along the straight edge and draw a parallel line as in the diagram. The use of the set-square reinforces the idea that lines between the parallel lines are perpendicular to both of the parallel lines. Draw arrows on the parallel lines to indicate that they are parallel.

Draw a straight line on the board and, using a large pair of compasses with the point on the line, draw arcs as in the diagram. Place a straight edge to just touch the arcs (the tangent to each arc) and draw the line. Draw arrows on the lines to indicate that they are parallel.

Demonstration 2

Draw the diagram on the board and bring students to the front to inspect angles and work out their sizes. With some students this will be straightforward revision and you can expect them to do the calculation and explain their answer.

For less successful students, give maximum assistance and help them do the calculations. Say the explanations for them to repeat. It is important that they speak the words and become familiar with how to explain what they are doing. They will not learn by merely listening to others, but by speaking full sentences and writing them in their books to learn. Less articulate students (and EAL students) need to be taught the correct language and need to practise speaking it to the class. They will participate in this activity provided they are confident that they have the correct words to speak.

After calculating all the angles with the whole class, clean the board and ask the students to repeat the exercise in their books. Assist the less successful students to ensure that all of the angles and explanations are correct.

Worked example

Ask the students:

> *What are we given? What do we know about the interior angles of a triangle? How can we write the sum of the interior angles of this particular triangle? How can we solve the equation?*

The example sets out the solution in exactly the style that students should write their answers in their books. Make sure that they always write the equals sign underneath the previous one.

Essential exercises

Students can work on Exercises 1 and 2 in pairs, groups or as a whole class, but insist that they explain how they worked out the angles. Get them to speak full sentences such as, 'These angles are equal because they are vertically opposite angles.' and not abbreviated phrases such as 'vertically opposite'.

Students may need help in constructing the equations in Exercise 2, and in solving them. You may need to provide some simpler examples using numbers first.

Challenging exercise

With some assistance, all students should be able to attempt Exercise 3. Do the question as a class puzzle with groups working together first, and then presenting their arguments at the front. As before, insist that they speak full sentences for their explanations.

Problem-solving exercise

Treat questions like this as a puzzle, with students inspecting the diagram and working like detectives. Get students to inspect the diagram, consider what they know, and provide reasons for their answers.

Plenary

Invite students to draw the examples (a) to (d) on the board and get them to explain what is meant by the terms such as 'alternate angles'.

Get students to sketch a triangle with interior angles $x°$ and $y°$, and mark the opposite exterior angle before writing down its value. Emphasise the importance of sketching before performing a calculation.

Worksheet 31 provides further practice in making a sketch from written information and then formally calculating implicit information.

Homework

Encourage students to use the *Glossary* when they cannot answer a question in the *Homework*.

Shape and Space

Teacher's Notes Teacher's Notes Teacher's Notes Teacher's Notes Teacher's Notes teach
acher's Notes Teacher's Notes Teacher's Notes Teacher's Notes Teacher's Not
acher's Notes Teacher's Notes Teacher's Notes Teacher's Notes Teacher's Notes Teacher's N

Shape and Space

 Angles in polygons

Goals

Once again, geometrical reasoning is used to calculate unknown angles and lengths. Explicit information is given, and geometrical properties are known. Implicit information can be deduced from this but the argument needs to be clear and well presented. Sketches and diagrams are essential to this work.

The sum of the interior angles of a triangle is a well-known fact but how can it be proved? The work in this lesson shows students how the knowledge they have gained about angles and parallel lines can be used to produce a proof for the angle sum of a triangle.

Using the property of the sum of the interior angles of a triangle, the students can deduce the sum of the interior angles of quadrilaterals, pentagons, and so on. From this they can derive a formula for the sum of the interior angles of any polygon. Similarly they can derive a formula for the sum of the exterior angles of any polygon.

All students need to see how, by working systematically and logically, these mathematical arguments can be constructed. Provide sufficient assistance to enable all students to gain some understanding of this process.

In recent years, teachers have frequently used software packages such as LOGO to introduce properties of angles of polygons. The problem with this approach is that the work is normally restricted to that of *regular* polygons rather than on *generalised* polygons. It is preferable that students develop the knowledge of the properties of general polygons first and then consider what this means for specific polygons.

Starter

The exercise in this lesson relies on students being able to divide polygons into triangles in a particular way. Ask students to inspect the polygons (What is a polygon?) and ask them questions.

How many sides has each polygon? What are the names of the polygons? Are they regular or irregular? How many triangles can you see? Are there any other shapes you can see?

Demonstration 1

Place three sticks on the floor in any position. Join them to make an open shape. Then join them to make a closed shape (a triangle). Give instructions to a student to walk around the shape and turn through the interior angles.

Walk forward to this vertex, turn through the interior angle, walk backwards to the next vertex and turn through the interior angle, walk forwards to the third vertex and turn through the interior angle, walk backwards until you reach the starting point.

Now give instructions for students to walk around the triangle and turn through the exterior angles. Get them to walk clockwise and then anticlockwise. As they walk forwards show how they turn through the angle from the direction they are facing to the direction of the next side of the triangle.

Erratum: Note that one of the angles in diagram (d) is incorrectly marked. The exterior angle marked at B should be between BC and AB produced.

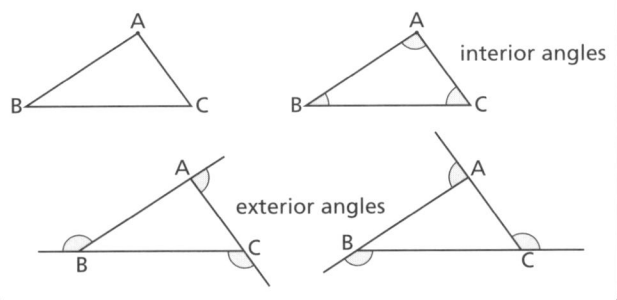

Demonstration 2

Discuss what is meant by 'Given △ABC. AB produced to D.' The term 'produced' is rarely used yet it is so efficient. To replace it we would need to say 'extend the line AB to D in the direction of AB'. **Worksheet 32** requires students to interpret instructions carefully (especially the word 'produce'). Most students will benefit from working through this worksheet.

Discuss exactly what has to be proved. Mark the exterior angle CB̂D with an arc, and mark the two interior angles with two and three arcs respectively.

Shape and Space

We want to prove that this angle [indicate the exterior angle] *is equal to this angle added to this angle* [indicate the two interior angles].

What do we know about angles on a straight line? They add up to 180°. So this exterior angle and this angle [indicate the third angle] *add up to 180°. What do we know about the sum of the interior angles of a triangle? They equal 180°. So these two interior angles and this third angle* [indicate the third angle again] *add up to 180°. So the exterior angle equals the sum of the two opposite interior angles.*

Worked example

Although this is a relatively simple example it is important that the students set out the answer with an explanation.

Essential exercises

Students know that the sum of the interior angles of a triangle is 180°, but they need to see if they can construct a proof of this for themselves. The first exercise provides the opportunity for this. Work through the proof step-by-step with the less successful students, and get them to copy it into their books. For the more successful students, get them to work in groups and ask a group to present their proof on the board.

When we construct geometrical proofs we sometimes have to look at a shape and imagine lines or curves that are not originally drawn. We do not want to complicate the diagram and so we have to consider what lines or curves we need to draw. In Exercise 2 we are told to use angles of a triangle to deduce something about the quadrilateral. But there are no triangles in the diagram and so we have to create some. The *Starter* has given the students the idea of how to do this. We can draw one of the diagonals to create two triangles and now the proof is straightforward.

Exercises 3 and 4 continue the pattern of visualising the shapes divided into triangles, and using the property about the sum of the interior angles of triangles to prove the sum of the interior angles of other polygons. The pattern leads to a generalisation. This generalisation can be explained by considering the geometrical properties of the shapes. This sort of reasoning is a good rehearsal for the requirements of GCSE coursework.

Challenging exercise

All students should attempt Exercise 5. Draw polygons on the ground and get students to start at a point on the perimeter and walk all the way around the edge of the shape until they return to the starting point. At each vertex mark the angle they turn through. Whatever the polygon, they will always turn through 360°.

Imagine a polygon with 100 sides, 1000 sides, 1 000 000 sides. As the number of sides increases to infinity, the shape approximates to a circle. As you walk around a circle you turn through 360°.

Problem-solving exercise

Students often study regular shapes before irregular shapes. They then have difficulty recognising that a shape like the one below is a hexagon.

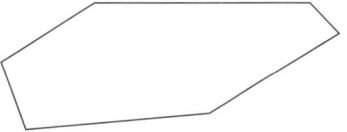

This lessons covers work with general polygons first before considering regular polygons. Students will use the properties of general polygons to discover the properties of regular polygons and to calculate their angles.

Plenary

Summarise the work done in the lesson and check the students' understanding of the sum of the exterior angles of polygons.

Homework

A regular hexagon has many useful properties. Students use the knowledge gained in the lesson to deduce these properties in the *Homework*.

Shape and Space

Shape and Space

Page 128 Geometrical reasoning

Goals

In previous lessons students have used geometrical reasoning to work out angles. In this lesson they use geometrical reasoning to detect what shapes are being discussed.

All the properties of shapes used in this lesson have been covered in earlier yearly teaching programmes. However, many of these will have been forgotten and may need revising. Display posters and models of shapes for students to see.

Once again, sketching is an important activity in building up a visual image of the shape in question. It is helpful to have models that students can take apart to see the original net that was used for its construction.

The exercises in this lesson focus on two-dimensional shapes. However, such shapes are only figments of our imagination prompted by pencil drawings on a page. Real-life shapes are all three-dimensional and so the *Goals* relate knowledge of shapes in two-dimensions to the ability to describe and draw nets of three-dimensional shapes.

Starter

Using two-dimensional drawings to represent three-dimensional objects requires some conventions. The word 'horizontal' comes from the word 'horizon' and the convention is to draw this parallel to the width of the page. A vertical line is represented as a line that is perpendicular to the horizontal.

A freehand drawing of a cube consists of four horizontal and four vertical lines joined by lines at an angle of about 45°. However, an isometric drawing of a cube has the four lines at 30°.

Students may need several attempts to make a freehand drawing of a square-based pyramid, to avoid getting lines that overlap.

Demonstration 1

The majority of students need convincing that the diagrams in this demonstration really do represent different views of a triangular prism. Get every student to construct the net of the prism using a ruler and pair of compasses. If they intend

making the shape as a solid they will need to consider cutting flaps to glue.

Ask every student to view their prism from the front, and sketch what they see. Now ask them to give the dimensions of the rectangle and get them to draw an accurate diagram of the front elevation. Repeat this with the view from the side and above (plan).

Repeat the process with other solids such as a tetrahedron, a square-based pyramid, a cylinder and a cone. Then invite the students to view shapes made with cubes, like the one in the *Goals* and get them to draw the front elevation, plan and side elevation.

Demonstration 2

Most polygons are identified as either 'regular' or 'non-regular', but the quadrilateral has fascinated people for centuries. The properties of the different types of quadrilaterals are worthy of further study.

The general name for a polygon with four sides is a 'quadrilateral'. A quadrilateral with no sides equal or parallel is a 'scalene quadrilateral'. As we begin to explore properties such as 'parallel sides' and 'equal sides', notice the logic of the language and the inclusive nature of the statements.

A **trapezium** is a quadrilateral with at least one pair of opposite sides parallel.

A **parallelogram** is a quadrilateral with two pairs of opposite sides equal and parallel. A parallelogram is therefore also a *trapezium*.

A **rectangle** is a *parallelogram* with its four angles right angles.

A **rhombus** is a *parallelogram* with four sides equal.

A **square** is a *parallelogram* with its four angles right angles and its four sides equal. A square is therefore both a *rectangle* and a *rhombus*.

The Venn diagram provides a visual image of the inclusive nature of these titles. A square is a rectangle, a rhombus, a parallelogram, a trapezium and finally it is a quadrilateral. It is a quadrilateral with the most specific properties.

Shape and Space: **Geometrical reasoning**

A useful way of thinking about this type of classification is to consider our own backgrounds. A person born in Crediton belongs to all of these groups: Devonshire, English, British, European, and a member of the human race. He will use the title that is the most appropriate for the context.

Worked example

Assist the students in reading the words and building up the diagram. What information is given? We know that the shape is a quadrilateral and the diagonals bisect each other at right angles. Since the diagonals bisect each other we know that the shape is a parallelogram. The additional fact that the diagonals bisect at right angles tells us that the shape is a rhombus. The sides AB and BC are therefore equal and the triangle is isosceles.

Essential exercises

In Exercise 1 take each clue in turn and gradually build up a picture. Students are often tempted to jump to conclusions before they have sufficient evidence. For example in part (a) they will often assume that four straight sides means a rectangle or square. Use sticks, and with the second clue place four different lengths of stick on the table as an open shape. The third clue closes the shape, and the fourth clue makes you exchange the sticks for four equal length sticks. Move the sticks around until the diagonals are different lengths. The last clue is actually redundant but confirms that the shape is a rhombus.

First of all, get the students to work individually on Exercise 2. Then get them to discuss their answers in groups, and finally ask groups to present their conclusions. Make sure that they explain and justify their decisions. Part (d) may take some discussion. A parallelogram does have the properties of a trapezium (two opposite sides parallel) and therefore has the sufficient conditions to be a trapezium. However the reverse is not true, a trapezium is not a parallelogram.

Challenging exercise

Exercise 3 is best done using sticks for the diagonals of the quadrilaterals. Read the descriptions with the class. Invite a student to show two sticks crossing as required.

The first description has the diagonals intersecting at right angles and one bisecting the other. Note that it does not say that the diagonals bisect *each other*, and so this cannot be assumed. The shape is therefore a kite. Parts (b), (c), (d) and (e) are all types of parallelograms because their diagonals bisect each other (parallelogram, rhombus, rectangle, square). Parts (f) and (g) are types of trapezia because the diagonals intersect each other in the same ratio (trapezium, symmetric trapezium).

Problem-solving exercises

In Book 1 students investigated triangles on a pin board. In Exercise 4 they investigate quadrilaterals on a pin board.

Students can waste a lot of time colouring in tessellations. Exercise 5 does not require the drawing or colouring in of tessellations but a scrutiny of why certain shapes will or will not tessellate.

Plenary

Summarise the work done in the lesson and ask students to complete the drawings in the *Goals*.

Homework

The *Homework* activity allows students to select shapes for themselves and be creative about the clues. It is likely that they will give more clues than are necessary. Challenge the class to write only the clues necessary to draw a particular shape.

Shape and Space

 Page 132 # Geometrical deduction

Students have been introduced to the idea of geometrical reasoning and deduction in previous lessons. They have been taught to inspect shapes and consider what they can see and what they already know, in order to work out further facts. This lesson builds on previous work and invites students to interrogate shapes in particular ways.

Work through the following with the class.

> *Look at a circle with centre O. What is a circle? What are the properties of a circle? A circle is a set of points equidistant from one point, its centre. Ah! So the clue is 'equidistant from one point'. We can draw any line from O to the circumference of the circle and it will always have the same length, that of the radius. But surely this is obvious? Yes, but a valuable property to consider when looking at shapes within circles.*

> *Draw two radii of a circle. Can you see an isosceles triangle? An isosceles triangle implies that there are two equal base angles that when added to the third interior angle gives a sum of 180°. We also know that if we draw a line from the centre of the circle to the mid-point of the base of the isosceles triangle it forms a right angle. We will remember all these things and make use of them when we need them.*

Starter

Draw a set of isosceles triangles of varying sizes and orientations on the board. Indicate the equal sides with dashes. Inspect each triangle in turn and indicate what information is 'given' or 'explicit'. Invite students to use arcs to indicate equal angles that they are able infer from the given information. Get the students to say 'I am given that these two sides of this triangle are equal. It is an isosceles triangle. I can infer that these two angles are equal.'

Demonstration 1

Draw a circle centre P on the board. Mark any two points A and B on the circumference of the circle. Join PA and PB. Indicate that PA is the radius of the circle and PB is the radius of the circle. Invite students to say what they know

about these radii and write PA = PB. Use dashes to indicate that the two lines are equal. Join AB and discuss triangle ABP. It has two equal sides. Therefore it is an isosceles triangle. Repeat for different positions of A and B.

Demonstration 2

Draw a circle on the board and mark four points P, Q, R and S on the circumference. Inspect shape PQRS: it has four straight edges; it is closed; all its vertices are on the circumference of a circle. PQRS is called a **cyclic quadrilateral**. This is a definition that needs to be learnt.

Draw another circle and mark three points A, B and C on the circumference. Mark a fourth point N inside the circle. Join AB, BC, CN and NA. Inspect shape ABCN: it has four straight edges; it is closed; not all of its vertices are on the circumference of a circle. ABCN is not a cyclic quadrilateral. Mark another point M outside the circle. Inspect shape ABCM. Again, ABCM is not a cyclic quadrilateral.

You can extend the work here to prove that opposite angles of a cyclic quadrilateral are supplementary. This is one of the questions in the *Challenging exercises* so you may wish to let the students attempt this before going through it with the class.

In the first diagram that shows a cyclic quadrilateral mark the centre of the circle C. Draw four equal radii CP, CQ, CR, and CS. You now have four isoceles triangles and you can mark the equal base angles with letters a, b, c, and d.

The sum of the angles of any quadrilateral is 360°.
So $2a + 2b + 2c + 2d = 360°$
or $a + b + c + d = 180°$

But $a + b + c + d$ is the sum of opposite angles of the cyclic quadrilateral (from inspection of the diagram).
So the sum of the opposite angles of the cyclic quadrilateral is 180°. Therefore the opposite angles of a cyclic quadrilateral are supplementary.

Worked example

Draw the diagram of triangle ABC, with AB produced to D on the board. Describe the diagram using those words. Ask the students what it is we are required to prove. (That an exterior angle of a triangle is equal to the sum of the two interior opposite angles.) Ask the students to supply the information they know (implicit information) about the interior angles of a triangle, and angles on a straight line. (This will provide the first two lines of the proof.) Write the complete proof on the board as you go through it with the students.

Essential exercises

The proof in Exercise 1 is normally stated as the theorem: 'The angle $A\hat{O}B$ at the centre of a circle is twice the angle $A\hat{P}B$ at the circumference subtended by the same arc AB'. It is an important theorem because it can be used to deduce many other theorems about angles in a circle. It is surprisingly easy to prove using basic knowledge of triangles and circles. The questions are designed to build up the proof in stages. When the students have completed the exercise ask them to help you reproduce the proof on the board.

Exercise 2 builds the proof that 'an angle in a semi-circle is a right angle' and the Exercise 3 builds the proof that 'angles in the same segment, subtended by the same arc, are equal'.

Challenging exercise

You may have demonstrated the first part of Exercise 4 as part of *Demonstration 2*. If so, get the students to reproduce the proof. Otherwise, challenge them to consider how they might begin, and then assist them with the proof.

The second part of Exercise 4 requires the students to consider the properties of a rhombus. Opposite angles of a rhombus are equal. If the sum of the opposite angles of the rhombus is 180° then each angle must be 90°. The rhombus must be a square to be cyclic.

All the interior angles of a rectangle are right angles. Opposite angles will always be supplementary and therefore any rectangle is a cyclic quadrilateral. Draw any rectangle. Draw its diagonals. Draw a circle, centre at the intersection of the diagonals such that it passes through each vertex of the rectangle. Check with different rectangles.

Problem-solving exercise

Discuss with the class how they might begin this investigation. Suggest that they work systematically and methodically. They may have access to suitable computer software to assist them in this task.

Suppose the circles have equal radii. Suppose they do not overlap. Suppose they just touch. Suppose they overlap just a little. Suppose they overlap so that the circumference of one passes through the centre of the other. Suppose ...
Now suppose the circles do not have equal radii. Suppose ...

Make sure that students use compasses and rulers to draw the diagrams of the different situations. Circles are not easy to draw freehand and sketches are likely to lead to incorrect assumptions.

Plenary

Students need to be aware that deduction is not something unique to geometry. We use logic and deduction in our everyday lives. Invite students to make up their own questions to ask the class.

Homework

The examples in the *Homework* use the properties of angles in a circle that the students have proved in the lesson. You may need to do some examples first with the class.

Worksheet 33 will be useful with your least confident students: it provides practice in ruler and compass work.

Shape and Space

Shape and Space

 Page 136 # Constructions and loci

Goals

The first two goals are in fact the same but expressed differently. The first refers to the completed object whilst the second refers to the properties of an ellipse.

We often talk about a circle, the finished object, but we often forget to refer to its construction as a set of points equidistant from a given point. Yet it is this property that we most often want to use, as seen in the previous lesson. It is this property of a circle that enables us to use a pair of compasses to construct perpendicular bisectors, angle bisectors and so on.

Consider the construction of the perpendicular bisector of line segment PQ. Normally we draw the arcs just long enough to be able to complete the construction. Suppose instead, that you drew the full circles. The diagram below is like those drawn in the *Problem-solving exercise* in the previous lesson. Students can see why the line RS is perpendicular to the line PQ.

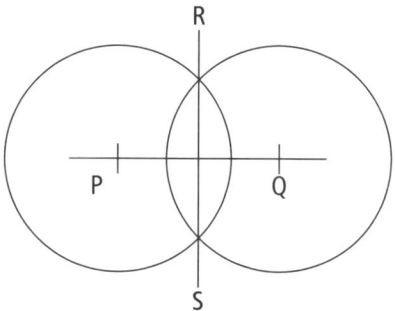

Starter

The two constructions in the *Starter* should be revision of work done in Book 1. However, you may need to demonstrate each of these to the class and set them examples to do as practice.

For question 1, first draw two identical intersecting circles, centres P and Q, as in the diagram above. Show how the line joining the centres of the circles is perpendicular to the line joining the points of intersection (PRQS is a rhombus and the diagonals of a rhombus bisect each other at right angles). Demonstrate how to use this fact to construct the perpendicular bisector of a line and show how short arcs are used to show where the circles intersect.

Indicate a point X on RS, the perpendicular bisector of PQ.

> *How far is X from P? How far is X from Q? [Draw the lines PX and QX.] What can you say about the angles that PX and QX make with the perpendicular bisector?*

Demonstration 1

The idea of a locus is well demonstrated by drawing an ellipse using a pencil, a piece of cotton and two pins. Students can see how the piece of cotton remains the same length and the pins stay the same distance apart. The shape drawn is therefore the locus of a point that moves so the sum of its distances from two fixed points is constant.

Place the pins a fixed distance apart. These represent the two fixed points. Attach the ends of the cotton to the two pins (the cotton should be longer than twice the distance between the two pins.) The cotton represents a fixed length. Place a pencil on the cotton and pull it tight so that both strands are coincident. Keeping the cotton taught, rotate the pencil around the pins until you return to the starting point. The shape you have drawn is an ellipse.

Provided you have not allowed the cotton to slacken as you do the drawing, the sum of the lengths of the three parts equals the length of the piece of cotton and is therefore constant. We say that an ellipse is 'the locus of a point that moves so that the sum of its distances from two fixed points is constant.

Demonstration 2

Constructing inscribed and circumscribed circles requires very careful drawing and accurate use of geometrical instruments. Make sure that the students bring compasses, rulers and sharp pencils to the lesson.

In previous lessons and in the *Starter* the students have seen that the line through the centre of a circle and through the mid-point of a chord is perpendicular to the chord.

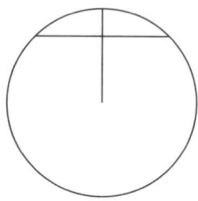

In the construction of the circumscribed circle we use this in reverse to construct the circle. Assist students in linking the facts about circles, chords and perpendicular bisectors of chords.

Draw any triangle. Construct the perpendicular bisector of all three sides. When constructed accurately, these three lines intersect at a point (The point can be inside or outside the triangle, or lie on one of the sides.). Using this point of intersection as the centre of the circle, draw a circle through each of the vertices. This is the **circumcircle**.

Draw any triangle. Construct the bisectors of each interior angle. When constructed accurately the three lines should intersect at a point. Using this point of intersection as the centre of the circle, draw a circle that just touches each side of the triangle. This is the **incircle**. Each side of the triangle is a tangent to the circle and the diagram can be used to show how the radii are perpendicular to the tangents.

Worked example

The example here shows how the same facts that have been used many times before can be used to find the exact centre of a circle. The perpendicular bisector of a chord passes through the centre. The perpendicular bisectors of two chords must therefore intersect at the centre.

Essential exercises

All of the exercises provide the students with practice in construction work. Make sure that they bring geometrical instruments and sharp pencils to the lesson. Insist that when compasses are used they draw clear arcs to indicate how they have achieved the construction.

Challenging exercise

Exercise 5 asks students to reproduce the constructions seen in *Demonstration 2*. Although they have seen the construction, they now have to follow the instructions carefully and accurately to achieve the same result.

Problem-solving exercise

Exercise 6 reinforces the idea that a locus is a set of points obeying a given rule. Before the students actually place counters according to the instructions in the question, ask them to visualise the final diagram in their imagination and draw a sketch. Then get them to check the actual result with counters and compare it to their sketch.

Invite students to make up their own rules for a partner to construct with counters.

Plenary

Summarise the work done in the lesson and discuss how to find the centre of a circle by drawing the perpendicular bisector of any two chords. This has been done in the *Worked example* using two chords that meet at a point on the circumference. Any two chords can be used and this could be used as an opportunity to investigate why this works.

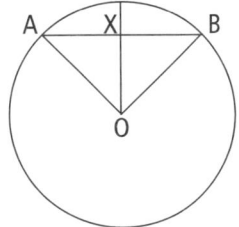

In the diagram above,
OA = OB (radii of the circle),
X is the mid-point of AB (given).
Triangles AXO and BXO are congruent (SAS)
Therefore $A\hat{O}X = B\hat{O}X$
$A\hat{O}X + X\hat{A}O = 90°$ (Angle sum of triangle ÷ 2)
Therefore $A\hat{X}O = 90°$

So the perpendicular bisector of any chord passes through the centre of the circle. The perpendicular bisectors of any two chords will intersect at the centre.

Homework

You may need to provide some hints for the students to be able to complete the constructions for homework. Revise the properties of the three shapes mentioned.

An equilateral triangle is a regular triangle with all sides equal.
A regular hexagon is a six-sided polygon with all six sides equal in length. A circle can be used to construct a regular hexagon.
An isosceles triangle has two sides equal and its base angles equal. 30° is half of 60°. Construct an angle of 60° and bisect it to get an angle of 30°.

Shape and Space

Shape and Space

Transformation geometry 1

Page 140

Goals

Students have studied reflections and rotations of shapes in previous years. They have drawn rotations and reflections by eye, and have constructed reflections using perpendicular bisectors. The most common mistakes in tests occur when reflections must be made in mirror lines that are not vertical or horizontal. This mistake is often caused by a lack of formalising the definitions of transformations.

The *Demonstrations* in this lesson are designed for students to construct transformations accurately using the full definitions. Students are expected to inspect shapes to check that lengths and angles are preserved, and to recognise that this means that objects and images are congruent to each other.

Students move on in this lesson to drawing shapes on rectangular axes, investigating combinations of transformations, and the effect transformations have on the coordinates of shapes.

It is unlikely that students will have spent much time on translations in earlier years. It is not until we start moving shapes around on rectangular axes that translations begin to make sense. Translations can be described by giving instructions to move shapes to the right or left and up or down but here vectors are used to provide this information efficiently and economically.

The word 'transformation' implies a change and students may expect a transformation to change a shape's appearance. However, rotations, reflections and translations are all **isometries**: object and image are congruent. The only change that takes place is the position of the image with respect to the object. The transformation 'enlargement' changes lengths but not angles (object and image are similar) and this will be studied in the next lesson.

This lesson formalises the definitions of certain transformations. A translation can be defined by a vector. A reflection can be defined by the equation of the axis of reflection. A rotation can be defined by the centre of rotation, the angle of rotation and the direction of rotation.

Starter

The activities in the *Starter* prepare students to scrutinise shapes in particular ways. When we study congruent or

similar triangles we need to be able to identify corresponding sides and angles.

The word 'corresponding' has been used earlier to describe angles made by a transversal crossing parallel lines. In this case the word is used to describe the relationship between an object and its image. When a line AB is transformed into a line A'B' then we say that A'B' corresponds to AB.

Draw the object and image. Consider A, B and C in turn, and note the image of each. Inspect each line and each angle, and identify the corresponding images.

Demonstration 1

Draw a grid on the board or OHT. Cut out a cardboard triangle ABC and stick it in place. Invite a student to follow instructions.

Translate the triangle twelve, three. That means move the triangle twelve places to the right and three places up. Now translate the triangle negative twelve, negative three. That means move the triangle twelve places to the left and three down. Triangle ABC is back where we started.

Repeat, but this time draw the object (triangle ABC) and the image (triangle A'B'C') after the first translation.

Is triangle ABC identical to triangle A'B'C'? Yes. Triangle ABC is congruent to triangle A'B'C'. Corresponding lengths are equal and corresponding angles are equal.

Repeat for different vectors. Invite students to give vectors followed by instructions. Give instructions to translate a shape and ask students for the vector that will return it to its original position. Each time note that the object and image are congruent.

Give instructions for students to translate the triangle with one vector followed by another translation with a different vector. Ask students to give a single vector to replace the two.

Demonstration 2

Although the accurate construction of a reflection was covered in the Book 1, students need to practise it several times.

In a previous lesson the students constructed a perpendicular bisector of a line segment. In this demonstration they have to construct the perpendicular to a line from a point in order to find the reflection of a point in a line.

> With centre A, and radius greater than the distance from A to the mirror line m, draw arcs on the line m to cut it in P_1 and P_2. With centre P_1 then P_2, draw arcs, the same length as before, to intersect at A'.
>
> Repeat the construction to find the image of B.

Essential exercises

All of the exercises explore the result of combining operations. Some students will be able to draw triangle ABC and its image after two transformations and visualise the single transformation that can replace them. However, you may need to conduct this as a whole-class activity, using a large grid and cut-out triangles.

Make sure that students describe the single transformation in full. In the first example they should not merely say that the single transformation is a translation but they should also provide the vector $\begin{pmatrix} 6 \\ 0 \end{pmatrix}$.

Exercise 2 has the result that the reflection in the y-axis followed by the reflection in the x-axis can be replaced by the single transformation of a rotation of 180° about the origin. This is the same result as that in Exercise 3 for the single transformation to replace two anticlockwise rotations of 90° about the origin.

Students may be surprised that reflections in a line are self-inverses. Take care with the translations where the inverse requires a change of sign.

Challenging exercise

In this exercise get the students to explain what happens to the coordinates of triangle ABC by writing sentences. Ask them to investigate different objects and make general statements. For example:

(a) When an object is reflected in the x-axis, its coordinates (x, y) become $(x, {}^-y)$.

(b) When an object is reflected in the y-axis, its coordinates (x, y) become $({}^-x, y)$.

(c) When an object is reflected in the line $y = x$, its coordinates (x, y) become (y, x).

And so on.

Problem-solving exercise

Exercise 8 is best completed with the whole class, using a large grid on the board or OHP. Ask students to look for single transformations first, and then to consider combined transformations. There will be several different ways of getting from the object to the image.

Plenary

Look at the vectors in the *Plenary*.

> Which pairs of vectors translate an object and then return its image to the position of the object? Consider reflecting an object in the x-axis. What reflection will return its image to the original position?

Consider further transformations and their inverses.

Homework

Before setting the *Homework* you may need to look at the example of, say, an irregular and regular hexagon.

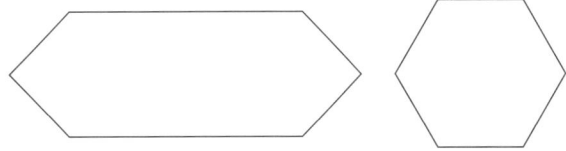

This irregular hexagon has two lines of reflection symmetry, and order of rotation symmetry two. The regular hexagon has six lines of reflection symmetry, and order of rotation symmetry six.

Teacher's Notes Teacher's Notes Teacher's Notes Teacher's Notes Teacher's Notes Teach
Teacher's Notes Teacher's Notes Teacher's Notes Teacher's Notes Teacher's Not
acher's Notes Teacher's Notes Teacher's Notes Teacher's Notes Teacher's Notes Teacher's Notes Teacher's N

Shape and Space

Transformation geometry 2

Page 144

Goals

The work on enlargements in this lesson is intended to prepare students for work on similarity in Book 3. The previous lesson focused on transformations of shapes where the object and image were congruent. With enlargements the object and image are similar but not necessarily congruent. The *Demonstrations* includes a shear transformation so that students can see a transformation where the image is neither congruent nor similar to the object.

Starter

The *Starter* revises plotting points, constructing triangles with sides of given lengths, and drawing linear graphs. With some students this might be a brief test of skills whereas with others you may need to demonstrate each of these before setting further examples for students to do for themselves.

Three coordinates define a unique triangle. Similarly, three lines of given length define a triangle unique in shape, but with any position. Two triangles with sides of the same length are **congruent** whereas two triangles with the same angles are **similar**.

Demonstration 1

You will see that this demonstration does not involve enlarging the triangle with a simple scale factor such as 2 or 3. This is deliberate. It is important to emphasise that we have to multiply lengths by the scale factor; simple enlargements encourage students to 'add on' rather than multiply. In this case the scale factor is 8 : 5. Discuss this scale factor. It is just greater than 1·5 but less than 2 so the image of the triangle will have lengths that are just over 1·5 times as long as the object.

Draw any suitable triangle ABC appropriately positioned on the board and mark a point P. Invite a student to come to the board and draw lines from P to each vertex and extend each line an appropriate distance. Measure PA, PB and PC. Get the students to multiply each length by the scale factor and check their results. Invite a student to measure the distances PA', PB' and PC' and draw the enlarged triangle. Measure the angles of the object and of the image, and confirm that they are the same. Use the word 'similar' to describe the two triangles.

Measure the sides of the enlarged triangle and check that it has been enlarged by the required scale factor. Get each student to draw a triangle and enlarge it by a given scale factor. For students with poor motor skills, provide them with a suitable triangle and centre of enlargement on paper and assist them in calculating the new lengths.

Demonstration 2

Show the students a pile of identical textbooks and note that the end shape is a rectangle. Keep the bottom book in place and gently push the pile sideways so that the end shape is a parallelogram. The shape has changed but the area remains constant. This is a **shear**.

A shear is a transformation where the image is neither similar nor congruent to the object. However, a shear does preserve area. Demonstrate this again by shearing a triangle as in the demonstration and noting that the perpendicular height of the triangle remains constant (it is the perpendicular distance between the parallel lines).

Imagine triangle ABC formed by row upon row of sticks that get shorter and shorter until the last one is just a dot. Push the sticks sideways so that they all move parallel to the base to form triangle ABC'. The area covered by the sticks has not changed.

Essential exercises

It is often difficult to prevent students from rushing in and answering questions before stopping to think. This habit is not helped by giving students timed tests that do not allow for thinking time. Students need to develop the disposition of contemplating pictures, diagrams and graphs and mentally noting what they see before trying to answer any questions.

In Exercise 1 the instruction asks students to 'Study the information in the diagram' and they are told that the diagram is not drawn to scale. Work with the whole class and ask them what they can see.

Look at triangle ABC. What are the lengths of the sides of the triangle? Triangle ABC has been enlarged to triangle A'B'C'. What is the scale factor of the enlargement? What is the image? What side in the image corresponds to side AB in the object? What is the length of this side? How did you work that out? What ...

Inspect the shapes for each exercise with the whole class before getting the students to answer the questions for themselves.

All of these exercises focus on linear lengths, scale factors, and the effect on angles when enlarging a shape. Area is not considered here but you may like to challenge the students to consider what happens to the area of a shape when it is enlarged.

The term 'similar' has not been used in the exercises because there are plenty of other terms that students need to become familiar with. However, you could look at the objects and images in each case and demonstrate how the image is similar to the object.

Challenging exercises

Exercise 4 looks at an enlargement on rectangular axes. When the centre of enlargement of the shape is the origin, the coordinates can easily be calculated when the scale factor is known. With scale factor s, the coordinates (x, y) become (sx, sy).

Exercises 5 and 6 address the notion of area of shapes when enlarged. You could extend this to consider the effect on volume when a solid shape is enlarged with a given scale factor. You could also demonstrate that mathematics can go beyond real life. We may not be able to visualise four- or five-dimensional shapes but we can imagine what the effect would be of enlarging a five-dimensional shape with a given scale factor. We can calculate the lengths, area, volume and some imaginary properties such as the 'troggle' and 'filume' of the image!

Exercise 7 uses the correct technical term for a transformation that can be performed in any order. Does an enlargement with scale factor m followed by enlargement with scale factor n give the same result as an enlargement with scale factor n followed by enlargement with scale factor m? This question can be extended to consider the combinations of other transformations and whether they are commutative.

If the linear scale factor of an enlargement is n, what is the inverse enlargement?

Problem-solving exercise

Exercise 8 applies what has been learnt about enlargements to a real-life situation. Such real-life examples help to reinforce the idea that all lengths are enlarged by

the same scale factor but all angles are preserved. This is why any photograph (the image) is similar to the original (real) object.

Plenary

The first two activities of the *Plenary* demonstrate the inverse transformation of an enlargement with scale factor 3. Ask the students to state the inverse transformation of (a) an enlargement with scale factor 10, (b) an enlargement with scale factor $\frac{1}{2}$, and so on.

Homework

The activity for the *Homework* links this work on enlargements with that on scale drawing. Once again the real-life situation reinforces the idea that angles are preserved under enlargements with right angles in the actual living room remaining as right angles in the scale drawing.

Shape and Space

 Page 148

Visualisation

Goals

Two-dimensional shapes only exist in the imagination. We can draw them on a page and we can cut out shapes that appear to be two-dimensional but now, of course they actually have a third dimension even though it may be very small. We can view a two-dimensional shape from various perspectives and describe what we see.

In comparison, three-dimensional shapes actually do exist. All of real-life is three-dimensional. However, no matter what perspective we take we cannot see all of a three-dimensional shape from one position. When we look at a three-dimensional shape our imagination usually completes the picture for us.

Close your eyes and imagine a tetrahedron. What you picture is likely to be a common two-dimensional representation of a tetrahedron.

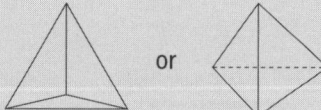

Now imagine that you are looking at a solid tetrahedron directly in front of one of its faces. What do you see? Now imagine that you are looking directly at one of its slant edges. What do you see? Now look down from directly above one of its vertices. What do you see?

These different views of a tetrahedron help us to build up the complete picture. If we have the front elevation, the side elevation and the plan of a shape we should be able to build a model of our shape.

Now imagine that the tetrahedron is made out of one piece of cardboard and carefully take it apart along its edges. What can you see? This is called the net of the tetrahedron. Is there only one possibility?

Now do the same visualisation of a square-based pyramid. What views of this pyramid distinguishes it from a tetrahedron?

Starter

We begin by visualising two-dimensional shapes and revising their names and properties.

The first activity is to sketch shapes, and the first shape is a regular hexagon. *What does 'regular' mean?* (All the sides are of equal length, and all the angles are of equal size.) *A regular quadrilateral is given a special name, what is it? And what is a regular triangle called?*

The second activity involves visualisation and not drawing. Imagine drawing a line from a vertex of an equilateral triangle to meet the opposite side at a right angle. Cut along the line. What is the shape you have cut out? Describe it.

The shape is a right-angled triangle. It is exactly half of the original triangle. It has one angle of thirty degrees and another angle of sixty degrees.

The third activity is to visualise bisecting an angle of an equilateral triangle, and cutting along the angle bisector. The result is, of course, the same as before.

The fourth activity results in three identical isosceles triangles, each with two angles of thirty degrees and one angle of one hundred and twenty degrees.

Demonstration 1

This demonstration provides an orthogonal (or orthographic) projection of a hexagonal pyramid. Orthographic projection always includes a plan and front and side elevations. Accurate drawing of the base allows accurate representation of the perceived foreshortening of the lines in the front and side elevations. It invites discussion of the appearance of lines in a two-dimensional representation.

Demonstrate drawing a hexagonal pyramid with perpendicular height 10 cm and each side of the hexagon 4 cm. Show students the step-by-step building up of the different elevations. To draw the plan construct the hexagon by drawing a circle of radius 4 cm and stepping round the circle in 4 cm chords. Of course, it matters where we start. If we intend the front elevation to be as shown we must ensure we start with a chord parallel to the lower edge of the page. Construction lines drawn through each vertex up the page now identify the perceived position on the front elevation of the vertices.

The perpendicular height of the cone drawn on the front elevation now fixes the remaining lines on that elevation. Projected horizontally, lines drawn from the plan fix all

necessary points on the side elevation. Ensure that the students appreciate the need for the construction line under the side elevation to be drawn at 45°. Discuss which lengths are 'true' lengths and which are distorted by 'foreshortening'.

Students should practise drawing these elevations for a range of simple three-dimensional shapes including a cone (in preparation for *Demonstration 2*).

Demonstration 2

This demonstration focuses on drawing an orthogonal projection for a truncated cone. Demonstrate drawing a cone of perpendicular height 10 cm and base radius 4 cm. The cone is initially drawn in full using construction lines. An oblique line drawn on the front elevation is sufficient to construct the defining points of the 'cut' on the plan and the side elevation (each is an ellipse). Vertical lines drawn from the left and right extremities of the oblique line on the front elevation appear as the left and right extremities of the cut on the plan. Horizontal lines drawn from the top and bottom extremities of the cut on plan appear at the sides of the cut on the side elevation. Horizontal and vertical lines locate the corresponding points on the plan. These defining points indicate the major and minor axes of the ellipses. (Note: so that the diagram in the Student's Book is not over complicated, some of these lines have been omitted from the drawing.)

Essential exercises

Ask the students to do Exercises 1 and 2 first by visualising the nets folded to make the solids, then get them to draw and cut out the nets and check whether they were correct.

For Exercise 3 use a set of solid shapes so that students can check that their first thoughts, when using their imagination, were correct. Help them to see that when they look at a square-based pyramid from above, the triangular sides do not appear the same size as the actual triangles. The slant edges appear to be shortened in length.

Students who experience difficulties with visualisation would benefit from building shapes, viewing them from various directions and describing what they see. Our imagination usually completes part of shapes that we cannot see. Drawing plans and elevations of shapes requires us to ignore our imagination and draw only what we can actually see.

Exercise 5 requires even more effort with the imagination. Inspect the drawing of a 3-D shape and imagine what it looks like in real life. Parallel lines in the drawing are also parallel lines in the real object. The drawing may not show angles as right angles but you can imagine those right angles in the real object.

Challenging exercises

Invite students to visualise the shapes generated in Exercise 6 and get them to discuss their answers in pairs or groups. Get them to check their answers by generating the shapes using plasticine.

Ask the students to discuss Exercise 7 and get them to sketch diagrams of their answers. Ask them to check if there is only one possible way of doing the cutting. Then get them to check their answers by cutting plasticine models.

Problem-solving exercises

Give the students sets of linking cubes for Exercise 8. Get them to make the shapes and to calculate the surface areas. Ask them to explain why they think they get their answers and get them to predict the shapes with smallest and largest surface areas for different numbers of cubes.

Exercise 9 may need to be done with plasticine. Get the students to work systematically by cutting off corner pieces that gradually get bigger. What happens when the cut gets to the middle of the edges? Can any more be cut off?

Exercise 10 is a puzzle that students enjoy solving. It requires students to work systematically. They could check their answers by making a cube and writing the letters on the faces.

Plenary

The first activity practises the visualisation of the net of a tetrahedron. Do all the nets produce a solid shape? Is it always the same?

The second activity requires students to consider the angle properties of a regular hexagon. If we place three regular hexagons together then the point at which they meet will have an angle sum of 360° and it would be impossible to fold this into three dimensions.

Homework

Ask students to do the *Homework* activity as a preparation for the next lesson. Give the students a set of cubes each and ask them to check their drawing against what they actually see. Invite students to present their answers at the board.

Your least confident students will benefit from using **Worksheet 34** for practice in sketching two-dimensional representations of three-dimensional shapes.

Shape and Space

Teacher's Notes Teacher's Notes Teacher's Notes Teacher's Notes
Teacher's Notes Teacher's Notes Teacher's Notes Teacher's Not
acher's Notes Teacher's Notes Teacher's Notes Teacher's Notes Teacher's Notes
Teacher's N

Shape and Space

Area and volume

Goals

Book 1 introduced students to the idea of measurement as comparison with a standard unit (the denomination). Teachers demonstrated with cards like these:

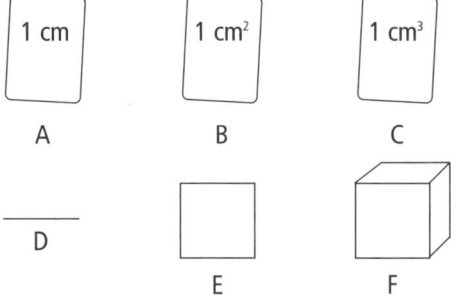

This emphasised that the unit of measure is a tangible thing. Measurement of the length of a piece of string consists of comparing it to 1 cm. Measurement of area compares a shape to 1 cm^2, and volume compares a shape to 1 cm^3.

In this lesson students revise their work on area before concentrating on the volume of prisms. Each prism in this family of solids can be seen to be layers of identical shapes.

Make a set of identical triangular layers 1 cm thick. If you use a right-angled triangle (say with measurements 9 cm, 12 cm and 15 cm) you can easily calculate the volume of each layer (54 cm^3 in this case).

[Place the first layer on the table.]
This prism has a volume of 54 cm^3.

[Place a second layer on top of the first.]
This prism has a total volume of 54 cm^3 × 2 = 108 cm^3.

Repeat with further layers emphasising that the volume is the number of cubic centimetres in each layer multiplied by the number of layers.

Starter

Before setting the activities in the *Starter*, you may need to discuss the meaning of the word 'prism'. It is not a word that we meet regularly and students often confuse prisms and pyramids. Get students to look up the word in the *Glossary*.

'A prism is a solid with uniform cross-section.' The word 'uniform' is used to describe the fact that wherever we take

parallel cross-sections we get the same shape. A cross-section is usually taken by cutting the shape parallel to its ends; and unless it is specified otherwise, we usually assume that the word 'cross-section' means that without qualification.

There are two standard ways of sketching prisms. They can be visualised as identical layers placed end to end vertically or horizontally. As a result we sometimes refer to the length of the prism and sometimes to the height of the prism. In both cases we are referring to the total measure of identical layers.

A rectangular prism is called a cuboid in maths, although the word is rarely used elsewhere. More generally it is called a box. When all the edges are equal we get a cube as in the third activity.

The fourth activity revises the area of a rectangle and the area of a parallelogram. Students may need some help with this.

Demonstration 1

Developing the formulae for the volumes of different prisms is straightforward for students who understand the basic idea that a prism has a uniform cross-section. We need to demonstrate this idea for a variety of solid shapes. Some students will be able to visualise cross-sections from the 2-D diagrams but many will need to see the actual shapes for themselves.

Make a set of prisms using plasticine or equivalent. Demonstrate cutting the prism parallel to the common face and get students to check that wherever you cut the prism the cross-section remains the same. Each face of the cross-section is congruent to the end faces. Show how a prism can be viewed in different positions so that the cross-section is sometimes horizontal, sometimes vertical or at whatever angle the prism is placed.

Cut a prism into centimetre slices parallel to the common face. Examine one slice and calculate the cross-sectional volume in cm^3. Pile up the slices and calculate the total volume of the prism. Get the students to visualise doing the same with the other prisms.

Now consider the general cases with side lengths labelled with letters and construct the formula for the volume of each prism in turn.

Shape and Space

Teacher's Notes   Teacher's Notes   Teacher's Notes   Teacher's Notes   Teacher's Notes   Teacher's N
Teacher's Notes   Teacher's Notes
Teacher's Notes   Teacher's Notes   Teacher's Notes   Teacher's Notes   Notes

Shape and Space: **Area and volume**

Demonstration 2

Get the students to make nets for different prisms. Examine each net and consider the shapes that make up the nets. Calculate the area of each component part to get the surface area of the solid shape.

Give some examples of shapes like those in the diagram where the lengths of the sides are not simple whole numbers. This will ensure that the students think more carefully about what they are doing. Working out the height of the triangle for the triangular-based prism will require measuring on a scale drawing because the students do not yet know Pythagoras' theorem.

Worked example

Students may know the formula for the volume of a cuboid as $l \times w \times h$. Here we are treating the cuboid as a rectangular prism and considering layers with the same cross-sectional area.

Worksheet 35 provides a great deal of practice in calculating area and volume. All students would benefit from using this sheet.

Essential exercises

These exercises are not just sets of calculations on area and volume. They all invite the students to think about what they are doing. Students should inspect the diagrams carefully for explicit and implicit information.

In Exercise 1 the shaded shape is a square, so only one side needs to be worked out in order to calculate the area. Exercise 2 can be worked out using a simple division. A number that does not divide without some thought has deliberately been chosen because otherwise the students may do the calculation intuitively without thinking.

Exercise 3 allows the students to be creative and design trapezia with their own measurements, provided they give the correct area. This is excellent practice of number work.

Exercises 4 and 5 give practice of calculating volume and surface area. Exercise 6 allows the students to be creative again, and revises work on factors. If they keep to whole numbers they will be limited with their answers.

Exercise 7 shows the students that the cross-section of a shape does not have to be a commonly known mathematical shape but, as in this case, can be a composite shape.

Challenging exercises

Exercise 8 provides a nice little puzzle. The area of the square with side d is clearly d^2 units squared. The other

square has a diagonal of length d. The students do not know Pythagoras' theorem and so they will have to draw both diagonals and recognise that the smaller square is equal to four right-angled triangles, each with area $\frac{d^2}{8}$. The area of this square is therefore $\frac{d^2}{2}$. The ratio of the areas of the two squares is 1 : 2.

Exercise 9 should be set out as two equations to be solved. Insist on this even though some students will be able to do the calculation mentally.

Problem-solving exercises

You may need to do Exercise 10 with the whole class. Get them to work out the volume of each cube before doing the subtraction. We know that students always want a numerical example and this is a good question to help them realise that sometimes we have to give answers using symbols.

Plenary

Examine the three diagrams carefully. The first diagram shows a water filled tank in the shape of a cuboid. We can calculate the volume of water in the tank. The second diagram shows the water taking the shape of a triangular-based prism. It has half the volume of the cuboid. The third diagram shows the water taking the shape of a trapezoidal prism. Its volume is equal that of the previous diagram, and it is also equal to the area of the trapezium $\times$ 3m. Let the area of the trapezium be A. We can write an equation for A and solve it.

Homework

Students may have done the max-box investigation before. (It is one of those investigations that can be repeated from time-to-time using different techniques.) At this stage the students could use a spreadsheet and look for maximum values. They could work out an algebraic formula and draw a graph. Later they can use calculus. The activity is far too long for one homework. They could begin to do it at home and complete it in class, or they could do the task spread across two homeworks.

Shape and Space

Shape and Space

Page 156 # Circles

Goals

The circumference and area of a circle were both introduced in Book 1. This lesson revises the two together, using the same visual images as before. If you know that the students did the measuring of the circumference and diameter of objects previously, then just use the pages as revision.

Analyses of national tests show that students regularly make mistakes in their circle work. It is important that students do some practical work to enable them to understand this mysterious thing called 'pi'.

When we develop the formula for the area of a rectangle, students can easily see that we are comparing the area of the rectangle to the area of, say, 1 cm². It is easy to visualise a rectangle filled with these units. We want to be able to visualise the area of a circle in the same way.

We divide the circle into an infinite number of sectors, cut them out, and piece them together again as a rectangle with known dimensions. The length of the rectangle is equal to approximately half the circumference of the circle and the width is approximately equal to the radius of the circle. The greater the number of sectors the closer we get to these measurements. This idea of a 'limit' is important to establish to assist students with maths they may meet later.

Starter

The symbol π (pi) is used to represent an infinite decimal (an irrational number). It is impossible to write an exact value for this number and so we use a symbol. We can then replace the symbol with a number once we have decided on the degree of accuracy required. We use the most appropriate approximation for π according to the situation.

The *Starter* emphasises what is being done when we approximate a decimal to a specified number of places. This is linked to the vocabulary 'rounding off a number' that is widely used.

> *Look at the first group of digits, 3·1. There is three and one tenth here. Look at the next digit (4 < 5) and this determines that the number π is closer to 3·1 than 3·2.*

> *Look at the second group of digits, 3·14. There is three and fourteen hundredths here. Look at the next digit (1 < 5) and this determines that the number π is closer to 3·14 than 3·15.*

> *Look at the third group of digits. There is three and one hundred and forty-one thousandths here. The number π is closer to 3·142 than 3·141.*

The second point for discussion is used to remind students that the diameter of a circle is twice the radius.

Demonstration 1

Ensure all students know what is meant by 'diameter'. Strengthen their understanding by clarifying that any circle has an infinite number of diameters. Show that the length of the diameter is the longest of any measurement taken 'across' the circle.

Draw an accurate circle on the board or OHP but do not mark the centre. Discuss with the students how to measure the diameter of the circle.

In earlier lessons students have used the construction of perpendicular bisectors of chords to find the centre of the circle. They could do this again here to find the centre, draw a diameter through it, and measure its length.

Alternatively they could use parallel rulers as in the diagram and measure the distance between them. They would not be able to draw the diameter on the circle using this method.

Discuss the limitations of each method and the degree of accuracy achieved. Discuss how accurate any measurement can be using a ruler and the naked eye.

For those students who have not covered work on the circumference and diameter in previous years, set the task of measuring the circumference (using string) and diameter of circles using objects such as tins.

Record the results and consider the relationship between the circumference and diameter. Establish that the circumference is approximately three times the diameter. Discuss the historical developments of this relationship and explain that better approximations are given by 3·1, 3·14, 3·142 etc and that this number cannot be worked out exactly. Hence the use of the symbol π.

Show the students a graph of $C = \pi d$ and discuss various points on the line. Ask them to imagine what circles are being suggested by given points on the graph.

Demonstration 2

This demonstration shows how a circle can be partitioned (the area has the same value but a different appearance). Successively large numbers of partitions are shown so that the movement can be seen towards the limit, an image with an area that can be calculated – with the ultimate image being one that has to be visualised.

Worked example

The example shows students how to set out calculations of the circumference and area of a circle, using the formulae derived previously and a given approximation for π.

Worksheet 36 gives further practice in calculations using π.

Essential exercises

It is assumed that the students have completed straightforward work on circles previously. The exercises here provide further practice, but each one allows the students to see maths as a puzzle. They have to inspect the diagrams, describe what they see (explicit information), and consider how to calculate what is asked for (the implicit information) using their knowledge of circles.

Set the exercises for the students to puzzle over individually. Then get them to share their answers in pairs or groups. Finally invite them to present their answers with explanations to the class.

Challenging exercises

These exercises are probably best done with the whole class unless you are working with a group of very confident students. They are not particularly difficult but the students may need some prompting at stages in the work.

Ask the students to discuss the exercises in groups, and then get students to come to the board to assist you in developing the solution. Invite other students to give instructions as you work.

Problem-solving exercise

This is a classic investigation that involves using and applying the knowledge of circles. Students can begin by calculating areas numerically. They can extend the problem

by letting x be the distance from one corner and generalising the solution. They could extend the problem even further by considering different shaped barns.

Plenary

The relationship between the angle at the centre of a sector, the radius r of the sector and the radius R of the base is fascinating.

In this example the length of the arc of the sector is $\frac{170}{360} \times 2\pi r$ and this is equal to the circumference of the base of the cone $2\pi R$.

So
$$\frac{170}{360} \times 2\pi r = 2\pi R$$
$$\frac{170}{360} \times r = R$$

The radius of the base of the cone is a little less than half the radius of the sector and so its diameter will be almost 5 cm.

In the second example the radius of the base of the cone is a little more than a third of the radius of the sector and its diameter will be almost 4 cm.

Confident students will be able to follow this reasoning, but with less confident students make the cones and measure the diameters.

Homework

This task allows students to be creative. Much of maths has 'correct answers' which need to be found, and this is an opportunity to allow students some freedom in using their skills in design whilst at the same time applying their knowledge of circles. It also gives students practice in using geometrical instruments.

Shape and Space

Teacher's Notes Teacher's Notes Teacher's Notes Teacher's Notes Teacher's Notes
Teacher's Notes Teacher's Notes Teacher's Notes Teacher's Notes Teacher's Note
acher's Notes Teacher's Notes Teacher's Notes Teacher's Notes Teacher's No

Handling Data

Introduction

Developing an understanding of handling data

In Book 1 students revised and consolidated work done in earlier years on discrete data. The book then introduced them to grouped data and continuous data. They were also introduced to some new mathematical terminology and statistical techniques. In Book 2 students revise the work from Book 1 and are introduced to some new techniques for interpreting data and comparing distributions. This includes an introduction to the language and ideas involved in statistics. The requirement to carry out a statistical enquiry for GCSE means that students need to be very confident in this work to achieve satisfactory grades. The actual mathematics involved is not difficult. It mainly entails applying the number work taught in *I See Maths* Books 1 and 2.

Comparing distributions

The statistics we calculate in our everyday lives are usually used for the purpose of comparison. We want to know which class did best in a test, or which form of travel is most popular. Manufacturers want to know the range of sizes in which to make clothes, and supermarkets want to know the types of food we like to eat.

Although averages can be useful, they can often hide certain facts about a distribution. For example, the mean wage can hide the fact that there may be a couple of people earning huge sums of money whilst the rest of the staff manage on the minimum wage. Additional information such as the **range** can be helpful but may still not give a very good picture.

Suppose we examine a set of data and then look more closely at a subset, the **inter-quartile range**. We begin to see how spread out the distribution is. A box-and-whisker diagram provides an excellent profile of the distribution. The mathematics is simple. We calculate the lower quartile, the median and the upper quartile, and then draw a simple diagram. Box-and-whisker diagrams can be drawn for two or more distributions using the same scale and they give us useful information for comparison. By introducing this work now, we can prepare students to use such techniques with confidence in later years.

Probability

The topic of probability is often taught separately, after teaching handling data. However, it is useful for students to be able to calculate probability when interrogating and interpreting data. For this reason probability has been given a prominent place at the beginning of this section.

Students need to understand the difference between theoretical and experimental probability. This was introduced in Book 1 and is revisited here to give it a more thorough treatment. We then extend the ideas to successive events in preparation for future work.

Working with large sets of data

Most students now have access to databases and spreadsheets on computers. Once students have become confident in using and applying the statistical techniques in this book, it is a good idea for them to apply their knowledge to large sets of data, preferably data that has been collected about themselves or their school or college.

Unfortunately computers are not as intelligent as we sometimes think! Most software packages will produce any diagram or graph at the touch of a button for any set of data. The computer does not consider whether the diagram or graph is appropriate or correct for that data. Students need to be trained to think for themselves when they use computers and to decide which diagram or graph is appropriate and correct for the data being represented.

Conducting a statistical enquiry

Students have spent time in the past collecting and representing data. They often do this without a reason (other than they have been asked do it for 'maths') and this can develop bad habits in this subject. They need to be trained in how to set up an enquiry by asking appropriate and relevant questions, and making a hypothesis. They need to know how to select an appropriate sample, and how to write questionnaires or interview questions. And finally, they need to know how to interpret and represent the data they collect, and how to communicate their results. The final lessons in this section prepare them for conducting such an enquiry.

Handling Data

Handling Data

 # Theoretical probability
Page 164

Goals

When we pick up a pack of playing cards we know that there are fifty-two cards in the pack provided we do not have any jokers. There are four suits, twelve picture cards and half the pack is red. Using this information we can calculate the probability of selecting a particular card when we take a card at random. For example, there are four queens and so the probability of selecting a queen is $\frac{4}{52}$ (the number of favourable outcomes divided by the total number of possible outcomes). This is known as **theoretical probability**.

By the end of this lesson the students should be able to understand the technical language of probability, and be able to calculate theoretical probabilities for given sets of data. This is mainly revision of work done in Book 1 (pages 200–207), but you may need to do the demonstrations from that book before moving on. In this lesson emphasise the correct language and terminology for probability.

Starter

Do not assume that all students have used ordinary playing cards. Show the class a pack of cards and invite students to give the names of the suits and the number of cards in each suit. Discuss what is meant by 'picture cards', and count out the number of each type and colour of card and make a record.

Although this may seem simple to some students it is important to establish the contents and nature of the data under consideration before calculating probability. For example, the first part of question 1 asks for the probability of selecting a red card. Work through question 1 with the class, for example:

1(a) *How many cards are there in the pack? Fifty-two. This means that there are fifty-two possible outcomes when I select a card at random. How many of the cards are red? Twenty-six. So there are twenty-six favourable outcomes. The probability of getting a red card P(red) = $\frac{26}{52}$. That is: the number of favourable outcomes divided by the total number of outcomes.*

Remind the students that probability can take any value from zero to one. If something is certain then the

probability of it happening is one. If something is impossible then the probability of it happening is zero. When we throw an ordinary die the outcome has to be one of the numbers from 1 to 6. The probability of getting any number from 1 to 6 is one. The probability of getting the number 7 is zero. If the probability of something happening is n then the probability of it not happening is $1 - n$.

Introduce the notation 3' to mean 'not three' for question 3 part (b). The probability $P(3) = \frac{1}{6}$ so the probability $P(3') = \frac{5}{6}$ (or $1 - \frac{1}{6}$).

Some students will benefit from some routine practice in calculating probabilities in straightforward contexts. Use **Worksheet 37** for this.

Demonstration 1

Inspect the sample set.

There are two red counters and three blue counters in this sample. How many different ways are there of selecting four counters from these five counters?
I could have one red counter and three blue counters like this. I could have … There are five different ways. [Work systematically and notice that this is the same as choosing to remove one counter.]

How many of the five ways of selecting four counters has three blue counters? Two of the five ways. We say that the probability of selecting three blue counters P(3 blue counters) = $\frac{2}{5}$.

Demonstrate how to work out each of the examples on the page. Start with a different sample set of counters, and again set out all the ways of selecting four at random. Get students to ask the questions.

Demonstration 2

In this example the variable is 'shoe size' and the population consists of the shoe size of six people. When working out the number of different ways of obtaining a random sample of five values of the variable, note the systematic way of recording results. Students must be

trained to work systematically, and find ways of recording that avoid duplication or omission. The mean of each sample is calculated and recorded.

Once we have recorded these results we can begin to ask questions. Three examples of questions are given on the Demonstration page. You could ask others such as what is $P(\overline{x} = 5\cdot8)$, $P(\overline{x} < 6)$, $P(\overline{x} < 6\cdot5)$?, and so on.

You can extend the problem by considering the random selection of samples containing four values of the variable. Writing these out systematically demonstrates that there are fifteen ways of selecting four values, with the mean ranging from 5·25 to 6·75. Invite the students to suggest questions, and get them to compare the probabilities of getting a certain mean from both types of sampling.

Worked example

The probabilities to be calculated in the *Worked example* follow the same reasoning as parts (b) and (e) in the *Starter*. Discuss why this is so with the class.

Essential exercises

Exercise 1 may need some revision of prime numbers, factors, multiples, etc. Scrutinise the numbers 1 to 6 and identify certain properties before asking the students to consider the required probabilities.

Exercise 2 should have been practised in the *Starter*, and Exercise 3 is similar to *Demonstration 1*, so both should be straightforward. Exercise 4 is similar to Exercise 1 but has larger numbers.

Exercise 5 requires the total number of students to be calculated before the question can be answered.

Challenging exercises

Introduce Exercise 6 by considering the probability of getting a 3 when rolling a die. What is the probability of not getting a 3? Demonstrate how this can be calculated by subtracting the first answer from 1.

The last part of Exercise 7 needs some interpretation.

P(green) = 0·1. That has the same value as $\frac{1}{10}$ and means that I would expect to get one green counter for every ten selections. I expect to have to draw about thirty counters to get three green counters.

Ask students to consider the same question for different coloured counters. Some are straightforward to calculate, such as the blue that will need approximately sixty draws. However, a yellow counter is expected to appear thirty-five

times in every one hundred draws or 3·5 times in every ten draws. Theoretically, a yellow will appear three times in approximately nine draws.

Problem-solving exercise

The minefield game is well known amongst school students. However, not all may have played it before, and you may need to explain it. Discuss how the probability of landing on a mine affects the level of difficulty of the game.

Plenary

Discuss with the students how they would select a random sample of three people from six. Consider ways such as making cards and putting them in a bag for selection.

Draw a table on the board with six columns. Invite students to show all the possible ways they can select samples of three from the given set of six people. Consider possibilities such as: 'Suppose A, B, C and D are female and E and F are male. What is the probability of selecting an all female sample?'

Set the questions in the *Goals* and invite students to present the answers at the board. Insist that the students explain their answers.

Homework

The statements in the *Homework* are intended to get students to consider whether there is any mathematical explanation for the statements, and whether the events are **dependent** or **independent** events. For example, the first statement cannot be reasoned mathematically. The probability of getting a six with an unbiased die is $\frac{1}{6}$ and does not change from person to person.

The second statement is different. The fact that it has rained for the last three days probably means that there is a particular type of weather front and the probability of it raining tomorrow depends upon statistical data that is used to predict the weather.

The third statement is similar to the one about throwing a die. The fact that there has been one plane crash does not alter the probability of the plane you are catching having a plane crash. They are independent events. This is also true of the last statement. We have to divorce our feelings about luck from the mathematical calculations.

Page 168

Probability from experimental data

Goals

The idea of experimental probability was touched on in Book 1. This book extends the idea and formalises the language and terminology. In almost all real-life situations we cannot calculate a theoretical probability because we do not have sufficient information. We use statistical data to help us calculate an experimental probability.

In industry the techniques of experimental probability are widely used. Manufacturers need to calculate the probability of producing faulty products, or the probability of measurements being within an acceptable range. Testing products is an expensive business and so they want to reduce the number of products they sample to a minimum, but still ensure the quality.

Suppose everyone in the class threw an unbiased die just five times. The outcomes would all be very different. However, should they throw their die a hundred times each then the proportion of outcomes for each number on the die (the relative frequency) would be close to the expected frequency. If we combined all the class results the proportions should be even closer to that expected. The more trials carried out, the closer the results come to the theoretical probability.

In this lesson the students compare the expected frequency with the actual outcomes of repeated trials. For example, they calculate that they would expect any number on a die to appear five times in thirty throws, and compare what actually happens when they throw the die thirty times. They also conduct experiments, or use experimental data, in order to make predictions based on the results.

Starter

By now students should be proficient in calculating theoretical probabilities. They all know that the probability of getting a '4' on a die is $\frac{1}{6}$. In this activity the students have to interpret this statistic and decide what it means in terms of actually throwing a die. Theoretically, we would expect to get each number on the die exactly once if we roll the die six times. We all know that this does not happen in real-life. That is the difference between theory and practice.

If we roll a die twelve times we would expect to get two '4s'. If we roll it one hundred and twenty times we would

expect twenty '4s'. If we roll it one hundred times we would expect $100 \div 6 \approx 17$ '4s'.

The third activity entails testing these expected outcomes and comparing the theory with experimental results.

This starter activity may take a whole lesson. Do not cut back on this work just to save time because it is vital that students get a good grasp of the difference between theoretical probability with expected outcomes, and experimental results.

Demonstration 1

This demonstration shows students how to use the results of trials to calculate experimental probability. They compare the observed frequency of favourable outcomes with the total number of outcomes.

First the students read the table of results and note the observed frequency for each possible outcome. Next they calculate the experimental probability using these results. They then use the theoretical probability to work out what they might have expected to get as outcomes.

These particular results indicate that the number 6 is appearing more often than expected. Can any conclusions be drawn from this? Is the die biased? In this case there have only been fifteen trials and more would have to be conducted in order to make any inferences or draw any conclusions.

Calculation of experimental probability from real experiments can be time consuming – so they are best done at home. **Worksheet 38** provides some contexts for routine practice of simple experiments.

Demonstration 2

In the previous lesson the students wrote down all the possible ways of taking a sample of five from a population of six people. From this they could calculate the probability of getting a sample with a particular mean. In this demonstration the same population is used but this time fifteen random samples have been taken and recorded.

Remind the students of the work they did in the previous lesson. Scrutinise the results of taking samples and note the

observed frequencies. Compare the experimental results with the expected frequency as calculated using the theoretical probability.

Note how there were more random samples with a mean greater than 6 than was expected. Discuss how this might affect a survey of average shoe sizes.

These ideas have been introduced before students move on to work on handling data. When students conduct an enquiry and collect data through sampling techniques get them to consider the probability of getting a representative sample.

Essential exercises

Work through the first exercise with the whole class. New terminology is introduced in this exercise that will need some explaining. **Relative frequency** records the total number of favourable outcomes compared with the total number of possible outcomes.

After the first set of ten trials the number of 'heads' (favourable outcomes) compared with the number of throws (possible outcomes) is $\frac{2}{10}$. After the second set of ten trials the total number of favourable outcomes compared to the total number of outcomes is $\frac{5}{20}$. Each total accumulates as more trials are conducted.

The exercise begins with a question asking students to calculate the theoretical probability of getting a 'head', followed by a question to calculate expected outcomes using this theoretical probability. Students then compare the experimental data with the theoretical expectations.

Discuss these results. After just ten trials the number of 'heads' is small. It would be easy to make the assumption that the coin was biased in favour of 'tails'. The third set of ten trials gives a very different result and on its own might indicate the opposite to be true. The relative frequency shows that the total number of 'heads' is approaching half the total number of trials. It is not until a total of fifty trials have been conducted that the total number of 'heads' gets close to the expected half of the total number of trials.

The second exercise shows how experimental probability can be used in the work-place. In this example there is no way of calculating the theoretical probability. However, certain standards are set by the industry, and the company will want the number of defective devices to be within given limits. These methods are widely used (using these and more sophisticated techniques) in quality assurance programmes.

Challenging exercises

Exercise 3 requires the use of computer software. In the absence of this, the actual experiment will have to be

conducted by the students. They will need to record their results as in Exercise 1 and conduct a large number of trials.

With some help, all students should be able to do Exercise 4. Once again the students use the experimental results to calculate the experimental probability. The only difference here is in the use of language and symbols. You may need to provide assistance in interpreting the question. Students need to become familiar with the different ways of expressing statistical questions. Mathematically capable students can still fail in tests if they do not understand what is being asked.

Problem-solving exercise

The students need to make a hexagonal spinner for the experiment in Exercise 5. This is good revision of constructing an accurate hexagon and drawing the diagonals. They then apply the knowledge they have acquired in the earlier exercises to compare the results for their spinner with the theoretical expectations. Get them to evaluate the accuracy of their construction using their results.

Plenary

Invite students to explain the difference between theoretical and experimental probability. Ask them to answer the questions in the *Goals*.

Homework

Students may find that the coin they use has been damaged in some way or they may decide that they have not been spinning it sufficiently. However, they may get perfect results! Discuss their results at the beginning of the next lesson. Ask them to consider whether one hundred trials were sufficient to make inferences such as these.

Handling Data

Page 172 Successive events

Goals

If I roll a die and then spin a coin the two events are independent of each other. Getting a 'head' on the coin is not dependent upon getting a specific number on the die. For every possible outcome on the die I can get every possible outcome on the coin. The best way to present all of these outcomes is in a two-way table that is referred to throughout *I See Maths* as a **possibility diagram** or **possibility space diagram**. An alternative term, sample-space diagram, is sometimes seen, although this implies the selection of a sample – which is not the case. These diagrams ensure that we include every possible outcome. If we were to draw up a list of possible outcomes it would be easy to omit some of them.

Possibility diagrams are excellent visual pictures of showing all the possible outcomes of two successive events. However, they cannot be extended to three or more successive events and so we need a more sophisticated diagram for these. **Tree diagrams** are very helpful in visualising many successive events and we introduce these here in preparation for later work.

In all of the examples in this lesson the successive events are independent of each other. You may wish to extend this work to dependent events for some students. Here is an example.

> *A bag contains three red counters, two blue counters and five yellow counters. I select one counter at random from the bag and keep it on the table. I select a second counter at random from the bag. What is the probability of getting two counters of the same colour?*

In this case, the second event depends upon the first event. If I selected a red counter the first time there would be only two red counters left in the bag, out of a total of nine counters for me to select from the second time. Get the students to draw a tree diagram for these successive events and calculate the probability of getting two counters the same colour.

Starter

The first activity in the *Starter* introduces the meaning of the word 'successive' so that students understand what is meant by 'successive events'.

The second and third activities revise work done in previous lessons. Make sure the students know this work and the associated language before moving on.

Demonstration 1

When we roll a die or spin a coin we call it an **incident**. When we record the result we call it a **trial**. It is important that students know these words. When we follow one incident with another we say that they are **successive incidents**. Similarly, when we record two successive incidents we call them **successive trials**.

When we identify a specific outcome as something we are interested in we call it an **event** and when one event follows another we call them **successive events**.

All of these words are used in everyday language. Although the mathematical meaning is the same as that in everyday life we are much more precise in how we use the words.

Invite students to give their own examples of incidents, trials and events and of successive incidents, trials and events.

Demonstration 2

Ask the students to help you make a systematic list of all twelve of the possible outcomes when you roll a die and spin a coin. Demonstrate the method you use to ensure that you include all possibilities. Demonstrate how you can record these results in a diagram called a 'possibility space diagram'.

Discuss how the possibility space diagram ensures you include *all* the possible outcomes. Explain that Diagram 1 and Diagram 2 show alternative methods of recording the information. The diagrams can then be inspected to find the number of occurances of the favourable outcome, and the probability can be calculated. In this case we can see there are 3 favourable outcomes in a total of 12 possible outcomes, hence the probability of getting an even number and a 'tail' is $\frac{3}{12}$ or $\frac{1}{4}$.

Worksheet 39 provides practice in drawing tree diagrams. All students will benefit from using this worksheet.

Handling Data

Essential exercises

There are different ways in which these possibility space diagrams can be completed. Exercise 1 shows one way (writing the pairs). Sometimes we just put a cross to indicate a combination. However, we are sometimes looking at the result of adding or subtracting the outcomes and we then need to put that result in the correct space.

Before doing Exercise 1, you may like to ask the students to make a list of all the possible results of throwing two coins. The most common mistake is to give HH, TT and HT without taking account of the order of the results. A quick experiment with coins quickly shows that the experimental probability of each result is not a third as expected but closer to $\frac{1}{4}$, $\frac{1}{4}$ and $\frac{1}{2}$. This can be explained by considering HT and TH as two separate results.

Show how recording these events in a possibility space diagram avoids omitting any of the possible results. Count all the possible outcomes and help students work out the probability of getting two 'heads', and so on.

Students who are successful with the first exercise should be able to do the second and third exercises without much help. Notice that in Exercise 3 the first card is replaced before a second is selected. This ensures that each event is independent. The diagram is not needed to answer the first two questions of Exercise 3. The probability that the first card is a '7' is $\frac{1}{10}$ and the probability that the second card is a '5' is also $\frac{1}{10}$. There are a hundred possible outcomes and only one of these gives a '7' followed by a '5'. There are seven favourable outcomes with a sum of twelve, giving a probability of $\frac{12}{100}$ (or 0·12 or $\frac{6}{50}$ or $\frac{3}{25}$).

Exercise 4 repeats the same process to provide practice in interpreting possibility space diagrams. However, the diagram is far too big to draw and the students have to work in their imagination. They need to formalise the idea that the total number of possibilities is the product of the number of the outcomes for each event. Students should then notice that:

$$P(\text{ace of spades}) = \frac{1}{52}$$

and P(ace of spades followed by ace of spades)
$$= \frac{1}{52} \times \frac{1}{52} = \frac{1}{2704}.$$

You may like to ask some further questions of your own for this possibility space diagram.

Challenging exercise

The tree diagram is introduced here in preparation for work in Book 3. Students may like to draw the possibility space diagram first and see how the two diagrams provide the same information. The tree diagram is not complete but again you may like to ask the students to do this so that they can see the strong links with the possibility space diagram.

Since the question is about the probability of getting a 'six' on a die, the tree diagram has been limited to providing just that information. The branches represent the probability of getting a 'six' and not getting a 'six'. This is an efficient way of setting out all the possibilities. You could extend the diagram to consider throwing three dice, and working out the probabilities of getting 'six' one, two or three times.

Problem-solving exercises

Recording results systematically is a skill that the students need to learn. They need to consider a method for doing this. Those who are confident with tree diagrams could set out the results in that way and the pattern for the total number of outcomes would be immediately apparent. The first two branches each have two branches and these four each have two branches. The sequence is 2, 4, 8, 16, … and the term-to-term rule is 'multiply by two'. Students studied sequences in Book 1 and earlier in this book, and should be able to work out that the nth term is 2^n.

Exercise 7 applies the students' knowledge of possibility space diagrams to a practical activity. Students could make the spinners and compare their results with the expected results.

Plenary

Check that students can answer the question in the first *Goal*. Discuss the second *Goal* using all the language introduced in this lesson.

Homework

The *Homework* is a typical question that is frequently set in national tests. Not all students will know what a fruit machine is, so go through this before setting the *Homework* .

Descriptive statistics 1

Goals

The world is full of data that has been collected and recorded in databases. This data is not very helpful in its raw state. We need to make sense of it by describing what we see and summarising what we see. Some of the simplest things we can do are to put the data in order, note the range of the data, and work out its middle value (the **median**). The data can be put in order using a **stem-and-leaf diagram**, and this also provides an initial visual image of the data. We can begin to compare two sets of data by setting them out on the same stem-and-leaf diagram.

Work on the range and median was covered in Book 1 (pages 184–191). Students should be familiar with these terms, and most will be confident in working out these statistics. The only new work here is the introduction of a stem-and-leaf diagram. Students may have seen these in other areas of the curriculum such as geography or biology. You could check with other departments in the school to see what has been covered.

Starter

The two sets of data in the *Starter* are provided to remind students of the method for calculating the median. The number of values of x in the first data set is twelve. The rank of the median is $(12 + 1) \div 2$, i.e. 6·5. In other words, the median is the value of x that is halfway between the sixth and seventh position (There is no actual value here, so we estimate it as 81).

In the second data set the number of values of x is eleven. The rank of the median is $(11 + 1) \div 2 = 6$. The median is at the sixth position and is 80.

In both of these cases the number of values of x is small and students could easily work their way in from the ends until they reach the middle value. However, this does not help when they have large data sets. Neither does it provide a basis for calculating the lower and upper quartiles and inter-quartile range. Students do not find this method difficult provided it is introduced early and used consistently.

The *Starter* revises all the vocabulary met in Book 1. Assist the students in using words like 'variable' and 'range' by getting them to answer the questions in full sentences. For

example 'The lowest value of the variable is 62, the highest value of the variable is 95 and the range of the data set is 95 take away 62 which is 33'.

Demonstration 1

The idea of lower and upper quartiles is introduced here in preparation for work in Book 3. It does not involve any difficult mathematics. The only difficult thing is the number of new words to remember.

When students are given data sets like those in the *Starter* they can see all the values of x in rank order, and they can easily work out the range and the median. When data is presented in a frequency table like that in *Demonstration 1* it can seem much more difficult to read. Before doing any calculations help the students read the table.

> *This is a frequency table for a data set. The variable is x and the values of x are in rank order. The frequency of the variable is $f(x)$. The value 155 occurs two times. Its frequency is two. The values 156 and 157 do not occur at all. Their frequency is zero. The value 158 …*
>
> *The total number of values of the variable x is twenty-three. The rank order of the median is $(23 + 1) \div 2 = 12$. Let us look for the twelfth value of x. There are two here, and one here makes three, and one here makes four …, and three here makes fourteen. The twelfth one is in here. [It is one of the three occurrences of 165.] The median value of x is 165.*
>
> *The rank order of the lower quartile is $(23 + 1) \div 4 = 6$. The sixth value of the variable x is 162. The rank order of the upper quartile is $(23 + 1) \div 4 \times 3 = 18$. The eighteenth value of the variable x is 167.*
>
> *I can draw a scale from the lowest value to the highest value. I can draw a scale from 155 to 171. I can draw a box on this scale from 162 to 165 and another box from 165 to 167. This is called a box-and-whisker diagram. Here are the boxes and here are the whiskers. I can see that the left-hand whisker is longer than the right-hand whisker. There are more values near the top end. The inter-quartile range is only five. Half of the values of x are bunched together between 162 and 167.*

Worksheet 40 provides practice in calculating 'the five number summary' and drawing a box-and-whisker diagram for a number of data sets.

Handling Data: **Descriptive statistics 1**

Demonstration 2

The first data set is the same one as in *Demonstration 1* but before being listed in rank order. Instead of rearranging the data set in rank order in a frequency table it is recorded in a stem-and-leaf diagram. The first two digits (the hundreds and tens) of the number are placed in the first column. The ones digits are placed in the second column in the order they occur in the data set, and then rearranged in rank order in the third column.

The advantage of recording results in a stem-and-leaf diagram is that it provides a visual image of the data. It is immediately clear that the majority of the values of x are in the range 160 to 170. The three statistics, (Q_1, Q_2, Q_3) can be calculated by counting along the rows. Check the results with the answers from *Demonstration 1*.

Another advantage of recording results in a stem-and-leaf diagram is that a second data set can be recorded with its rows on the left (see Student's Book 2, page 179, Exercise 7), and an initial comparison can be made.

The second data set in this demonstration has values identical to the first data set in all but place value. (Divide each value in the first data set by ten.) The lower quartile, median and upper quartile are all a tenth of those from the first data set.

Worksheet 41 will be useful for most students to practise the routine of using a stem-and-leaf diagram.

Essential exercises

The first exercise provides practice in calculating the rank position of the median. Get students to write down their working.
Example: Sample size $n = 15$
      Rank position of median $(15 + 1) \div 2 = 8$

Exercise 2 is revision of work done in Book 1. Students may need help with part (e).
    Place the data set in rank order.
    ¯1, ¯1, ¯1·5, ¯2, ¯3, ¯3, ¯4, ¯6, ¯8, ¯9
    Sample size $n = 10$
    Rank position of median $= (10 + 1) \div 2 = 5\cdot5$
    Median $= ¯3$
    Range $= ¯1 - ¯9 = 8$

The sample size in Exercise 3 is seventy-five.
    Lowest value 57
    Highest value 127
    Rank position of median $= (75 + 1) \div 2 = 38$
    Median $= 88$
    Range $= 127 - 57 = 70$

Extend the exercise by using the data set to calculate the lower and upper quartiles and draw a box-and-whisker diagram. Describe what you see.

In Exercise 4 draw the stem-and-leaf diagrams for the two data sets 'back-to back' (as on page 179 of the Student's Book). Circle the medians and indicate the positions of the mean values. Describe what you see.

Challenging exercises

Exercise 5 extends the work in the *Essential exercises* to include the drawing of box-and-whisker diagrams. Discuss the two data sets.

Exercise 6 is extension work and should not be attempted by all students. It presents a real challenge! When information is provided in a frequency diagram we do not have sufficient detail to calculate exact statistics. We can only estimate the values. The diagram begins with $x = 4$ mm and ends at $x = 6\cdot5$ mm. We can estimate the range to be $6\cdot5$ mm $- 4$ mm $= 2\cdot5$ mm.

The sample size is one hundred. The rank position of the median is $(100 + 1) \div 2 = 50\cdot5$. The first two columns represent 26 results $(8 + 18)$. The median lies in the third column, somewhere between 5 and $5\cdot5$. To be precise, it is the $24\cdot5$th result $(50\cdot5 - 26)$ in this column. The value of x can be estimated to be 5 mm $+ \frac{24\cdot5}{40} \times 0\cdot5$ mm $\approx 5\cdot3$ mm.

Problem-solving exercise

Exercise 7 shows how the ideas practised in the *Essential exercises* can be applied to a real-life example. Discuss the results with the students and decide what can be inferred from the statistical data.

Plenary

Set the questions in the *Goals* to check that the students understand how to calculate the range and the median, and get them to draw a stem-and-leaf diagram.

Discuss how you would arrange the recording of data for the second activity of the *Plenary*.

The two box-and-whisker diagrams for each of the data sets in *Demonstration 2* should be identical (adjusted by a power of ten).

Homework

This activity would be of greater interest if you collect data from the class and get the students to compare the heights of boys and girls. You could collect the data for the whole year group and compare the results of each tutor group.

Handling Data

 Page 180 Descriptive statistics 2

Goals

Students were taught how to calculate the mean value of a set of data in Book 1 (pages 180–183). In this lesson we move on to using an assumed mean so that the calculations are made simpler. This is mainly practice in number work, but the use of an assumed mean can help some students understand what they are doing when they calculate the mean.

Book 1 introduced the symbols $\bar{x}$ and Σ for 'mean' and 'sum' respectively. These are used again in the demonstrations for this lesson, but not in the exercises. It is left to the teacher to decide whether to insist on students using these symbols but it should be encouraged, since regular use does breed familiarity and confidence.

The fact that students are usually very confident in the basic work on calculating the mean is used in this lesson to introduce them to some harder ideas. They have already considered how to estimate the median from a frequency diagram (Student's Book 2, page 179, Exercise 6) and here they will be looking at how to estimate the mean from similar information. Although this is not essential work at this stage, introducing these ideas now will help students later on. It also provides a challenge rather than merely repeating earlier work.

Starter

The *Starter* begins with basic revision and then moves on to revise the mean and the difference from the mean. The symbols $\bar{x}$ and Σ are revised. Part (e) asks for a calculation of the difference from the mean for each variable. You might find it helpful to draw a grid and complete these differences in a row below the x-values:

x	362	364	370	372	372	380	382	...
$x - \bar{x}$	⁻16	⁻14	⁻8	⁻6	⁻6	2	4	...

The total of the differences from the mean should, of course, be zero. Discuss this result and ask whether this will always be the case. An understanding of this will prepare students for calculating standard deviation in Book 3.

Worksheet 42 provides practice in calculating deviations from the mean. This work will consolidate the fact that $\Sigma(x - \bar{x}) = 0$ for all data sets. This sheet is suitable for less confident students who need basic arithmetic practice and experience of the implication of $\Sigma(x - \bar{x}) = 0$.

Demonstration 1

The use of calculators has made working out the mean an almost effortless task. However, we still have to enter every number (accurately) and we can make this easier by assuming the mean to be a particular value and only entering the differences.

The first table in *Demonstration 1* provides an explanation of why we can use an assumed mean. The mean of the top set of five numbers is 4. Each entry in the lower data set is *exactly* ten more than the set above. The mean value of the lower data set is also *exactly ten more* than the mean of the other data set. We could have worked out the mean of the second data set by merely adding ten to the first answer.

The second and third tables show how we can treat a data set in different ways. Part (b) considers each number as a sum of $20 + x$ and part (c) considers each number as $30 + x$. Ask students for other ways of writing the numbers. They could choose any start number such as $10 + x$, or $5 + x$, and so on. The choice is arbitrary.

Part (d) shows how the ideas in the first three parts can be used as an aid to calculating the mean. Again get students to choose a different assumed mean and see that they get the same result. When the assumed mean is provided for the students to use, they sometimes think that there is something magical about the choice. Emphasise that we try to pick a number that is most appropriate for the set of data.

Demonstration 2

Data is rarely presented in its raw form as in the figures at the top of *Demonstration 2*. It is normally presented in frequency tables. Because students learn to calculate the mean by 'add 'em up and divide by the number' they often make the mistake of adding the list of values of x and dividing by the number of values of x in the table, instead of taking into account the frequency of the values of x. This demonstration can be used as a reminder of how to calculate the mean from a frequency table.

In the example here we present the data set in a horizontal table. Students can easily be thrown when data is presented in different ways. Make sure that they see data in horizontal and vertical tables.

In this example the variable x is the test score. Assist students in making the connection between the raw data at

Handling Data

Handling Data: **Descriptive statistics 1**

the top of the page and the first two rows of the frequency table. The scores have been recorded in descending order.

> *What is the highest score? 90. How many nineties are there? One. What is the next score? 86. How many? One. The next? 84. How many? Three. The next? …*
>
> *Let the assumed mean be 80. Subtract the assumed mean from each value of x. [10, 6, 4, 2, 0, ⁻2, ⁻10] We need to multiply this difference by the frequency. [10, 6, 12, 4, 0, ⁻4, ⁻10] Now we must calculate the mean of these differences. $18 \div 12 = 1·5$. The actual mean is $80 + 1·5 = 81·5$.*

Get students to check the result by using the raw data to calculate the mean. Which is the most efficient method? For this size of data set it is probably just as easy to calculate the mean using the raw data. However, with large sets of data, or if x is a value with a large number of digits, the use of the assumed mean is likely to be more efficient.

Worked example

This shows a method for working out the mean of a set of data, using an assumed mean.

Essential exercises

The first exercise is straightforward practice in calculating the mean with raw data. It is also practice in manipulating positive whole numbers, decimals, fractions and negative numbers. Students can elect to use an assumed mean to do these calculations if they wish.

Exercise 2 can be seen as three puzzles to be solved using knowledge of the mean. Part (a) requires the knowledge that if the mean of three numbers is 13 then their sum is $3 \times 13 = 39$. If two of the numbers are 9 and 13 then the third number must be 17. Another way of solving this puzzle is to notice that one of the values is the same as the mean. The third number must be as much above 13 as 9 is below. $13 + 4 = 17$.

Part (b) of Exercise 2 provides different information about a data set of three. The youngest person is 30 and the range is 24 so the oldest person must be $30 + 24 = 54$. Now the question follows as in part (a). Part (c) of Exercise 2 poses a different problem. This is one way to find the solution:

> *The mean of Joel's scores is 18 so the mean of Sarah's scores is 18. The range of Sarah's scores is $2 \times 12 = 24$. Sarah's scores must be symmetrical about 18 so the smallest is $18 - 12 = 6$ and the largest is $18 + 12 = 30$. Check the mean – 18.*

Exercise 3, part (a) may need some working through with the class. It is tempting to find the mean of the five given numbers but this is wrong because you are finding the mean of only five people, not fourteen people. The students

must first calculate the sum of the first ten peoples' heights ($10 \times 173·6$ cm), then add on the four new heights, and finally divide the result by fourteen.

Part (b) of Exercise 3 is similar in that the total of the percentage scores has to be calculated for each class before a year average can be calculated. This is best explained by noting that each class has a different number of pupils and this gives each class average a different weighting.

Challenging exercises

Students need to recognise the difference between 'calculate' and 'estimate'. In these exercises an exact answer cannot be calculated because we do not have the raw data. Interrogate the given data in Exercise 5:

> *Look at this first column. [$145 \leq x < 150$]. There are two students with heights in this range. What might the heights of these students be? Could they both be 145 cm? Yes. Could they both be 150 cm? No, because that height is not included in this range. Could they be …?*

Inspect each entry. Estimate the range. $175\text{cm} - 145\text{cm} = 30\text{cm}$. There are 30 children, so the median will be at the $(30 + 1) \div 2$ th position (15·5th position). This is in the third column. An estimate of the median is $155 \text{ cm} + \frac{6·5}{9} \times 5 \text{ cm} = 158·6 \text{ cm}$. We estimate the mean by considering the midpoints of each range of values. We look at 147·5 cm, 152·5 cm, 157·5 cm, and so on. We calculate: $(147·5 \text{ cm} \times 2 + 152·5 \text{ cm} \times 7 + 157·5 \text{ cm} \times 9 + 162·5 \text{ cm} \times 8 + 167·5 \text{ cm} \times 3 + 172·5 \text{ cm} \times 1) \div 30$.

It is very easy for students to confuse all the things that begin with the label 'frequency'. We have 'frequency table', 'frequency diagram' and 'frequency polygon'. It is only through regular use that students will become familiar with this language. Demonstrate how to draw a **frequency polygon** with the first set of data in Exercise 6 and let the students complete the second one on the same axes.

Problem-solving exercise

Exercise 7 shows how the knowledge gained in this and the previous lessons can be applied to a real-life situation.

Plenary

Check that students understand how to calculate the mean in each case.

Homework

The *Homework* is an extended piece of work that can be set over a couple of weeks. It could be continued in class and set as a practice coursework in preparation for GCSE.

Handling Data

 Page 184 # Interpreting data 1

Goals

Students studied the interpretation of data in Book 1 (pages 164–171). They have also studied much of this in earlier years. We have to be careful not to present just more of the same or they will lose interest. The next set of lessons allows students to use and apply their knowledge of handling data to some real-life problems.

Work on estimating the mean has been included because this is far more likely to be met in real-life than the simple calculation of the mean from raw data. By considering midpoints and multiplying by the frequency, students are reminded how to read frequency tables. They also get a better understanding of class intervals.

Starter

This work revises work done in previous lessons and reinforces the language and symbolisation of statistics. A sample has been selected at random from a population. The variables x and y represent age and test scores respectively.

Get the students to do the questions first on their own, and then get them to present their answers on the board, ensuring that they explain their reasoning.

Demonstration 1

A set of raw data is provided and the students have to decide what to do to make sense of it. The two variables are the same as those in the *Starter* (the data set in the *Starter* is a sample from this population). The first thing to do is to use a recording system that shows the data more simply. A frequency table could be used but here we have used a stem-and-leaf diagram. Figure 2 shows that the ages are bunched mainly in the twenties, so a further diagram in Figure 3 separates out the data into groups below and above the halfway mark. We can now see the population is mainly of people in their late teens or early twenties. We can see also that there are forty-eight values of x and y.

What do these stem-and-leaf diagrams tell us? We can see that more than half the students were in their twenties. Figure 3 shows that no student was under 17 years and none older than 42 years. The median is at the $\frac{49}{2}$ th person, and is 22, and so we can say that approximately 50% of

the students were younger than $22\frac{1}{2}$ years (assuming that in any normal population the birthdays would be spread evenly throughout the year).

The lower quartile is 20 years ($\frac{49}{4}$ th person) and the upper quartile is $29\frac{1}{4}$ years ($\frac{3}{4} \times 49$ th person) so 50% of students have ages within this range (the inter-quartile range).

The statistics calculated here can be seen visually. We could continue to work out the actual mean for both sets of data using the raw data. You could do this so that you can later compare the actual mean with the estimated mean (which is worked out in *Demonstration 2*).

Demonstration 2

Suppose the same data had been recorded in frequency tables like those on page 185 of the Student's Book. The data has been grouped in groups of three in both cases, and the frequency recorded as $f(x)$. Now we cannot calculate the actual mean value because we do not have sufficient data. We have to 'estimate' the mean using the mid-values. An additional column has been created to record mid-value of $x \times f(x)$. Invite students to explain how each entry in this column has been calculated. For example, 18 is midway between 17 and 19 and $18 \times 10 = 180$.

The estimated mean is calculated by finding the sum of the mid-value of each group multiplied by the frequency of that group, $\Sigma[\text{mid-value of } x \times f(x)]$, and dividing by the number in the population (48). Students who completed the *Challenging exercises* in the previous lesson will have seen this done already.

Compare the estimated means with the actual means. **Worksheet 43** provides additional practice in this for all students.

Essential exercises

The first exercise shows how three TV regions chose to represent the results of a survey using three different types of diagrams. Discuss which diagram gives the best visual image. Each type of diagram has its own merits but can also be misleading. The information in the diagrams needs careful scrutiny before any comparisons can be made.

The numbers taking part in the survey in each region are different, and care needs to be taken when making

 **I See Maths** Book 2

comparisons. The purpose of the exercise is to get students to see why it is necessary to use something like percentages that compare outcomes with a specified number (100) in order to make comparisons. The exercise is good practice on manipulating fractions, ratios and percentages.

Exercise 2 demonstrates that when representing different sized data sets with pie charts the circle should be drawn such that the radius is proportional to the square root of the sample size. All too often we ignore this requirement.

Challenging exercise

Exercise 3 again presents two sets of data in different forms. In one we have a frequency table and in the other we have a frequency diagram. This work will reinforce the meaning of these words.

Note that we do not have sufficient information to calculate exact statistics for these data sets. We have to estimate the values as best we can. The students will need to decide what degree of accuracy to use in their answers, and whether they are going to give answers as tenths (and hundredths?) of minutes or whether they are going to convert the answers to minutes and seconds.

Make sure that the box-and-whisker diagrams are drawn to the same scale so that the two data sets can be compared.

Problem-solving exercise

Exercise 4 does not ask students to make any specific calculations. They have to inspect the data sets and decide what calculations might help them in planning a holiday. The students may come up with different answers, and this is fine provided they can justify their recommendations.

This is what real-life is like. We are not given helpful hints about what statistics would be useful but instead we have to consider which of the available statistics would be relevant. Discourage students from duplicating work such as representing the data in several different forms. In GCSE students are penalised for producing redundant information.

Plenary

In *Demonstration 2* the values are grouped in class intervals of three. The first set of values is {17, 18, 19}. If we double this class interval to 6 we would include the values {17, 18, 19, 20, 21, 22}. The mid-value of this class interval would be 19·5. Note how the last set of values will include {41, 42, 43, 44, 45, 46} if we want to maintain the size of the interval. However, we know that the value in this interval is actually less than 43 so this is bound to skew the

result. Use these class intervals to work out an estimate of the mean. How does this compare with the result in *Demonstration 2*. You could also consider what would happen if the class intervals started {15, 16, 17, 18, 19, 20}, and so on.

Suppose we have class intervals to include {17, 18, 19, 20, 21, 22, 23, 24, 25} then the mid value is 21. Use class intervals like this to estimate the mean. This time the last class interval ends at 43 and we have not had to create new values to keep the intervals equal in size.

Repeat with class intervals like this {17, 18, 19, 20, 21, 22, 23, 24, 25, 26, 27, 28}. Note that the last class interval will have to be {41, 42, 43, 44, 45, 46, 47, 48, 49, 50, 51, 52} Consider how this will affect the estimates of the mean.

Homework

Your students have probably seen compound bar charts before, but they are presented here just in case they have not. Compound bar charts are sometimes used in national tests so students need to be able to recognise and interpret them.

Handling Data

Page 188 Interpreting data 2

Goals

It is often assumed that high correlation between two variables proves that one causes the other. In medicine, for instance, it might be assumed that a high correlation between smoking and heart disease proves that smoking causes heart disease. A statistician would not make this assumption. High correlation might be sufficient to provoke a hypothesis about causation; but that hypothesis would have to be explored in medical research, not statistics.

This lesson is largely about scatter diagrams as an image of presence or absence of correlation. It is important, however, that students appreciate what kind of data they are dealing with when they create scatter diagrams. A scatter diagram is drawn using **bi-variate** data. There are two variables. Although this sounds obvious, it does need making clear that the data they have used until now (in bar graphs and frequency diagrams, and when calculating the mean, and so on) is **uni-variate** (with an associated function called the frequency). This is the difficulty: early introduction of statistics, when algebraic confidence is incubating, lacks some of the technical vocabulary that would clarify it. However, all is not lost. The previous focus on uni-variate data can be clarified by emphasising the nature of bi-variate data. You will see that this is the major focus in the *Starter*.

There is a second important matter. The idea of correlation is not as clear in scatter diagrams as is often assumed. Introduction to correlation really needs some version of a correlation coefficient to clarify it – and *Pearson's product moment correlation coefficient* is very useful. This is usually referred to as **Pearson's r**. Although the demonstrations do not depend on this, the next few paragraphs consider a more accurate view of correlation that you may choose to include in your teaching.

When we deal with scatter diagrams as shown in the demonstrations, the **line of best fit** is very important; it helps to estimate an unknown value of one variable from a known value of the other variable. The line of best fit (at this stage we will deal only with a straight line) has an equation of the form $y = rx + c$ in which the gradient, r, is related to the correlation coefficient. In fact, if we use standardised scores (z scores) for the two variables, the gradient of the line of best fit **is** equal to r. It can be seen immediately that the line of best fit can be more accurately drawn if we know r. It is also the case that the line of best fit goes through the point $(\overline{x}, \overline{y})$. With this information we

can accurately draw the line of best fit. Of course, we have not dealt with z scores yet, but with carefully chosen raw data, we approximate to this.

When we inspect a bi-variate data set as in Figure 1 of the demonstrations, we can see that an increase in x is associated with an increase in y; in fact, if you tell me a value of x I can be completely confident that I can tell you the corresponding value of y. Now look at Figure 2. On the whole, when x increases then y also increases, but the inference is not so reliable. Tell me a particular value of x and I cannot now be as confident that I can tell you the corresponding value of y. We say that Figure 1 has two variables that are perfectly correlated; Figure 2 has two variables that are not so well correlated. We can measure the correlation! Just type the bi-variate data set in a spreadsheet; ask it to calculate PEARSON and it will give you the measure. Try it with the data set for Figure 1: $r = 1$ (this is perfect correlation). Try Figure 2: $r = \cdot 7$ (a high-ish correlation, but less than $r = 1$). Pearson's r is a measure of correlation (not a basic measure, but a derived measure. see **Worksheets 44** to **46**).

If you introduce these ideas to your students, they will be able to draw their own scatter diagrams from the data sets provided; calculate the mean of x and the mean of y, calculate Pearson's r for the bi-variate data set; and draw the line of best fit (which will be fairly accurate, because the data had been carefully chosen).

Take courage! Do it! Otherwise, use the demonstrations as suggested below. In either case, **Worksheets 44** to **46** will be useful for your most confident students.

Starter

Enable students to make sense of the term 'bi-variate data'. Link it to other uses of the prefix 'bi'; and notice how it is sometimes attached to a noun (as in bicycle) and sometimes to an adjective (as in bifocal). The English language is rather careless in the way it allows 'bi' to consort with both nouns and adjectives; but it does give us the opportunity to utilise the idea of explicit and implicit information. Look at the grid of words using 'bi' meaning 'two'. In 'bicycle' it is explicit that we are to think about a cycle; but it is implicit that it has two wheels rather than two saddles. However, in 'bi-focal lenses' it is explicit that we are talking about lenses, but 'bi' does not refer to the number of lenses; it refers to the fact that each lens has more than one focus (each lens has two). This is fairly explicit, but you have to know that 'focal' is linked to 'focus'. Examine each entry in turn. Get to the point where 'bi-variate distribution' is to be understood as a distribution that involves two … well, 'variate' is suggestive of 'variable' – so we can deduce that we are looking at something that has two variables.

Look at question 2:

> *Look at the variable x for respondent b. What is x? What is the frequency of that value of x? The table does not tell us that: it is not a frequency table. It tells us, instead, that, in one case, when $x = 41$ then $y = 71$. It lists two variables. … etc.*

Suppose we wanted to know whether certain test scores depended on the age of the person taking the test. Can we say that younger people performed better than older people or vice versa? We need to plot a person's age against their test score to see if there is any correlation.

Inspect the two data sets and ask students to calculate the mean of each set. Draw a grid on the board and draw x- and y-axes to represent age and test scores respectively. Invite students to come to the board and plot the points (x, y). Plot the point representing the two means in a different colour.

The points on this graph are very scattered. What can we infer from this diagram? Older people do seem to be achieving better scores 'on the whole' than younger people. There is a general trend for older people to perform better than younger people. We can just about draw a line to represent this trend so there does appear to be some positive correlation between older people and higher scores.

Demonstration 1

Inspect the graph and discuss what you see. In Figure 1 all of the points, including the point representing the means, lie on the line $y = x + 1$. As x increases so y increases. There is an exact linear relationship between x and y so there is perfect correlation between x and y. In this case it is **positive correlation**.

Demonstration 2

Figure 2 shows a set of points that indicate positive correlation. As x increases then y tends to increase. We say that there is positive correlation between the variables. We can draw a line of best fit to indicate this relationship. This line will pass through the point (10·1, 9·5) representing the mean of each set of data.

Figure 3 shows a set of points that are scattered randomly all over the graph. There is clearly no obvious relationship between the two variables. We say that there is no

correlation and we cannot draw a line of best fit. The final figure shows a set of points where, as x increases y decreases. We say that there is **negative correlation** between the variables. We can draw a line of best fit to indicate the relationship. This line will pass through (9·9, 9·1) representing the mean of each set of data.

Essential exercises

Students are led through Exercise 1 step-by-step as they inspect the data sets, draw a scatter diagram and interpret what they see. Most students should be able to do this work without much help.

Exercise 2 allows the students to interpret a set of data on their own. They should follow a similar method to that used in Exercise 1.

Challenging exercise

Exercise 3 is straightforward and should be done by all students without assistance. They may need some help with part (e) if it has been a while since they studied linear graphs.

Problem-solving exercise

In Exercise 4 students are not specifically directed to look for links between any particular variables. They are asked to consider what comparisons might be sensible, and decide which variables they will use. This exercise would be of more interest if you produce sets of data about their own class or year group. The exercise uses a sample of data for only ten students. You could use large data sets and a spreadsheet to provide more realistic diagrams.

Plenary

Since this topic is fairly straightforward, the students can be creative and design or collect their own bi-variate distributions and write about them.

Homework

Arm-span and height are almost always linked. Get students to collect the measurements as they are working on the exercises. Discuss the results at the beginning of the next lesson.

Handling Data

Handling Data

Page 192 Planning an enquiry

Goals

The four-point plan for conducting an enquiry is:

1. Planning an enquiry

2. Collecting data

3. Representing data

4. Communicating results

This lesson focuses on the first point, 'Planning an enquiry'. You may want to take all four lessons together and get students to do their own enquiry following the four-point plan. The latter part of the summer term is an ideal time for such an activity.

Students studied setting up an enquiry in Book 1 (pages 192–195). They practised one of the most important features of any statistical enquiry, that of framing a hypothesis. This is a rather difficult concept that needs representing to students in a principled way so that it can be developed later into the famous statistical notion of 'null hypothesis and alternative hypothesis'. You may need to revisit the earlier work before embarking on this lesson.

Students should not present a hypothesis based merely on opinion or prejudice. They should be able to give some justification for their hypothesis by citing some prior evidence. Such evidence could be the results of a pilot study, personal observations of certain events, newspaper reports and so on.

Once students have decided what it is they are going to study they have to decide what sample to select, how big a sample to select, and what method of sampling to use. We introduce three types of sampling in this lesson: random sampling, stratified sampling and quota sampling. Students have to decide which method is most appropriate for their enquiry. The question of what size sample to take cannot be decided by some formula: students must consider what size sample they can reasonably cope with, and whether this allows them to undertake the kind of sampling (stratified; quota; and so on) that they need for the work.

The exercises are somewhat unusual in this section. They model the *types* of questions students should ask when setting up an enquiry. It is expected that students will ask their own questions in preparation for their own enquiry.

Starter

The *Starter* reminds students of the terms 'variable', 'sample of a variable' and 'random sample of a variable'. Discuss ways in which a random sample can be selected. Look at computer programs that generate random numbers. Students may have used these in other areas of the curriculum such as geography.

Discuss how to select random numbers from a bag.

> *Suppose we put the numbers 1 to 30 in a bag. Select a number. Should that number be replaced? If we replace the number then every number has an equal chance of being selected but we may select the same number twice. If we do not replace the number then each successive selection increases the probability of a number being selected. We could ignore or include repeated numbers. We must decide which method we are going to use before conducting the enquiry.*

Looking at word or sentence lengths is a popular enquiry for GCSE coursework. Selecting a sample of text can be done in several ways. Students have to decide whether they want to analyse consecutive words in random sentences, or random words. A chunk of text could be selected by randomly selecting a page. Alternatively, one sentence could be selected at random from each of say, fifty pages. What method would they use to choose a page, sentence or word at random? Discuss the different ways of selecting text.

Demonstration 1

This first demonstration provides an overall picture of how to conduct a statistical enquiry. Although this lesson focuses on the first point of the plan, students can see what it is they are going to do. They need to have some idea of where they are going and what they have to do.

At this stage you may wish to get students to consider what topic they would like to study. Get them to work in groups discussing the topic and thinking about what they might select as a focus. Get them to read about their topic using the library and the Internet.

Demonstration 2

Discuss what is meant by 'a hypothesis'. Be specific that a hypothesis is a statement. But be equally clear that the

Handling Data

Handling Data: **Planning an enquiry**

statement is not a guess, and it is not a belief or a prejudice; it follows from some evidence. Explain that reading about their topic might provide the students with some evidence upon which to base their hypothesis.

The example on page 193 of the Student's Book shows a newspaper report on students suffering spinal injury from carrying heavy bags. This newspaper report provides some initial evidence on which to base a hypothesis. The statement in the headline needs closer scrutiny. What does the statement mean by 'heavy'? How heavy are students' bags? What do students carry in their bags? Are students required to carry certain books to school? Do some year groups carry more than others in their bags?

Initial observation and informal questions lead the students in this demonstration to form a hypothesis that Y8 and Y10 carry about the same mass and the Y8s think that it is too much. There is no investigation into whether this results in spinal injury.

What data do they need to collect to test this hypothesis? Who or what will they test it on? What size sample will they use? (They must decide what they can reasonably cope with.) How will they select their sample? Will the sample be representative of the year groups selected? Will it be representative of the school? Will it be representative of students across the country? These are all questions the students need to ask.

Discuss the different ways in which samples could be taken. If certain year groups and possibly tutor groups are selected then the sample is stratified. If the sample is selected to have equal numbers of boys and girls then it is a quota sample by sex.

Essential exercise

Three statements have been selected from newspaper articles for discussion in Exercise 1. Study the types of questions that are modelled in the exercise. Ask students to pose their own questions related to each statement. Get them to consider other statements they may have read in newspapers or heard on the radio or TV.

The students could select any of these statements as the basis for their own enquiry or they could find topics of their own. Collect newspaper cuttings that might act as stimuli for an enquiry.

Challenging exercise

The six statements provided in Exercise 2 are given to enable students to practise setting up an enquiry and making appropriate plans. It is not expected that they will write essays on the subject but should set out a list of activities to be executed at the start of a project. They do

not have to imagine that *they* will conduct the enquiry but need to think what a team of researchers might do.

For example, part (a) might be a team of government scientists looking for links between the incidence of leukaemia and the proximity to mobile phone masts. First, they would need to find out what the incidence of leukaemia is across the whole population. If this information is not already available then they may need to find this out for themselves before looking at any particular location. Next, they would have to decide on the location (the area to be considered) and the data that has to be collected. The students can then consider whether the whole population is scrutinised or whether a sample would be sufficient, and so on.

Problem-solving exercise

Exercise 3 provides practice in deciding how to select appropriate samples for the enquiry suggested. In some cases the student may begin by considering members of the population that they would *not* wish to sample. For example, perhaps a survey about how people will vote in an election should not include people under eighteen, and a survey about 'senior citizens' and pensions should not include people below pensionable age.

Plenary

Discuss the purpose of selecting samples, and ask students to suggest whether samples you suggest are representative of the populations. To what extent can results from samples be used to generalise?

Homework

It is expected that students will use the work in these lessons to set up their own enquiry and carry it out over an extended period. This first *Homework* is designed to get them thinking of their enquiry. You could provide the students with a planning sheet to complete and hand in for comments before proceeding. Discuss the limitations of a statistical enquiry and the dangers of making statistical inferences from small samples.

Handling Data

 Page 196 # Collecting data

Goals

This lesson focuses on the second point for consideration when conducting a statistical enquiry: collecting data. Having made a hypothesis and selected what type of sample is needed, the students need to decide how they are going to collect the data.

In the example about school bags this might include weighing school bags and recording the results. Students have been taught earlier how to make tally charts and how to complete a frequency table. First, students have to decide whether the data is discrete or continuous. In this case it would be continuous data. Will every result be recorded separately or will the frequency table be designed to catalogue the masses within a range of values? The latter would be preferable but the range will have to be agreed.

Another aspect of this enquiry requires collecting students' opinions and this requires questionnaires or interviews. Questionnaires are widely used in statistical surveys but all too often we put too much faith in the results. Questions have to be carefully worded to avoid bias. They also need to be designed to obtain the information required. This may seem obvious but when you look at a range of questionnaires you can see that this is not such an easy task. Collecting factual information in this way can be successful, but we need to take care when we are canvassing opinions. In all cases it is difficult to know the extent to which respondents answer truthfully.

Students could collect data through observation. For example they could find a suitable location and observe students passing at certain times of the day. In the bag enquiry they could record the frequency of students looking tired or struggling with their bags. However, this data is subjective, and should not be used on its own but to support harder evidence.

Starter

The number of male and female students has been recorded in a table. Ask your students to suggest ways of selecting a representative sample. This is revision of work done in the previous lesson.

Demonstration

What makes a good question for a questionnaire? Study the questions on page 196 of the Student's Book.

Do you carry too much weight?
This question is suggestive. It puts the idea into the respondent's mind that their bag might be too heavy. What is meant by 'too much weight'? For some students merely carrying a bag would be too much!

Is your bag too heavy?
Again this is suggestive. Too heavy for one person may be light for another.

Do you like carrying your bag?
This is not a relevant question. Liking to carry a bag is not related to a measure of heaviness.

Don't you think that we have to carry too much to school?
This question is suggestive. It implies that the questioner wants a positive answer. It includes the words 'to school' that implies that the institution is responsible for the amount being carried in a bag.

Is it right that you have to carry so much to school each day?
This question does not only suggest that the students carry too much but it also suggests that this is a moral issue by considering the rightness of the act.

How often do you carry a school bag weighing about as much as the one you are carrying today?
There is no suggestion in this question that the bag being carried is light or heavy. It is objective and only asks the respondent a factual question without asking them to make a judgement.

How much of what you have in your bag is essential for today?
Although this is mainly a factual question the respondent might give an emotional response if they feel guilty about carrying non-essential items. It might be better to ask if they are likely to need everything they are carrying in their bag that day.

Have you ever suffered from back pain?
This is a factual question but it does not differentiate between an occasional twinge and severe back pain. It could be improved by providing a list of graded examples.

Discuss the validity of questionnaires and interviews. How honest are people when they give answers? Does this vary with the type of question? Is an interview more intimidating? Do students feel obliged to give certain answers to some questions (for example on smoking, drinking or taking drugs)?

Handling Data

Introduce the idea that there is often already a bank of data that can be used in a statistical enquiry. It might be possible to obtain class sizes and lists in order to select samples.

Now that the students have this data they can see that each year group has a different number of students. In order to get a truly representative sample they should select the correct proportion of males and females from each year. Having decided to select a total of 30 students from each year group they then have to calculate the number of males and females needed. The calculations are demonstrated on page 197 of the Student's Book.

Having decided on the composition of the sample, the students now have to organise the collection of data. In the demonstration the students decide to select every fifth student who approaches their 'station'. Discuss the limitations and difficulties they might meet using this method. What about uncooperative students? What if they do not have sufficient respondents? Will the location of their 'station' influence the outcome?

Essential exercises

Organise the students into groups to discuss the questions in Exercise 1. Get them to decide which questions should and should not be used. Invite them to present their answers to the class with explanations and justifications. Invite them to consider questions of their own that would be suitable for the surveys suggested.

Get students to work in pairs designing questions for the six surveys in Exercise 2. They could make posters of their questionnaires, and when they are displayed the rest of the class can judge which are the best.

Challenging exercises

Exercises 3 and 4 are designed to get students discussing the validity of results, and the possibility of using results to generalise to a wider population. It is important that your students develop an analytical disposition with regard to statistical enquiries. They will be bombarded with the results of surveys in their future life and they need to be able to judge when to question the validity of the results.

Problem-solving exercises

Exercises 5 and 6 provide practice in designing and conducting some simple surveys. Encourage the students to imagine they are working for a company that has been employed to carry out these surveys. Role-play is something they are likely to be familiar with in other areas of the curriculum and it can motivate the students to produce a well presented report.

Plenary

Discuss the different types of sampling techniques. Ask students to suggest possible surveys and which technique would be appropriate for each.

Homework

The *Homework* activity is designed to check that the students have understood the principles of writing questionnaires. They do not need to write many questions but they must ensure that the questions are not suggestive, are unbiased, and obtain the relevant information.

Handling Data

Handling Data

 Page 200 # Representing data

Goals

This lesson focuses on the third point for consideration when conducting a statistical enquiry: representing data. Drawing statistical diagrams and graphs has been rehearsed many times in this book and in Book 1. Students have had plenty of experience of this work. However, they usually draw the diagrams and graphs according to instructions in the text and not as the result of deciding on what is the most appropriate diagram or graph.

In this lesson the students are asked to consider the most appropriate representation of the given data. Although the exercises instruct the students to use specified representations, time should be given to discussing the appropriateness of the representation.

Students will have to produce a statistical piece of coursework for GCSE. The criteria include selecting an appropriate representation, explaining and justifying the representation, suggesting alternative or improved representation, and not duplicating or providing redundant representations. Students need practice in applying this knowledge in preparation for this coursework task.

All examiners have seen the results of a survey presented in a tally chart, a frequency table, a bar chart, a pie chart and a pictogram without any commentary linking them to the question under consideration. This is wasted effort on the part of the students and not only will such work gain no credit but the student will probably be penalised for producing redundant and irrelevant information. Good coursework marks are dependent on good teaching by the teacher and good preparation by the student.

Starter

The activity in the *Starter* revises work done in earlier lessons on continuous data. The purpose of the task is to remind students of some of the statistical techniques they are able to apply to their data.

What might be an appropriate mass for a student's bag? 4kg? 10kg? Use scales to determine the mass of one student's bag and use this to get the class to estimate the mass of some more. This is a good exercise in estimating masses.

Discuss whether the data is discrete or continuous. Get the students to use the invented set of data to do the

calculations in the *Starter*. Invite students to present their answers. Discuss the degree of accuracy to use for the answers.

Demonstration

Students invariably want to calculate the mean of a set of data. It is something that they are familiar and comfortable with, and they do the calculation without any thought as to whether it is appropriate. Work in previous lessons has highlighted the fact that when a set of data has some values way outside the general range, the mean is not a good summary.

The median can often provide a better summary, and when used alongside the lower and upper quartiles it can give a good profile of the data set. A box-and-whisker diagram can be drawn with this data and provides a good visual image of the data set.

The mode, however, is rarely useful unless we are looking at the most popular or most common item in a survey. Similarly, scatter diagrams and looking for correlation is only appropriate when we have bi-variate data.

When the data set consists of continuous data there is little choice in the type of diagram we use. We can draw a frequency diagram or a frequency polygon. Later we shall see how we can also draw a histogram but this needs an understanding of frequency density.

A simple but effective diagram is the box-and-whisker diagram (or box-and-whisker plot) but this would not be needed in addition to one of the other diagrams. It is the quality of the interpretation of these diagrams that is important and not the quantity of diagrams.

Essential exercises

You can find a vast amount of data about people's ordinary lifestyles on the worldwide-web. The government publishes tables of such information each year. When the students have completed these exercises get them to find a source of data, and select some data to represent.

Exercises 1 and 2 provide practice in drawing diagrams and graphs for discrete data. Exercise 3 provides practice in representing continuous data.

Handling Data

Challenging exercises

Exercise 4 leaves the choice of suitable class intervals to the students. Get them to discuss the most appropriate class interval before embarking on the exercise. Although the data is discrete in its raw form it is treated like continuous data when it is grouped into class intervals.

Exercise 5 provides an example of a pie chart. Students should not find this difficult but it is surprising how many students forget how to calculate the sizes of the angles. Demonstrate how to draw the table with an extra column for the angle and an extra row for the totals.

Problem-solving exercise

By now the students should be confident in statistical techniques. This is an opportunity to let them choose their own topic for investigation. You will need to ensure that all students have access to the Internet, and you may want to suggest specific websites to access.

Plenary

Make sure that all students can answer the first question in the *Plenary*. The answer is in the text and has been repeated on several occasions. How do students decide whether a variable is discrete or continuous? In this case it is simple because the mass has been measured and not counted so it is continuous.

Homework

The questions for homework are revision and follow on from the *Plenary*. Students should be confident in the language here. Ask students to explain and justify their answers.

Handling Data

Communicating results

Goals

This lesson focuses on the fourth point for consideration when conducting a statistical enquiry: communicating results. This work links clearly with the previous lesson on representing data. However, it is the commentary that accompanies the diagrams, graphs and calculated statistics that is emphasised here. It is essential that students consider their audience when reporting a statistical enquiry, and present a logical argument justifying their conclusions.

When the students set up an enquiry they pose questions and state a hypothesis. When they communicate their results they need to ensure that they have tested this hypothesis and can relate their results to the initial questions. There is little point in producing fancy diagrams and graphs that do not relate to the question being asked.

Statistics used to be a subject that was not taught until students began a university course. Over the years it has been introduced into school maths curricula, first at A level and then at GCSE. It now permeates the whole curriculum from ages 5 to 19. The actual mathematics involved is not difficult. Most of the techniques need little more than knowledge of basic number facts. However, the technical terms are numerous and need to be introduced early and used regularly to develop the required confidence and familiarity.

Technology has made it possible to deal with large sets of data, and statistics is used so widely in real-life that students need to have a good working knowledge of the subject. However, the familiarity that students now have with statistical techniques does not necessarily mean that they are able to use statistical data effectively. This lesson focuses on explaining and justifying results to do just that.

Starter

Previous lessons have instructed students to calculate the median and lower and upper quartiles, and to use this information to draw a box-and-whisker diagram. The first part of the *Starter* is asking students to remind themselves what calculations are needed for this type of diagram.

The second question in the *Starter* asks students to justify when they would use a stem-and-leaf diagram. Although textbook exercises frequently get students to draw these for

a single set of data they are more effective when used for two sets of data back-to-back. They can then be used to compare the two sets of data so that the range and spread-out nature of the values of the variable can be considered.

You could extend the *Starter* by asking the students to justify the use of other techniques and diagrams. For example, ask them when they would use a frequency table, frequency diagram or frequency polygon. When would they use a scatter diagram? This is an opportunity to consolidate the learning from previous lessons.

Demonstration

Students should be encouraged to return to their original question or hypothesis at all points of their enquiry. It is particularly important to return to it when writing the report and communicating results. There will have been a lot of additional information discovered whilst doing the enquiry, but students should stick to the question in hand.

When students have been working in class they know that you, the teacher, knows what they have been doing, and this often leads to abbreviated explanations. They need to consider whom the report is for. They could imagine presenting their work to the manager of a company or to the governors of a school. At some stage they will also have to consider that the report may be being written for an examiner who will be looking for particular aspects to be included in the work. Although we do not wish to be constantly preparing students for tests, it is important that they know what is needed in a piece of coursework.

Finally, students need to consider the actual presentation of their work. This is an opportunity for students to put their knowledge of technology to good use. They should be encouraged to use a word processor or presentation software to produce a well-presented report. They can use spreadsheets and computer-generated diagrams, but they will have to take particular care over the mathematical accuracy of diagrams and graphs produced in this way.

A statistical report is only as good as the quality of argument constructed. There must be a commentary that links diagrams and graphs to the original question or hypothesis. Any deductions or inferences must be justified using the statistics that have been calculated. Personal opinions should be avoided unless there is evidence to support them.

Students should consider ways in which their enquiry could be improved. Could they have selected a different or larger sample? Was the sample sufficiently representative of the population? Was the enquiry limited by time and resources? Were the diagrams or graphs produced the most appropriate for the data collected? Is any of the information redundant? What more could be done to answer the question?

Students must not assume that a diagram can speak for itself. On the other hand, lengthy essays stating the most obvious conclusions are also not required. Good mathematical arguments are elegant, concise, economical, logical and efficient. A tall order!

Essential exercise

Get the students to work in groups. Ask them to discuss the diagrams and what information they think can be read from them. Ask the students to produce a group report using all the information provided.

The class can imagine that they are working for a company which has been given the task of interpreting the data for the headteacher and governors. The results of the survey are to be used in deciding school policy for the coming year. What advice might the company give the governors about these students?

You could replace the data in this exercise with some real data collected from a group of twenty students in your school. Students can then consider how representative the data is, and what the results infer about students in the school.

Challenging exercise

Students need practice in making statistical inferences using diagrams and graphs. This exercise provides just a few examples of making statements about data. Ask students what further statements could be made.

Problem-solving exercise

Throughout this work on statistics we have encouraged students to consider the best ways of representing data. In this exercise students scrutinise two diagrams that are deliberately drawn to misrepresent the data. It is very important that students realise that statistics can be use to misinform people, particularly when profit may be the key factor for consideration.

Plenary

The students have now covered all the points in the four-point plan for conducting a statistical enquiry. Summarise all of these points and ask the students to explain the significance of each point.

Homework

Get your students to write a report based on the data provided in the *Homework*. There are two scatter diagrams about thirty students. What can be deduced from the information, and what useful further data could have been collected? Any inferences must be backed by evidence and explained and justified.

Students could be asked to prepare a two-minute presentation to deliver at the beginning of the next lesson. Talking about their work is excellent preparation for writing about their work. Invite other students to ask questions of the presenter. These questions should indicate whether the original presentation was sufficiently well explained.

Using and Applying Mathematics

Introduction

Maths is a subject that is exciting and interesting in its own right. We want students to enjoy doing maths for the sheer pleasure of engaging in stimulating intellectual activity. This is what school learning is all about. For every subject on the curriculum students inspect data, categorise it, use logic and reasoning and turn it into information. They learn what it is like to think as a scientist, an artist, a writer, a mathematician and so on. The processes involved in such study can be applied to solving all types of problems, and this section focuses on those processes.

Each set of exercises in the first part of the Student's Book is written under specific topic headings and each set includes an exercise on 'problem-solving'. These exercises assist the students in seeing the relevance of that topic in terms of other areas of mathematics or in everyday life. They will know that if the topic is fractions then they will be applying their knowledge of fractions. However, in real situations we are not given such hints. We have to decide what maths is appropriate to apply. In this section students will need assistance in making such decisions.

This section contains:

- An introduction to using and applying maths
- Using and applying maths to everyday life
- Using maths to investigate
- Working like a detective
- Using maths across the curriculum.

The debate about where to place 'using and applying' in the mathematics curriculum has been going on since the introduction of the National Curriculum. The 1999 version of the Mathematics National Curriculum includes using and applying in each section of the programme of study, to show an integrated approach. Meanwhile, the attainment target Ma1 remains unchanged as a separate target.

The National Strategy *Framework for Teaching Mathematics* sets out a separate section on 'using and applying mathematics to solve problems' in the yearly teaching programmes and corresponding examples. There is clearly a case for both an integrated approach and separate study.

Problem solving

The first spread introduces students to the idea of 'using and applying mathematics' using the words of the *Framework for Teaching Mathematics*. It is helpful for students to know these words because they will have to achieve certain levels of competence in these areas in order to gain a good grade at GCSE. It also helps them to see that maths is not just about content but also about process.

We provide the students with a framework for solving problems using mathematics. It might seem obvious to the students that they should read the question carefully, yet this is one of the major causes of errors.

The 'Frogs' investigation is well known. It involves swapping coloured counters following given rules. It is a good example for demonstration purposes because the students have to break the problem down, work systematically, record results and look for patterns. It also offers plenty of opportunities for extending the problem.

Confirm what has to be done in exchanging counters, and write down any rules on the board. Get the students to act out the movement for the exchange of two counters and record each move as they go. They will have to think about how they will represent the space. Ask them to explain any patterns of movement and any system they may have developed. Get them to check that they do have the least number of moves.

Record the number of moves in a table. Move on to three counters of each colour and again get students to act out the moves. They will need to develop a system to ensure that they do the exchange in the least number of moves.

Continue to act out the exchange of counters for four and then five counters. Get the students to suggest what the smallest number of moves will be, and then test their suggestion. Now interrogate the table of results. Can they make a conjecture about the least number of moves for six counters of each colour? Can they find a rule? How many moves would be needed for n counters of each colour?

Now invite students to suggest alternative investigations. They could change the number of counters of each colour, change the shape of the array of counters (circular, rows arranged as a cross etc.) and consider changing the rules for the moves.

Page 214 ## Using maths in everyday life

Some people think that the only reason for learning maths is so that we can solve problems in our everyday life. This is a very limited view, yet it is often the one that students give when asked about their attitudes towards the subject. The majority of problems will inevitably involve the application of basic numeracy to quantities such as money or measurement.

The hardest part of solving real-life problems is in identifying the explicit and implicit information, and in deciding on what maths to apply. The students will need lots of assistance to achieve this at this stage. Evaluation reports conducted in the early years since the introduction of the Numeracy Strategy identified this area as especially weak at KS2.

There is a tendency to assume that because the questions are posed in real-life contexts the students will find them easy. However, the opposite tends to be the case because first the students have to make sense of the problem before they can work at the solution. You will need to demonstrate how to make sense of the text, how to identify the information, and how to begin the solution.

The demonstrations are designed to show students how to read problems, and how to set out their solutions to the problems. Mistakes are so easily made when students omit certain steps in their solutions.

Demonstration 1 shows how to apply logical thinking. One girl pays £1·20 more than the other, and this is a difference of 5% on the original price. This is the only clue to the original price. If we know 5% of something, we can calculate 100% of that thing. This is the key to the solution: knowing that the original price must be 100%.

Exercise 1 is straightforward application of knowledge of percentages. The second exercise requires the application of logic. The students have not yet been taught how to set up a problem like this as two simultaneous equations. They have to consider different combinations of tea and biscuits in order to solve the problem. They may try to estimate the cost and try to work out the answer using trial and improvement. Encourage them to consider the solution like this:

> *Triple the first order: three teas and six biscuits would cost £4·62. Compare this with the second order. Two biscuits must have cost 84 pence. That makes the tea in the first order 70 pence.*

Get the students to write out their solution in full and ask them to draw diagrams where appropriate.

Ask the students to work on the problems in pairs, and then invite them to present their solutions on the board. Working together helps the students gain in confidence and provides

opportunities for them to interrogate the text with peer support.

Students could set out their solutions as posters to present to the class. Talking about the way they went about solving the problems is an important stage of their learning. This work is especially important in preparing students for GCSE coursework.

Page 218 ## Using maths to investigate

Mathematical investigations and puzzles should be stimulating and enjoyable for all students. However, it is crucial that they are given sufficient support to start the work, whilst leaving enough for them to tease out for themselves. This balance of assistance is vital in ensuring that students do not get lost in a fog or, alternatively, feel that they have not had the opportunity to think for themselves.

This demonstration is a good example of a problem that very quickly becomes too complex to be drawn accurately. It is easy to count the number of crossing points with one, two, three and then four straight lines although the four straight lines need careful drawing so that none of the crossing points are coincident.

Five straight lines are very difficult to draw for this investigation, but can be used as a check for the rule. The number of crossing points can be justified by considering the geometrical properties of the shapes. This is an important point because the students would be unable to prove the result algebraically.

The method of differences is often used to determine the algebraic rule for the nth term. In this case, all of the second differences are identical so the rule will be quadratic. This is beyond the students' capabilities at present, however they may recognise the pattern of numbers as the 'triangle numbers' and may already know the nth term.

All of the investigations in the exercises lend themselves to extensions. Encourage the students to consider their own 'what if …?' questions. All students should be able to complete these investigations.

Page 222 ## Working like a detective

Geometry provides one of the richest sources for maths problems. Inspecting diagrams and identifying the explicit and implicit information is just like looking for clues. It is just like working like a detective.

Get the students to draw the diagram in *Demonstration 1*. Select any appropriate radius for the large circle. Ask the

Teacher's Notes   Teacher's Notes   Teacher's Notes   Teacher's Notes
Teacher's Notes   Teacher's Notes   **Using and Applying Mathematics**
Teacher's Notes

students to work out the radius for the four smaller circles. This will help them to see the relationship between the larger and smaller circles. Now work through the solution with the whole class. If students find working with letters difficult, use the actual measurements of the circles drawn. A delightful result!

Demonstration 2 poses a challenge. Students may have constructed angles of 90°, 45° and 60° but now they have to consider ways of constructing an angle that at first sight does not seem obvious. Read through the instructions on page 223 of the Student's Book and get the students to follow the constructions. Now ask them to do the construction themselves. Ask them to think of other angles they could construct using the commonly known constructions.

Exercise 1 draws on a range of knowledge about shapes. The circle has been folded to give a square and most students will quickly see how to fold the circle again to give an octagon using the lines of symmetry.

To make the equilateral triangle, first determine the centre of the circle by folding as for the square. Next, fold the circle so that a point on the circumference just touches the centre. Repeat twice more (using the point on the circumference as the end of the next fold-line) and you have the triangle. Discuss with the class why this works. Now consider how the folds can be used to make the hexagon. Return to the equilateral triangle and fold **four circles** to make the tetrahedron.

Exercise 3 is a challenge. Construct the perpendicular bisectors of two chords of the arc. The centre of the circle is at the intersection of the perpendicular bisectors.

Geometry is a subject that brings together knowledge from different areas of the maths curriculum. Exercise 4 draws on knowledge of the area of a circle together with that of fractions and ratio. First work out the area of the circle with radius 3 cm. You could leave this as 9π cm². Discuss the benefits of leaving the area in this form rather than substituting an approximation for π. What fraction of the circle has an angle at the centre of 30°. The ratio is 30 : 360. The fraction is of the circle is $\frac{1}{12}$. The area of the sector is $\frac{1}{12}$ of 9π cm². The area is $\frac{3}{4}\pi$ cm².

Get the students to make the cylinder in Exercise 5. Students often find it difficult to make the connection between the circumference of the circular base and the length of the rectangular net.

Exercises 6 is an introduction to Pythagoras' theorem. The practical activity provides a visual image of the rule that they will use in Book 3.

 Page 226 **Maths across the curriculum**

It has often been said that students can walk from a maths lesson where they have been successful at drawing and interpreting graphs to a science lesson where they look completely bemused by the same graph. They just do not make the essential links and connections between the maths in a maths lesson and maths in other areas of the curriculum. One way of helping them overcome this difficulty is to address some of the other subjects during maths lessons. In this lesson we look at a topic in geography.

We have addressed the subject of scale on pages 116–119 of the Student's Book. The first demonstration revises this work within the topic of map reading. Discuss this with the Geography Department to see what they would expect the students to know.

All of the exercises are straightforward and follow on from the demonstrations. Use local maps and identify the different features by considering the contour lines.

Using and Applying

Teacher's Notes Teacher's Notes Teacher's Notes Teacher's Notes
Teacher's Notes Teacher's Notes Teacher's Note
acher's Notes Teacher's Notes Teacher's Notes Teacher's Notes
Teacher's No

National Curriculum Tests

Introduction

These sample tests provide questions like those the students will meet in national test papers. They have a different appearance because they are not spread out with space provided for answers. At some stage, the students will need to practise using a typical paper so that they know where to put their answers.

National tests do not assess all that has been learnt in a yearly programme. They test a limited set of content written in a particular style. They are snapshots of what a student can do unassisted on any particular day, to be compared with other students nationally. We must be careful not to place too much emphasis on such tests, but recognise a broader profile of the student using data gathered as work is completed in class.

Mental-arithmetic tests

Proficiency and speed in mental arithmetic is desirable but not as essential as some would make out. Progress in maths can be achieved without this asset, but will be slower and less efficient. Regular mental and oral work throughout lessons will help pupils improve in this area. In particular, this work helps students listen and concentrate on what is being said.

Students must learn to be absolutely silent during mental arithmetic tests. For some this is not easy! In such cases begin with five questions and gradually build up the test until the students can manage to concentrate for all the questions.

Go over the answers to the questions in detail and ask students to write out the answers to questions they could not do. Get the students to set themselves specific targets for improvement.

Preparing for tests

Students need to be taught how to set their answers out on test papers. Two examples are given on how to set out numerical calculations neatly. Students need to practise answering questions on plain paper.

The tests in the book are designed to take about fifty minutes. However, it is preferable to assist students in doing well and feeling successful rather than doing the questions at speed. As they become more familiar with such tests they will be able to do more of the questions in the given time.

Non-calculator tests

The first set of tests is for use without a calculator. The emphasis is on written methods and therefore there will be marks awarded for the workings. The questions assess students at levels 4 to 6 of the National Curriculum. On the whole, the questions begin at the lower levels and get increasingly more difficult.

Some students do not do themselves justice in tests because they have not developed the necessary test techniques. They need to be taught to do all the questions that they know they can do first. Often they can do questions near the end even if they have struggled with earlier questions.

Next, they should go back systematically and attempt any of the questions they missed out. Finally, they should read the questions again and check through their answers *carefully*. This is difficult to achieve in a short time limit but with practice it is manageable.

Although we attempt to make links and connections between and within maths as we teach, we still teach maths by topics. Tests, on the other hand, mix up topics and contexts so that students really have to stop and think about what they are doing.

Contextualising maths can actually make it more difficult, and not easier as many people think. The language used in the question can be confusing and non-technical terms may be used. The first time you do these tests with the students make sure that you give plenty of time to go through them and get the students to do corrections. They need to see model answers with neat working out.

Some people argue that students should not sit tests that assess areas of work not covered in lessons. In maths this would assume that some students are denied certain areas of the curriculum. It was noted earlier that all students should be taught the content of this book. Differentiation should be by the levels of assistance given and not by selection of content. However, some extension work has been provided for those students who are well advanced in their learning. Meanwhile the content in the tests should be familiar to all students. That is not to say that they will all be able to do the tests unassisted, but they will have an opportunity to attempt any of the questions.

We believe that weaker students should be assisted in doing these tests so that they can be successful. Students'

marks can be annotated to show they were achieved with a level of assistance. This has been shown to improve motivation and self-esteem. Failure and low marks are calculated to disillusion and de-motivate students.

All the tests require the use of rulers, protractors and pairs of compasses. Students should have this equipment with them for every lesson. Drawings and graphs should always be done in pencil.

Students often get questions wrong because they do not understand the instructions. They need to know that there are different ways of asking the same question. For example Test A1, question 3 asks 'What proportion of …'. This could have said 'What fraction of …', 'What percentage of …' or 'What is the ratio of …'. Get students to consider what is being compared. In this case it is the number of students who are very confident in maths to the total number of students. That is 10 to 30 and this can be written as 10 : 30, $\frac{10}{30}$ or $\frac{1}{3}$.

There are often several ways of working out the answer to a question. Look at Test A1, question 7(b). Students are given that 10% of a number is 64. From this they can see that 5% of the number is 32 and $2\frac{1}{2}$% of the number is 16. From this they can work out the answers to the questions. However, they could say that, given 10% is 64 then the number is 640. From this they can calculate each percentage in turn. Get students to use different methods and discuss the benefits of each.

Some questions test more than one area of knowledge. For example, Test A1, question 14 tests whether students can accurately substitute values into an algebraic expression as well as understanding that two brackets together means they are to multiply. It also tests whether students can do the calculation without a calculator. Impress on the students the need to write down each step so that they can gain credit for the parts they can do, otherwise one simple error in the final calculation can lead to zero marks.

Calculator tests

Students often believe that when they use a calculator in a test they do not need to write down their method and working. This is far from the truth. There is always a risk when using a calculator that one will make careless errors, so it is almost more important to set out the method neatly in this paper than the non-calculator paper.

Two examples of solving problems have been given as model answers. The equals sign should always line up neatly and every step should be shown.

Questions like those in the tests need rehearsing. We often try to dissuade students from using a calculator in lessons yet they really need to have plenty of practice in doing basic operations.

The first question in each of these tests is typical of national test questions. They look simple but the very first answer requires using inverse operations. Advise the students to work out the last number first using a calculator so that they become familiar with the rule. Then get them to work out the first number using a function diagram (see Student's Book 2, pages 88–89).

Many of the questions in national tests require an ability to read and comprehend. When someone speaks questions like those in question 2 it is easier to picture the operations than when you have to read them. Get students to develop the good practice of letting the unknown number be x. For example Test B1, question 2:

> Let the number be x.
> Then $4.5 \times x = 54$, so $x = 54 \div 4.5 = 12$.

The questions on each test are similar. This means that you can do the first test together as a class if you wish to prepare students for the types of questions they will get. It is always better to give students confidence in these questions by pointing out the sorts of errors that are commonly made.

Look, for example, at the tenth question in each test. It is a question on probability. In each case the probability of an event is given as a decimal and the first question asks for the probability of the event not happening. Take care! Make sure that the students write down their working. The answers are respectively: $1 - 0.08 = 0.92$; $1 - 0.05 = 0.95$ and $1 - 0.005 = 0.995$.

Whenever students get stuck on a question refer them back to the text. For example, the nineteenth question always asks for a percentage increase and decrease. Refer them to pages 68–75 in the Student's Book.

Worksheets

Introduction

Each topic in *I See Maths* is supported by visualisation. It is the basis for understanding. There is also a need for routine practice so that facts and skills can be consolidated for easy access. Some students do this very rapidly, and seemingly instinctively. For others, it is a long and laborious process that needs specific attention. When students have almost immediate recall of facts and skills, it supports their understanding. When they do not have immediate recall it is tempting, but wrong, to concentrate entirely on memorisation of facts and skills. These students need 'understanding' and 'routine practice' to support each other: they proceed hand in hand. This is the purpose of the worksheets in this section. Photocopy them and use them for the supportive routine practice that most students need.

Using the worksheets

The majority of worksheets provide additional examples to support specific pages in the Student's Book. The Teacher's Notes indicate the appropriate use of the relevant worksheet.

The first set of worksheets help in reviewing the work covered in Book 1. There may be some students who have not used the first book and others who need extra help with some of these earlier ideas. For example, Worksheet 1 provides extra straightforward examples of addition and subtraction of fractions and decimals.

For those students who need reminding of multiplication tables, Worksheet 3 provides some 'torture squares'. These are simple multiplication grids with the numbers deliberately jumbled up to ensure that students do not merely use patterns to complete them. Students can make up their own torture squares to set each other – they will probably be much harder than any you would set!

Teaching the relevant mathematics

The worksheets are designed for practice of facts and skills. There will be students who need some specific teaching to help them make sense of what is required. The important idea is that all learners need assistance to do things they cannot do alone, and progress involves the gradual removal of that assistance.

One example of this can be seen in Worksheet 9 on factors and multiples. This topic is normally introduced in Primary school, where factors are always assumed to be positive whole numbers. The link between this early work and the idea that any number 'x' can be a factor needs careful teaching. For example, the term $2x$ has many different factors. The obvious ones are 2, x and $2x$. However, we could also have $\frac{1}{2}$ and $4x$, since $\frac{1}{2} \times 4x = 2x$. There is an infinite number of different factors when we consider any two pairs of numbers whose product is $2x$. This demonstrates why we need to state clearly what sort of answers would be acceptable, and encourage the students not to make assumptions.

Mastery of the worksheets

When students struggle with a worksheet, they should be given assistance to complete it, but they need to get to the point where they can work through it more or less independently. Students can do the worksheet again and practise it to the point of mastery. It is this continuing practice that is especially important for homework. When students have already worked the worksheet fairly laboriously, with assistance, they can work at it again to become faster or more accurate. There should be no concern at repeating the same worksheet: the worksheets are written to be worth mastering.

Extension worksheets

A few of the worksheets have been designed to provide extension work. In particular, the worksheets supporting handling data (Worksheets 37–46) give further practice in some of the harder topics in statistics. The new requirement for a piece of coursework at GCSE in handling data means that we need to ensure that students are familiar with sufficient statistical techniques to apply to their enquiry. The actual mathematics used is not particularly difficult but the notation can seem daunting to some students. The more often they see the notation and use it, the more familiar it will become and this will lead to greater confidence.

Worksheets

Name ....

Class ....

Date ....

Book 1 Review: **Addition and subtraction of fractions and decimals**

1 (a) $\frac{3}{5} + \frac{4}{5} =$ (b) $\frac{2}{7} + \frac{4}{7} =$ (c) $\frac{5}{9} + \frac{2}{9} + \frac{7}{9} =$ (d) $\frac{2}{3} + \frac{4}{3} =$

    (e) $\frac{5}{13} + \frac{6}{13} =$ (f) $\frac{4}{11} + \frac{5}{11} =$ (g) $\frac{3}{4} + \frac{7}{4} + \frac{1}{4} =$ (h) $\frac{5}{6} + \frac{7}{6} =$

2 (a) $\frac{8}{5} - \frac{3}{5} =$ (b) $\frac{11}{7} - \frac{5}{7} =$ (c) $\frac{5}{9} - \frac{2}{9} =$ (d) $\frac{8}{3} - \frac{1}{3} - \frac{2}{3} =$

    (e) $\frac{17}{13} - \frac{9}{13} =$ (f) $\frac{7}{11} - \frac{1}{11} =$ (g) $\frac{7}{4} - \frac{6}{4} =$ (h) $\frac{17}{6} - \frac{7}{6} - \frac{4}{6} =$

3 (a) $\frac{2}{10} + \frac{5}{10} =$ (b) $\frac{7}{10} + \frac{9}{10} =$ (c) $\frac{16}{100} + \frac{8}{100} =$ (d) $\frac{54}{100} + \frac{31}{100} =$

       $\cdot2 + \cdot5 =$ $\cdot7 + \cdot9 =$ $\cdot16 + \cdot08 =$ $\cdot54 + \cdot31 =$

    (e) $\frac{9}{10} - \frac{7}{10} =$ (f) $\frac{12}{10} - \frac{8}{10} =$ (g) $\frac{19}{100} - \frac{12}{100} =$ (h) $\frac{74}{100} - \frac{65}{100} =$

       $\cdot9 - \cdot7 =$ $1\cdot2 - \cdot8 =$ $\cdot19 - \cdot12 =$ $\cdot74 - \cdot65 =$

4 (a) $\frac{21}{10} + \frac{33}{10} =$ (b) $\frac{96}{10} + \frac{59}{10} =$ (c) $\frac{231}{10} + \frac{456}{10} =$ (d) $\frac{824}{100} + \frac{326}{100} =$

       $2\cdot1 + 3\cdot3 =$ $9\cdot6 + 5\cdot9 =$ $23\cdot1 + 45\cdot6 =$ $8\cdot24 + 3\cdot26 =$

    (e) $\frac{85}{10} - \frac{63}{10} =$ (f) $\frac{72}{10} - \frac{29}{10} =$ (g) $\frac{37}{10} - \frac{8}{10} =$ (h) $\frac{119}{100} - \frac{87}{100} =$

       $8\cdot5 - 6\cdot3 =$ $7\cdot2 - 2\cdot9 =$ $3\cdot7 - 0\cdot8 =$ $1\cdot19 - 0\cdot87 =$

Worksheet 2

Name ....

Class ....

Date ....

Book 1 Review: Subtraction as the inverse of addition

1 Complete these sentences.

(a) If $6 + 3 = 9$, then (i) $9 - 3 = $ ___ , and (ii) $9 - 6 = $

(b) If $12 + 7 = 19$, then (i) $19 - 7 = $ ___ , and (ii) $19 - 12 = $

(c) If $54 + 63 = 117$, then (i) $117 - 63 = $ ___ , and (ii) $117 - 54 = $

(d) If $8·5 + 2·3 = 10·7$, then (i) $10·7 - 2·3 = $ ___ , and (ii) $10·7 - 8·5 = $

(e) If $9·6 + 13·8 = 23·4$, then (i) $23·4 - 13·8 = $ ___ , and (ii) $23·4 - 9·6 = $

(f) If $5·47 + 3·65 = 9·12$, then (i) $9·12 - 3·65 = $ ___ , and (ii) $9·12 - 5·47 = $

2 Complete this table.

x	3·7		9·9		14·85	19·57	0·85	39·7
y	5·8	4·6		7·23		34·65		
$x + y$		10·3	13·6	19·38	20·06		0·99	87·09

3 Complete this table.

x	77·9	86·5	42·81			93·2	19·37	42·6
y	30·8			32·7	75·5			
$x - y$		23·4	12·05	26·8	84·9	6·4	5·09	33·34

4 Complete these sentences.

(a) If $16 - 5 = 11$, then $11 + 5 = $

(b) If $76 - 49 = 27$, then $27 + 49 = $

(c) If $4·8 - 2·9 = 1·9$, then $1·9 + 2·9 = $

Letts I See Maths Book 2

Name ....

Class ....

Date ....

Book 1 Review: **Torture squares!**

Complete these tables.

×	3	7	5	6	9	8	2	4
2								
4								
3								
7								
5								
8								
6								
9								

×	6	2	9	3	5	7	4	8
3								
9								
6								
4								
2								
5								
7								
8								

×	9	2	8	3	7	4	6	5
5								
7								
3								
9								
2								
8								
6								
4								

×	8	7	6	5	9	4	3	2
0								
3								
5								
7								
8								
1								
10								
9								

×	11	0	30	5	6	7	80	25
2								
40								
5								
7								
6								
8								
3								
60								

×	15	20	300	40	7	80	9	·1
8								
2								
4								
7								
1								
0								
10								
50								

Book 1 Review: **Equivalent forms**

1 Write the following vulgar fractions as decimal fractions.

(a) $\frac{3}{10}$ (b) $\frac{7}{100}$ (c) $\frac{12}{10}$ (d) $\frac{43}{100}$

(e) $\frac{8}{1000}$ (f) $\frac{39}{1000}$ (g) $\frac{405}{1000}$ (h) $\frac{601}{10}$

2 Write the following vulgar fractions as decimal fractions.

(a) $\frac{2}{5}$ (b) $\frac{7}{20}$ (c) $\frac{13}{25}$ (d) $\frac{34}{50}$

(e) $\frac{3}{4}$ (f) $\frac{1}{2}$ (g) $\frac{21}{15}$ (h) $\frac{18}{24}$

3 Write the numbers in questions 1 and 2 as percentages.

4 Write the following numbers as percentages.

(a) $\frac{79}{100}$ (b) $\frac{7}{5}$ (c) $\frac{19}{10}$ (d) $\frac{3}{1000}$

(e) $\frac{12}{16}$ (f) $\frac{28}{56}$ (g) $\frac{3}{8}$ (h) $\frac{100}{100}$

5 Write the following numbers as decimal fractions.

(a) 50%   (b) 20%   (c) 75%   (d) 5%

(e) $2\frac{1}{2}$%   (f) 100%   (g) 247%   (h) 0·5%

Book 1 Review: **Algebraic addition**

1 Circle each term in the following expressions.

(a) $3 + 4 \times 5 - 2 \times 9$

(b) $8 \times 3 + 14 + 8 - 3 \times 4$

(c) $2 \times 3 \times 4 + 7 \times 4 \times 9$

(d) $159 + 633 - 96 \div 3$

(e) $(2 + 3) \times 8 + 15$

(f) $71 - (13 - 5) \div 4$

2 Circle each term in the following expressions.

(a) $2x + 7y - 5z$

(b) $x \div 3 + 5y + 8x$

(c) $14x - 3xy + 17y$

(d) $19 + 5x - 7$

(e) $98xyz + 76xy - 54yz$

(f) $41x - 33 + 17x$

3 Inspect the term $3x$.
Circle any terms that are 'like' the term $3x$ in the following expressions.

(a) $5 + 6x + 2y - 3z$

(b) $3 + 7x - 4a + 5x$

(c) $x + 3$

(d) $19 - 13x + 15y - x$

(e) $\frac{x}{4} + \frac{2x}{5}$

(f) $18 - \frac{9x}{10}$

4 Simplify the following expressions by collecting together like terms.

(a) $6x + 7x + 8$

(b) $5 + 7x - 3x + 9$

(c) $\cdot 8x + \cdot 7x + \cdot 2$

(d) $14x + 2y + \frac{x}{2}$

Worksheets

Name ....

Class ....

Date ....

Book 1 Review: **Solving equations**

1 Solve the following equations.

(a) $x + 5 = 8$

(b) $x + 7 = 19$

(c) $x + 4 = 13$

(d) $23 + x = 45$

(e) $99 + x = 102$

(f) $x + 103 = 227$

2 Solve the following equations.

(a) $x + 3 \cdot 2 = 4 \cdot 8$

(b) $7 \cdot 5 + x = 19 \cdot 6$

(c) $x + 4 \cdot 9 = 21 \cdot 7$

(d) $x + \frac{3}{5} = \frac{7}{5}$

(e) $\frac{7}{10} + x = \frac{12}{10}$

(f) $\frac{3}{11} + x = \frac{14}{11}$

3 Solve the following equations.

(a) $x - 4 = 10$

(b) $x - 7 = 21$

(c) $x - 5 = 15$

(d) $x - 2 \cdot 4 = 3 \cdot 7$

(e) $x - 3 \cdot 8 = 9 \cdot 7$

(f) $x - \frac{4}{5} = \frac{7}{5}$

4 Solve the following equations.

(a) $3x = 18$

(b) $5x = 20$

(c) $7x = 21$

(d) $10x = 80$

(e) $4x = 8$

(f) $9x = 81$

5 Solve the following equations.

(a)  $\frac{x}{4} = 2 = 3$

(b) $\frac{x}{3} = 5 = 4$

(c) $\frac{x}{8} = 6 = 9$

(d)

(e)

(f)

    Letts **I See Maths** Book 2

Book 1 Review: **Triangles and quadrilaterals**

1 (a) Name each triangle below, using the words 'scalene', 'isosceles', or 'equilateral'.

(b) Name each triangle below, using the words 'acute-angled', obtuse-angled', or 'right-angled'.

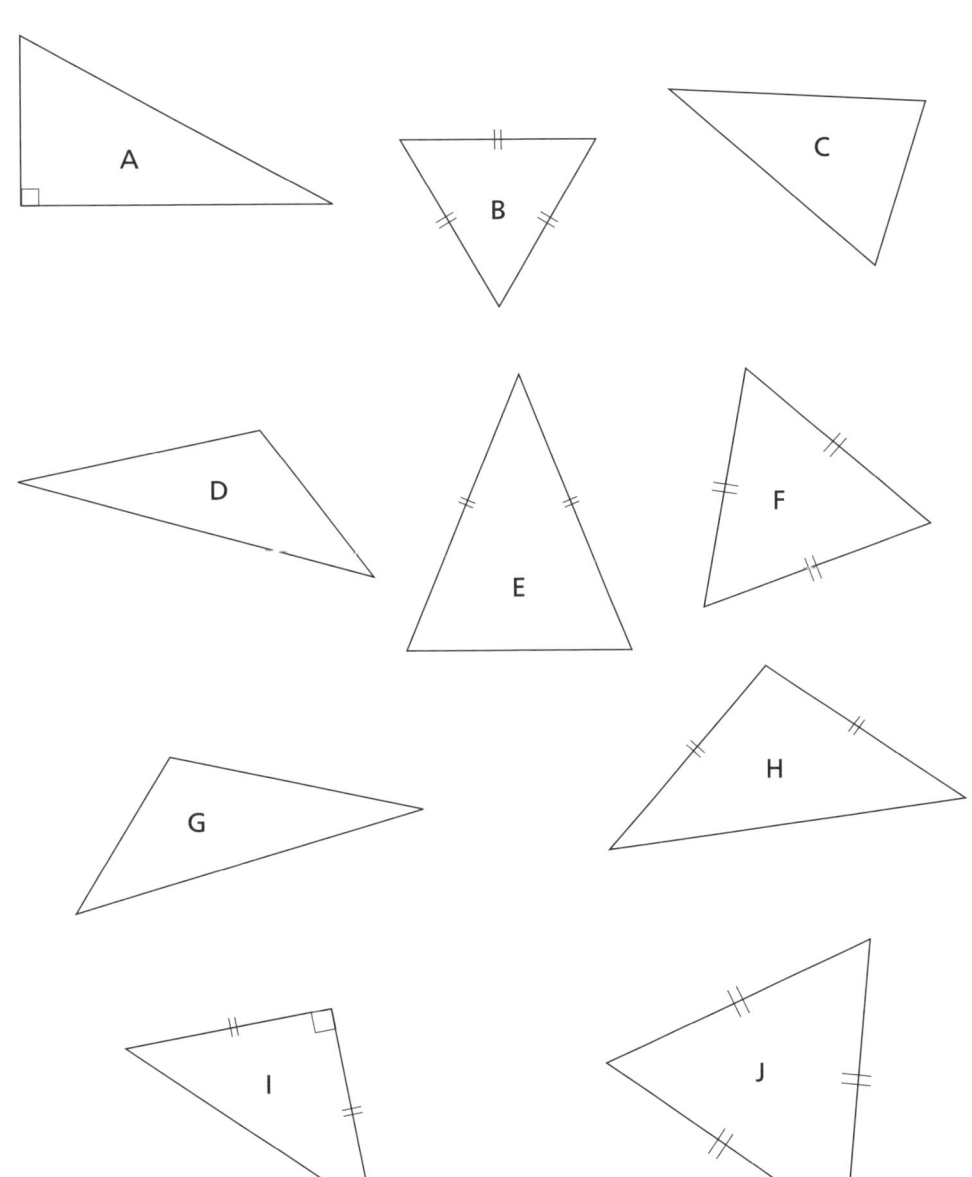

Number and Algebra: **Factors and multiples 1**

1 Write down all the whole number multiplication pairs for each of the following numbers.

(a) 16   (b) 25   (c) 49   (d) 15

(e) 24   (f) 29   (g) 32   (h) 100

2 Write down all the whole number factors of each of the following numbers.

(a) 12   (b) 20   (c) 23   (d) 87

(e) 36   (f) 99   (g) 121   (h) 196

3 Write down all the prime factors of each of the following numbers.

(a) 26   (b) 35   (c) 42   (d) 32

(e) 14   (f) 88   (g) 200   (h) 46

4 Write each of the following numbers as the product of its prime factors.

(a) 16   (b) 28   (c) 17   (d) 56

(e) 81   (f) 144   (g) 45   (h) 169

5 Work out the highest common factor (HCF) of each of the following sets of numbers.

(a) {8, 12, 16}   (b) {140, 294, 308}   (c) {60, 90, 75, 105}

© Letts Educational 2003

Letts I See Maths Book 2

Name ....

Class ....

Date ....

Number and Algebra: **Factors and multiples 2**

1 (a)   One factor of $2x$ is 2. What is the other factor?

(b)   One factor of $3xy$ is x. What is the other factor?

(c)   One factor of xyz is z. What is the other factor?

(d)   One factor of $56xy$ is $7xy$. What is the other factor?

(e)   One factor of $21x^2$ is $7x$. What is the other factor?

(f)   One factor of $5ab$ is $5b$. What is the other factor?

2   Write down the highest common factor of each of the following sets of terms.

(a) $\{2x, 2y\}$ (b) $\{5x, 7x, 9x\}$ (c) $\{6x, 10x, 18x\}$

(d) $\{xy, xz\}$ (e) $\{5xy, 7xy, 13xy\}$ (f) $\{14xy, 21xy, 35xy\}$

3   Factorise the following expressions. The first one is done for you.

(a) $6x + 8 = 2(3x + 4)$ (b) $9x + 15$

(c) $3x + 7xy$ (d) $20 + 4x$

(e) $ax + ay$ (f) $4 + 8x + 10y$

(g) $15xy + 10xz + 20xt$ (h) $14ax + 22bx + 39cx$

Worksheets

Number and Algebra: **The commutative law**

1 Check that the following statements are true.

$3 + 2 = 2 + 3 = 5$ and $3 \times 2 = 2 \times 3 = 6$ Addition and multiplication are commutative.

$3 - 2 \neq 2 - 3$ and $3 \div 2 \neq 2 \div 3$ Subtraction and division are NOT commutative.

2 True or false?

(a) $6 + 7 = 7 + 6$

(b) $43 + 71 = 71 + 43$

(c) $17 - 8 = 8 - 17$

(d) $4 \times 9 = 9 \times 4$

(e) $3 + 8 + 9 = 3 + 9 + 8$

(f) $4 + 5 \times 7 = 5 \times 7 + 4$

(g) $9 - 3 + 5 = 9 - 5 + 3$

(h) $8 \div 4 = 4 \div 8$

(i) $3 + 10 \div 5 = 10 \div 5 + 3$

3 Addition is commutative. You can rearrange sums to make them easy.

For example:
$$2 + 9 + 3 + 8 + 1 + 7 + 5 = 2 + 8 + 9 + 1 + 3 + 7 + 5$$
$$= 10 + 10 + 10 + 5$$
$$= 35$$

Rearrange the following sums and then work them out.

(a) $5 + 8 + 6 + 7 + 5 + 1 + 2 + 9 + 4$

(b) $7 + 9 + 2 + 3 + 6 + 1 + 8 + 5$

(c) $72 + 31 + 87 + 28 + 13 + 69 + 6 + 13$

(d) $0.8 + 0.4 + 0.1 + 0.3 + 0.6 + 0.2 + 0.9$

(e) $459 + 218 + 306 + 782 + 541 + 694$

(f) $9x + 2x + 7x + 5x + x + 3x + 5x$

© Letts Educational 2003

Letts I See Maths Book 2

Name ....

Class ....

Date ....

Number and Algebra: **Order of operations**

In the absence of brackets, multiplication and division take precedence over addition and subtraction.

1 Work out the values of the following expressions.

(a) $5 \times 6 + 7$

(b) $3 + 4 \times 8$

(c) $2 \times 6 + 3 \times 8$

(d) $9 + 4 \times 5 + 7$

(e) $17 - 3 \times 5$

(f) $4 \times 8 - 3 \times 2$

(g) $8 \div 2 + 5$

(h) $7 + 9 \div 3$

(i) $25 \div 5 - 16 \div 4$

2 Work out the values of the following expressions.

(a) $(4 + 3) \times 6$

(b) $(7 - 5) \times 8$

(c) $(90 - 10) \div 8$

(d) $3 + (5 + 2) \times 4$

(e) $24 - (9 - 4) \times 7$

(f) $5 \times (2 + 4) + 19$

(g) $32 \div (16 \div 8)$

(h) $3 + 6 \times (9 - 4)$

(i) $45 \div (9 + 6)$

3 Place brackets in the following expressions, where necessary, to make them correct.

(a) $4 + 4 \times 4 + 4 = 36$

(b) $4 + 4 \times 4 + 4 = 64$

(c) $4 + 4 \times 4 + 4 = 24$

(d) $4 + 4 \times 4 - 4 = 28$

(e) $4 + 4 \times 4 - 4 = 4$

(f) $4 + 4 \times 4 - 4 = 16$

4 Use the four operations (+, −, ×, ÷) and brackets to make each of the numbers from 0 to 50 using exactly four 4s.

Number and Algebra: **Multiplication**

Use the grid method to calculate these multiplications.

47 × 63

×	40	7	
60			
3			
		Answer	

82 × 53

×	80	2	
50			
3			
		Answer	

77 × 64

×	70	7	
60			
4			
		Answer	

39 × 28

×	30	9	
20			
8			
		Answer	

58 × 62

×	50	8	
60			
2			
		Answer	

48 × 29

×	40	8	
20			
9			
		Answer	

Letts **I See Maths** Book 2

Worksheets

Name ....

Class ....

Date ....

Number and Algebra: **Decimal multiplication**

1 Complete the following multiplications tables.

$\frac{1}{10} \times 0 =$

$\frac{1}{10} \times 1 =$

$\frac{1}{10} \times 2 =$

$\frac{1}{10} \times 3 =$

$\frac{1}{10} \times 4 =$

$\frac{1}{10} \times 5 =$

$\frac{1}{10} \times 6 =$

$\frac{1}{10} \times 7 =$

$\frac{1}{10} \times 8 =$

$\frac{1}{10} \times 9 =$

$\frac{2}{10} \times 0 =$

$\frac{2}{10} \times 1 =$

$\frac{2}{10} \times 2 =$

$\frac{2}{10} \times 3 =$

$\frac{2}{10} \times 4 =$

$\frac{2}{10} \times 5 =$

$\frac{2}{10} \times 6 =$

$\frac{2}{10} \times 7 =$

$\frac{2}{10} \times 8 =$

$\frac{2}{10} \times 9 =$

$\frac{3}{10} \times 0 =$

$\frac{3}{10} \times 1 =$

$\frac{3}{10} \times 2 =$

$\frac{3}{10} \times 3 =$

$\frac{3}{10} \times 4 =$

$\frac{3}{10} \times 5 =$

$\frac{3}{10} \times 6 =$

$\frac{3}{10} \times 7 =$

$\frac{3}{10} \times 8 =$

$\frac{3}{10} \times 9 =$

2 Complete the following equations. The first one has been done for you.

(a) $\frac{1}{10} \times 2 = \frac{2}{10}$ (b) $\frac{2}{10} \times 6 =$ (c) $\frac{7}{10} \times 9 =$ (d) $\frac{3}{10} \times 8 =$

·1 × 2 = ·2   ·2 × 6 =   ·7 × 9 =   ·3 × 8 =

(e) $\frac{4}{100} \times 6 =$ (f) $\frac{3}{1000} \times 8 =$ (g) $\frac{6}{100} \times 4 =$ (h) $\frac{7}{100} \times 7 =$

·04 × 6 =   ·003 × 8 =   ·06 × 4 =   ·07 × 7 =

3 Complete the following equations. The first one has been done for you.

(a) $\frac{2}{10} \times \frac{6}{10} = \frac{12}{100}$ (b) $\frac{7}{10} \times \frac{3}{10} =$ (c) $\frac{2}{10} \times \frac{8}{10} =$

·2 × ·6 = ·12   ·7 × ·3 =   ·2 × ·8   =

(d) $\frac{3}{100} \times \frac{2}{10} =$ (e) $\frac{3}{100} \times \frac{2}{100} =$ (f) $\frac{3}{100} \times \frac{2}{1000} =$

·003 × ·2 =   ·03 × ·02 =   ·03 × ·002 =

Name ....

Class ....

Date ....

Number and Algebra: **Making connections**

1 Given that **6 × 7 = 42**, complete the following equations.

(a) 60 × 7 =   (b) 600 × 7 =   (c) 6 × 70 =   (d) 6 × 700 =

(e) 60 × 70 =   (f) 600 × 70 =   (g) ·6 × 7 =   (h) 6 × ·7 =

2 **16 ÷ 4 has the same value as 160 ÷ 40. Match the pairs of expressions that have the same value in the two lists below.**

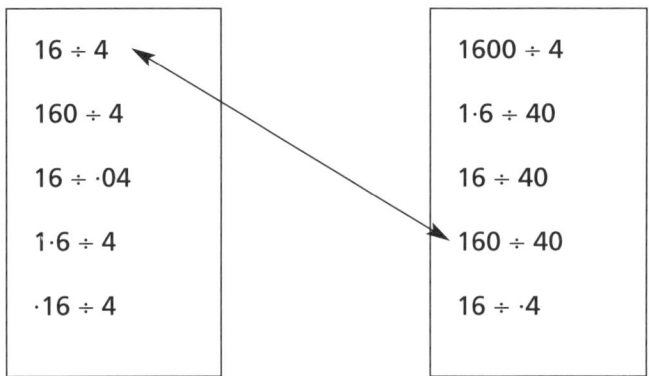

16 ÷ 4   1600 ÷ 4

160 ÷ 4   1·6 ÷ 40

16 ÷ ·04   16 ÷ 40

1·6 ÷ 4   160 ÷ 40

·16 ÷ 4   16 ÷ ·4

3 Given that **2·4 × 6·3 = 15·12**, complete the following equations.

(a) 24 × 63 =   (b) 24 × 6·3 =   (c) 15·12 ÷ 6·3 =   (d) 15·12 ÷ 2·4 =

(e) ·24 × ·63 =   (f) 15·12 ÷ 63 =   (g) 15·12 ÷ 24 =   (h) 240 × 630 =

Letts **I See Maths** Book 2

Name ....

Class ....

Date ....

Number and Algebra: **Powers and roots**

1 **Work out the following expressions.**

(a) $2 \times 2 \times 2 \times 2 \times 2 \times 2$ (b) $4 \times 4 \times 4$ (c) $5 \times 5 \times 5 \times 5$

(d) $3 \times 3 \times 3 \times 3 \times 3$ (e) $10 \times 10 \times 10 \times 10 \times 10$ (f) $9 \times 9 \times 9$

2 **Simplify the following expressions.**

(a) $13 \times 13 \times 13 \times 13$ (b) $87 \times 87 \times 87 \times 87 \times 87 \times 87$

(c) 159×159 (d) $105 \times 105 \times 248 \times 248 \times 248$

(e) $17 \times 17 \times 17 \times 17 \times 31 \times 31 \times 31$ (f) $2 \times 3 \times 3 \times 3$

3 **Simplify the following expressions.**

(a) $p \times p \times p \times p$ (b) $x \times x \times x \times x \times x \times x \times x$ (c) $a \times a \times a \times a \times a$

(d) $b \times b \times c \times c \times c \times d$ (e) $x \times x \times x \times x \times y \times y$ (f) $a \times a \div b \div b \div c$

4 **Simplify the following expressions.**

(a) $a^2 \times a^3$ (b) $x^6 \times y^2 \times x^5$ (c) $a^4 \times b^2 \times b^7$ (d) $p \times p^2 \times p^3$

(e) $a^6 \div a^2$ (f) $x^5 \times x \div x^3$ (g) $p^{11} \times p^3 \div p^7$ (h) $x^4 \times y \div x$

Worksheet **16**

Number and Algebra: **Approximation**

1 Write each of the following numbers to 1 d.p.

(a) 3·762   (b) 25·182   (c) 203·556   (d) 9·092

(e) 106·899   (f) 69·83   (g) 4·97   (h) 2·009

2 Write each of the following numbers to the nearest ten.

(a) 54   (b) 39   (c) 248   (d) 307

(e) 1005   (f) 9·8   (g) 28·99   (h) 14·8

3 Write each of the following numbers to the nearest tenth.

(a) 3·77   (b) 8·19   (c) 32·26   (d) 7·55

(e) 4·029   (f) 57·093   (g) 206·99   (h) 0·076

4 Write each of the following numbers to 3 significant figures.

(a) 23·652   (b) 307·951   (c) 0·003 462 2   (d) 0·080 07

(e) 40 096·98   (f) 200·8   (g) 1198   (h) 3 675 293

Letts **I See Maths** Book 2

Number and Algebra: **Recurring decimals**

1 Write each of the following vulgar fractions as decimal fractions.

(a) $\frac{1}{3}$ (b) $\frac{1}{6}$ (c) $\frac{5}{6}$ (d) $\frac{1}{7}$

(e) $\frac{2}{7}$ (f) $\frac{3}{7}$ (g) $\frac{5}{7}$ (h) $\frac{1}{11}$

2 Investigate what happens when you write the following vulgar fractions as decimal fractions.

(a) $\frac{1}{9}, \frac{2}{9}, \frac{3}{9}, \frac{4}{9}, \frac{5}{9}, \frac{6}{9}, \frac{7}{9}, \frac{8}{9}$

(b) $\frac{1}{13}, \frac{2}{13}, \frac{3}{13}, \frac{4}{13}, \frac{5}{13}, \frac{6}{13}, \frac{7}{13}, \frac{8}{13}, \frac{9}{13}, \frac{10}{13}, \frac{11}{13}, \frac{12}{13}$

3 Write the following recurring decimals as vulgar fractions.

(a) $0 \cdot \dot{6}$ (b) $0 \cdot \dot{1}\dot{8}$ (c) $1 \cdot \dot{6}$ (d) $0 \cdot \dot{2}\dot{7}$

4 Explain how you would convert the following recurring decimals to vulgar fractions.

(a) $0 \cdot \dot{8}5714\dot{2}$ (b) $0 \cdot \dot{0}4761\dot{9}$

Worksheets

Name ....

Class ....

Date ....

Number and Algebra: **Addition of negative numbers**

1 Complete the following equations.

(a) ⁻3 + ⁻5 =

(b) ⁻2 + ⁻7 =

(c) ⁻8 + ⁻11 =

(d) ⁻4 + ⁻9 =

(e) ⁻15 + ⁻7 =

(f) ⁻10 + ⁻3 =

(g) ⁻13 + ⁻15 =

(h) ⁻24 + ⁻31 =

(i) ⁻72 + ⁻108 =

2 Complete the following equations.

(a) ⁻6 + ⁻8 + ⁻4 =

(b) ⁻1 + ⁻5 + ⁻11 =

(c) ⁻2 + ⁻3 + ⁻7 + ⁻4 =

(d) ⁻44 + ⁻18 + ⁻21 + ⁻36 =

(e) ⁻99 + ⁻99 + ⁻99 =

(f) ⁻4 + ⁻96 + ⁻300 =

3 Complete the following equations.

(a) 1 + ⁻1 =

(b) 2 + ⁻2 =

(c) 6 + ⁻3 =

(d) 6 + ⁻8 + 4 =

(e) 10 + 14 + ⁻22 =

(f) ⁻100 + 100 + ⁻40 =

4 Complete the following equations.

(a) ⁻76 + ⁻83 + 123 + 75 =

(b) 87 + ⁻39 + ⁻26 =

(c) ⁻66 + ⁻92 + ⁻65 + 319 =

(d) 54 + ⁻81 + 152 + ⁻38 =

(e) ⁻40 + ⁻70 + 110 =

(f) 0 + ⁻7 + ⁻11 + 16 =

Letts I See Maths **Book 2**

Worksheets

Name ....

Class ....

Date ....

Number and Algebra: **Subtraction of negative numbers**

1 Complete the following equations.

(a) ⁻7 – ⁻5 =

(b) ⁻8 – ⁻2 =

(c) ⁻23 – ⁻16 =

(d) ⁻44 – ⁻9 =

(e) ⁻38 – ⁻19 =

(f) ⁻100 – ⁻99 =

2 Complete the following equations.

(a) ⁻21 – ⁻10 – ⁻6 =

(b) ⁻35 – ⁻20 – ⁻3 =

(c) ⁻81 – ⁻12 – ⁻7 =

(d) ⁻99 – ⁻99 – ⁻99 =

(e) ⁻47 – ⁻6 – ⁻14 =

(f) ⁻55 – ⁻50 – ⁻5 =

3 Complete the following equations.

(a) 32 – ⁻6 =

(b) ⁻81 – 7 =

(c) ⁻44 – 23 =

(d) 100 – ⁻100 =

(e) ⁻21 – 77 =

(f) ⁻21 – 101 =

4 Complete the following equations.

(a) ⁻79 – ⁻19 – 6 =

(b) 36 – ⁻14 – ⁻9 =

(c) 456 – ⁻238 – 92 =

(d) ⁻11 – ⁻15 – 18 =

(e) ⁻21 – 16 – ⁻7 =

(f) ⁻501 – ⁻500 – 9 =

Worksheets

Number and Algebra: **Multiplication and division of negative numbers**

1 Complete the following equations.

(a) $^-8 \times 3 =$ 　　　　(b) $^-6 \times 5 =$ 　　　　(c) $^-9 \times 7 =$

(d) $^-4 \times 6 =$ 　　　　(e) $^-5 \times 8 =$ 　　　　(f) $^-7 \times 7 =$

2 Complete the following equations.

(a) $9 \times ^-3 =$ 　　　　(b) $7 \times ^-5 =$ 　　　　(c) $6 \times ^-4 =$

(d) $5 \times ^-8 =$ 　　　　(e) $6 \times ^-6 =$ 　　　　(f) $10 \times ^-9 =$

3 Complete the following equations.

(a) $^-8 \times ^-4 =$ 　　　　(b) $^-6 \times ^-3 =$ 　　　　(c) $^-9 \times ^-9 =$

(d) $^-4 \times ^-5 =$ 　　　　(e) $^-5 \times ^-6 =$ 　　　　(f) $^-7 \times ^-8 =$

4 Complete the following equations.

(a) $^-8 \div ^-4 =$ 　　　　(b) $^-56 \div ^-7 =$ 　　　　(c) $^-45 \div ^-9 =$

(d) $^-8 \div 4 =$ 　　　　(e) $^-56 \div 7 =$ 　　　　(f) $^-45 \div 9 =$

5 Complete the following equations.

(a) $2 \times 3 \times ^-5 =$ 　　　　(b) $^-2 \times 3 \times 5 =$ 　　　　(c) $2 \times ^-3 \times 5 =$

(d) $^-2 \times ^-3 \times 5 =$ 　　　　(e) $^-2 \times 3 \times ^-5 =$ 　　　　(f) $2 \times ^-3 \times ^-5 =$

Letts I See Maths **Book 2**

Name ....

Class ....

Date ....

Number and Algebra: **Addition and subtraction of fractions**

1 Complete the following equations.

(a) $\frac{3}{5} + \frac{4}{5} =$

(b) $\frac{4}{7} - \frac{2}{7} =$

(c) $\frac{5}{9} + \frac{7}{9} =$

(d) $\frac{2}{13} + \frac{3}{13} =$

(e) $\frac{12}{87} - \frac{5}{87} =$

(f) $\frac{9}{131} + \frac{17}{131} =$

2 Complete the following equations.

(a) $\frac{2}{3} + \frac{5}{6} =$

(b) $\frac{7}{8} - \frac{3}{4} =$

(c) $\frac{2}{7} - \frac{5}{21} =$

(d) $\frac{9}{32} + \frac{7}{8} =$

(e) $\frac{47}{50} - \frac{77}{100} =$

(f) $\frac{7}{20} + \frac{9}{120} =$

3 Complete the following equations.

(a) $\frac{2}{3} + \frac{3}{4} =$

(b) $\frac{3}{5} - \frac{2}{7} =$

(c) $\frac{5}{7} + \frac{2}{3} =$

(d) $\frac{1}{4} + \frac{2}{9} =$

(e) $\frac{9}{11} - \frac{5}{9} =$

(f) $\frac{1}{2} - \frac{2}{7} =$

4 Complete the following equations.

(a) $4\frac{5}{6} + 3\frac{1}{6} =$

(b) $2\frac{3}{8} - 1\frac{5}{8} =$

(c) $9\frac{1}{5} - 2\frac{3}{5} =$

(d) $2\frac{1}{2} + 4\frac{1}{3} =$

(e) $5\frac{4}{7} - 1\frac{1}{8} =$

(f) $6\frac{3}{7} + 4\frac{2}{9} =$

5 Complete the following equations.

(a) $2\frac{1}{2} + 1\frac{1}{4} + 4\frac{2}{3} =$

(b) $3\frac{1}{5} + 2\frac{1}{3} + 4\frac{7}{10} =$

Worksheets

Number and Algebra: **Multiplication and division of fractions**

1 **Complete the following equations.**

(a) $\frac{2}{3} \times 4 =$

(b) $\frac{3}{5} \times 8 =$

(c) $\frac{4}{7} \times 6 =$

(d) $\frac{1}{2} \times 9 =$

(e) $\frac{7}{9} \times 5 =$

(f) $\frac{7}{10} \times 4 =$

2 **Complete the following equations.**

(a) $\frac{3}{5} \div \frac{1}{5} =$

(b) $\frac{8}{15} \div \frac{4}{15} =$

(c) $\frac{6}{10} \div \frac{3}{10} =$

(d) $\frac{1}{2} \div \frac{1}{2} =$

(e) $\frac{4}{3} \div \frac{2}{3} =$

(f) $\frac{9}{5} \div \frac{9}{5} =$

3 **Complete the following equations.**

(a) $\frac{2}{5} \times \frac{5}{7} =$

(b) $\frac{2}{3} \times \frac{3}{7} =$

(c) $\frac{3}{10} \times \frac{10}{12} =$

(d) $\frac{3}{4} \times \frac{4}{9} =$

(e) $\frac{5}{6} \times \frac{6}{7} =$

(f) $\frac{5}{8} \times \frac{8}{15} =$

4 **Complete the following equations.**

(a) $\frac{2}{3} \times \frac{6}{7} =$

(b) $\frac{1}{2} \times \frac{4}{5} =$

(c) $\frac{4}{5} \times \frac{3}{10} =$

(d) $\frac{2}{10} \times \frac{3}{10} =$

(e) $\frac{5}{9} \times \frac{4}{7} =$

(f) $\frac{7}{10} \times \frac{9}{100} =$

5 **Complete the following equations.**

(a) $\frac{3}{5} \times \frac{2}{3} \times 4 =$

(b) $\frac{3}{4} \times \frac{4}{5} \times 7 =$

Name ....

Class ....

Date ....

Number and Algebra: **Percentages 1**

1 Write the following vulgar fractions as percentages.

(a) $\frac{1}{2}$ (b) $\frac{1}{4}$ (c) $\frac{3}{4}$ (d) $\frac{2}{5}$

(e) $\frac{4}{10}$ (f) $\frac{3}{20}$ (g) $\frac{17}{50}$ (h) $\frac{19}{25}$

2 Write the following decimal fractions as percentages.

(a) 0·34   (b) 0·56   (c) 0·09   (d) 0·005

(e) 1·23   (f) 4·08   (g) 1·7   (h) 0·045

3 Write the following percentages as decimal fractions.

(a) 76%   (b) 90%   (c) 7%   (d) 0·5%

(e) 103%   (f) 245%   (g) $9\frac{1}{2}$%   (h) $\frac{1}{4}$%

4 Work out 10% of each of the following quantities.

(a) 50 pence   (b) £5   (c) £500   (d) £5000

(e) £6·70   (f) £23·80   (g) £45·24   (h) £542·20

5 Work out 5% of each of the following quantities.

(a) £19·40   (b) £26·80   (c) £37·40   (d) £19·90

(e) £8·90   (f) £23·30   (g) £460·50   (h) £290·00

Number and Algebra: **Percentages 2**

1 Complete the following sentences. The first one has been done for you.

(a) To work out 23% of a quantity using a calculator, multiply by 0·23.

(b) To work out 75% of a quantity using a calculator, multiply by …

(c) To work out 5% of a quantity using a calculator, multiply by 0…

(d) To work out 17·5% of a quantity using a calculator, multiply by 0…

2 Work out the following percentages.

(a) 15% of 300   (b) 34% 0f 600   (c) 9% of 150

(d) 12% of 225   (e) 56% of 420   (f) $\frac{1}{2}$% of 50

3 Work out the following percentages using a calculator.

(a) 30% of 96   (b) 17·5% of 84   (c) $12\frac{1}{2}$% of 178

(d) 2·25% of 46   (e) 19·4% of 75   (f) 22·5% of 276

4 Work out 5% of each of the following numbers.

(a) 96   (b) 124   (c) 328

(d) 584   (e) 1260   (f) 4760

Letts **I See Maths** Book 2

Worksheets

Name ....

Class ....

Date ....

Number and Algebra: **Percentage increase and decrease**

1 **Complete the following sentences. The first one has been done for you.**

(a)   To increase a quantity by 15% multiply by 1·15.

(b)   To increase a quantity by 34% multiply by …

(c)   To increase a quantity by 7% multiply by …

(d)   To increase a quantity by $\frac{1}{2}$% multiply by …

2 **Complete the following sentences. The first one has been done for you.**

(a)   To decrease a quantity by 15% multiply by 0·85.

(b)   To decrease a quantity by 34% multiply by …

(c)   To decrease a quantity by 7% multiply by …

(d)   To decrease a quantity by $\frac{1}{2}$% multiply by …

3 **Work out the following.**

(a)   Increase £20 by 5%   (b) Increase £15 by 25%   (c) Increase £65 by 2%

(d)   Decrease £20 by 5%   (e) Decrease £15 by 25%   (f) Decrease £65 by 2%

4 **What single calculation would you do to work out the following?**

"Increase a quantity by 15%, then increase the result by 15%, then increase this new result by 15%."

Worksheets

Number and Algebra: **Algebraic expressions**

1 Circle each term in each of the following expressions.

(a) $5 + 7 \times 9$

(b) $3 \times 4 + 5 \times 2$

(c) $8 + 5 \times 3 + 7 \times 6$

(d) $2 \times 5 \times 3 + 7 \times 9 - 9$

(e) $8 \div 3 + 7 \div 9$

(f) $4 \times 6 - 8 \times 9 - 4 \div 3$

2 Simplify the following expressions.

(a) $2x + 5x + 7x$

(b) $9x - 4x + 7x + 8$

(c) $19x + 7 + 4x - 4$

(d) $3a + 7b + 8a - 4b$

(e) $7x + 8y + 9x + 4y$

(f) $17 - 5x + 3y + 9$

3 Multiply out the brackets and simplify the following expressions.

(a) $2(3x + 4y) + 7(5x + 6y)$

(b) $3(5x - 2y) + 5(3x + 3y)$

(c) $6(2x + 8y) + (9x + 5y)$

(d) $4(5 + 7x) + 8(7 - 2x)$

4 Factorise the following expressions.

(a) $5xy + 3x$

(b) $2ax + 3ay$

(c) $10bx - 5by$

(d) $2x + 2y + 2z$

(e) $6xy + 9xz$

(f) $14axy - 7bxz$

Letts I See Maths Book 2

Name ....

Class ....

Date ....

Number and Algebra: **Solving linear equations 1**

1 **Work out the value of x in each of the following equations.**

(a) $x + 7 = 18$ (b) $x + 12 = 35$ (c) $x + 19 = 42$

(d) $16 + x = 18$ (e) $13 + x = 47$ (f) $45 + x = 103$

2 **Work out the value of x in each of the following equations.**

(a) $x - 4 = 7$ (b) $x - 8 = 15$ (c) $x - 17 = 58$

(d) $x - 23 = 81$ (e) $x - 44 = 76$ (f) $x - 99 = 99$

3 **Work out the value of x in each of the following equations.**

(a) $2x = 8$ (b) $5x = 15$ (c) $8x = 64$

(d) $10x = 120$ (e) $25x = 100$ (f) $50x = 450$

4 **Work out the value of x in each of the following equations.**

(a) $2x + 9 = 19$ (b) $4x + 5 = 17$ (c) $9x + 12 = 75$

(d) $7x - 3 = 32$ (e) $8x - 7 = 65$ (f) $4x - 23 = 25$

Worksheets

Number and Algebra: **Solving linear equations 2**

1 Work out the value of x in each of the following equations.

(a) $14 - x = 9$ (b) $27 - x = 20$ (c) $36 - x = 21$

(d) $99 - x = 67$ (e) $1 - x = \frac{1}{2}$ (f) $3 - x = {}^-2$

2 Work out the value of x in each of the following equations.

(a) $x \div 2 = 10$ (b) $x \div 5 = 7$ (c) $x \div 9 = 6$

(d) $\frac{x}{3} + 8 = 11$ (e) $\frac{x}{5} + 9 = 17$ (f) $\frac{x}{7} - 5 = 2$

3 Work out the value of x in each of the following equations.

(a) $2x + 4 = x + 9$ (b) $5x + 7 = 3x + 13$ (c) $4x - 2 = 3x + 4$

(d) $8x - 7 = 6x + 3$ (e) $7x - 14 = 5x + 4$ (f) $9x + 10 = 10x + 2$

(g) $3x + 8 = x + 12$ (h) $2x + 8 = 5x - 22$ (i) $4x + 6 = 5x - 6$

4 Work out the value of x in each of the following equations.

(a) $3 + 2(3x + 4) = 5x + 15$ (b) $\frac{x}{5} + 7 = x - 5$ (c) $\frac{3x}{7} + 5 = x - 11$

(d) $\frac{3x}{2} = \frac{5x}{2} - 4$ (e) $\frac{3x}{4} = 2x - 10$ (f) $\frac{4x}{5} = \frac{3x}{2} - 7$

Letts **I See Maths** Book 2

Worksheets

Shape and Space: **Using formulae**

> These five formulae are often used. You should learn to recognise them and know what the symbols mean without being told.
>
> Discuss each of these formulae and make sure you know everything about them.
>
> For example:
>
> $P = 2l + 2w$ P is the perimeter of a rectangle. The length of the rectangle is l and the width of the rectangle is w.
>
> (i) $P = 2l + 2w$ (ii) $A = lw$ (iii) $A = \pi r^2$ (iv) $d = st$ (v) $D = \dfrac{M}{V}$

1   Use $P = 2l + 2w$.
   - (a)   Find the value of P when $l = 7 \cdot 2$ and $w = 4 \cdot 3$.
     If the unit of l and w is cm, what is the unit of P?

   - (b)   Find the value of P when $l = 64 \cdot 2$ and $w = \cdot 05$.
     If the unit of l and w is inches, what is the unit of P?

2   Use $A = lw$.
   - (a)   Find the value of A when $l = 5 \cdot 2$ and $w = 1 \cdot 3$.
     If the unit of l and w is km, what is the unit of A?

   - (b)   Find the value of A when $l = 27 \cdot 2$ and $w = \cdot 15$.
     If the unit of l and w is m, what is the unit of A?

3   Use $A = \pi r^2$.
   - (a)   Find the value of A when $r = 4 \cdot 6$.
     If the unit r is mm, what is the unit of A?

   - (b)   Find the value of A when $r = 17 \cdot 23$.
     If the unit of r is hm, what is the unit of A?

4   Use $d = st$.
   - (a)   Find the value of d when $s = 52$ and $t = 3 \cdot 6$.
     If the unit of s is km/h and the unit of t is h, what is the unit of P?

   - (b)   Find the value of d when $s = 54 \cdot 2$ and $t = \cdot 05$.
     If the unit of s is cm/s and the unit of t is s, what is the unit of d?

5   Use $D = \frac{M}{V}$.
   - (a)   Find the value of D when $M = 14 \cdot 2$ and $V = 4 \cdot 3$.
     If the unit of M is g and the unit of V is cm³, what is the unit of D?

   - (b)   Find the value of D when $M = 64 \cdot 2$ and $V = \cdot 05$.
     If the unit of M is kg and the unit of V is m³, what is the unit of D?

6   For each of these formulae, make the letter in brackets the subject of the formula.

   (a) $P = 2l + 2w$; (l)   (b) $A = lw$; (l)   (c) $A = \pi r^2$; (r)   (d) $d = st$; (s)   (e) $D = \frac{M}{V}$; (M)

Name ....

Class ....

Date ....

Worksheet 30

Shape and Space: **Electrical units**

> **Look at this simple circuit.**
>
> **Electromotive force (e.m.f.) is measured in volts.**
> **We use the symbol V for e.m.f.**
>
> **Current is measured in amps. We use the symbol i for current.**
>
> **Resistance is measured in ohms. We use the symbol R for resistance.**
>
> $$i = \frac{V}{R}$$

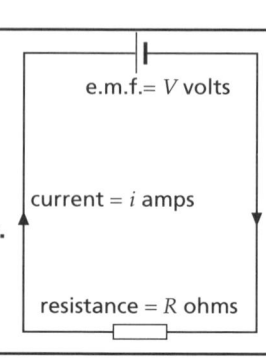

e.m.f.= V volts

current = i amps

resistance = R ohms

1 Discuss why we sometimes say 'volts per ohm' instead of 'amps'.

2 Calculate the current in each of these circuits.

(a)

e.m.f.= 12 volts

current = i amps

resistance = 2 ohms

(b)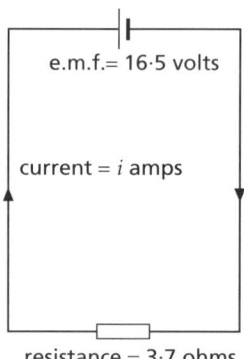

e.m.f.= 16·5 volts

current = i amps

resistance = 3·7 ohms

(c)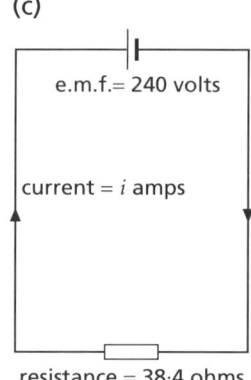

e.m.f.= 240 volts

current = i amps

resistance = 38·4 ohms

> **Look at this simple circuit.**
> **The power generated by the cell is measured in watts.**
> **We use the symbol P for power.**
>
> $$P = iV$$

e.m.f.= 240 volts

current = i amps

3 Calculate the power generated by the cell in each of these circuits.

(a)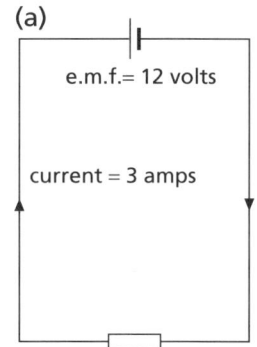

e.m.f.= 12 volts

current = 3 amps

(b)

e.m.f.= 240 volts

current = 6·3 amps

(c)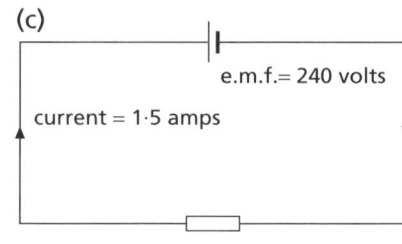

e.m.f.= 240 volts

current = 1·5 amps

Worksheets

Letts **I See Maths** Book 2

Name ....

Class ....

Date ....

Shape and Space: **Practice in sketching**

> A *sketch* is a drawing that uses given information to build a picture of a shape.
> It can be drawn freehand but should indicate measurements.
>
> A *diagram* is a neat drawing indicating all known information.
> It should be drawn with a straight edge where appropriate.
>
> A *construction* is an accurate drawing of a shape using exact or scaled measurements.
>
> Geometrical instruments such as a ruler, a set-square,
> a pair of compasses and a protractor should be used where appropriate.

1 Make sketches of these shapes.

(a)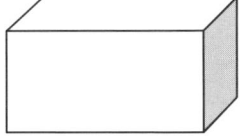

(b)

(c)

2 Sketch triangle ABC with AB = 4 cm, BC = 5 cm, CA = 6 cm.

3 Sketch triangle ABC with AB = 4·3 km, BC = 5·2 km, CA = 5·9 km.

4 Sketch a triangular prism. The cross-section is an equilateral triangle
with side = 4 cm. The length of the prism is 12 cm.

Worksheets

Name ....

Class ....

Date ....

Shape and Space: **Interpreting instructions**

> A *sketch* is a drawing that uses given information to build a picture of a shape.
> It can be drawn freehand but should indicate measurements.
>
> A *diagram* is a neat drawing indicating all known information.
> It should be drawn with a straight edge where appropriate.
>
> A *construction* is an accurate drawing of a shape using exact or scaled measurements.
>
> Geometrical instruments such as a ruler, a set-square,
> a pair of compasses and a protractor should be used where appropriate.

This is line segment AB.

This is line segment AB produced to P.

This is line segment BA produced to Q.

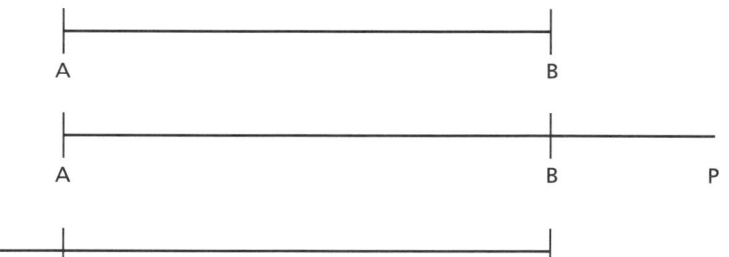

Follow these instructions.

1   Sketch △ABC with AB = 4·5 cm; BC = 7·3 cm; CA = 5 cm.

Produce AB to P; produce BC to Q; produce CA to R.
Let $C\hat{B}P = x°$; let $Q\hat{C}A = y°$; let $R\hat{A}B = z°$.
Calculate $x + y + z$.

2   Construct △ABC with AB = 4·5 cm; BC = 7·3 cm; CA = 5 cm.

Produce AB to P; produce BC to Q; produce CA to R.
Measure $C\hat{B}P$. Measure $Q\hat{C}A$. Measure $R\hat{A}B$.

3   Draw a circle of radius 3 cm and use it to construct a regular hexagon ABCDEF.

Produce AB to P; BC to Q; CD to R; DE to S; EF to T.
Measure an interior angle.
Measure an exterior angle.

Name ....

Class ....

Date ....

Shape and Space: **Ruler and compass constructions**

A *sketch* is a drawing that uses given information to build a picture of a shape.
It can be drawn freehand but should indicate measurements.

A *diagram* is a neat drawing indicating all known information.
It should be drawn with a straight edge where appropriate.

A *construction* is an accurate drawing of a shape using exact or scaled measurements.

Geometrical instruments such as a ruler, a set-square,
a pair of compasses and a protractor should be used where appropriate.

1 **Use this sketch to make your own construction.**

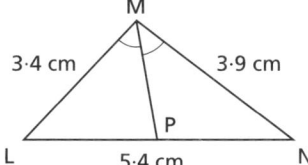

2 **Use this sketch to make your own construction.**

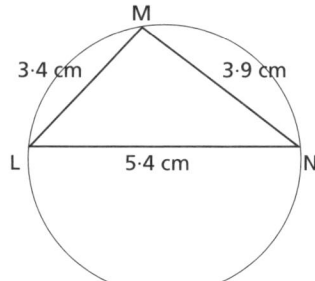

(LN is not a diameter of the circle.)

3 **Follow these instructions to make a sketch, and then construct the diagram.**

Draw two non-parallel line segments PQ = 4·5 cm and QR = 5·7 cm. Draw the
perpendicular bisector of PQ and the perpendicular bisector of QR. Let the two
bisectors meet at W. With W as centre and radius WP draw a circle. Check that the
circle you have drawn is the circumcircle of △PQR. Measure the radius of the circle.

Shape and Space: **Sketching 2-D and 3-D shapes**

1 **Sketch the following shapes:**

(a)   an isosceles triangle

(b)   a pyramid with a square base

(c)   a rhombus

(d)   a cylinder

(e)   a cone

(f)   two circles intersecting at A and B

2 **Sketch a copy of this truncated cone.**

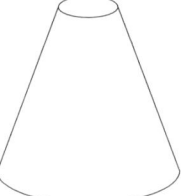

3 **Make a sketch of this cube with its corners removed.**

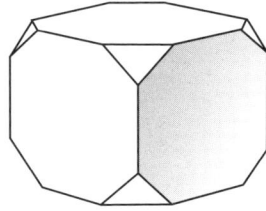

Letts **I See Maths** Book 2

Worksheets

Shape and Space: **Area and volume**

1 Calculate the area of each of these triangles.

(a)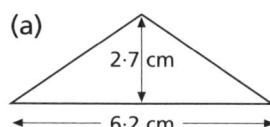

(b)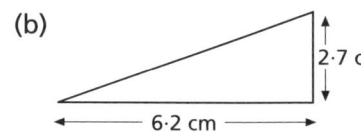

(c)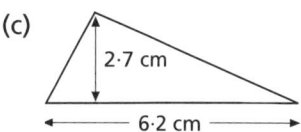

2 Calculate the area of each of these triangles.

(a)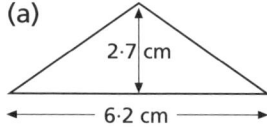

(b)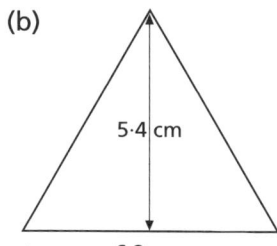

(c)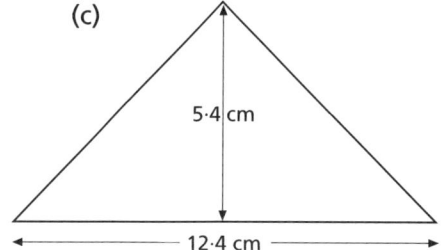

3 Sketch a cuboid 3·2 cm by 4·5 cm by 7·2 cm. Calculate its volume.

4 What is half the volume of a cuboid 3·2 cm by 4·5 cm by 7·2 cm?

5 What is the volume of this shape?

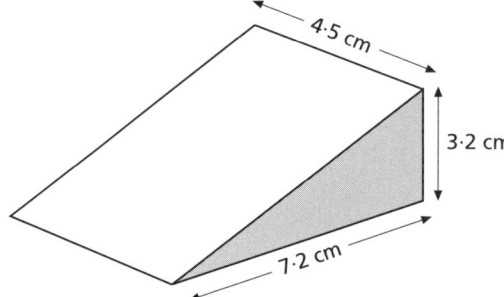

Worksheets

Name ....

Class ....

Date ....

Shape and Space: **Circumference and area of a circle**

Circle: $C = \pi d$ Circle: $A = \pi r^2$ Cylinder: $V = \frac{4}{3}\pi r^3$

$\pi = 3{\cdot}14159 \dots$

1 **Work out the circumference and area of each of the following circles, giving your answers correct to 1 decimal place.**

(a) $d = 5{\cdot}73$ cm   (b) $r = 5{\cdot}64$ cm

2 **Look at this cylinder.**

(a)   Calculate the total surface area.

(b)   Calculate the volume.

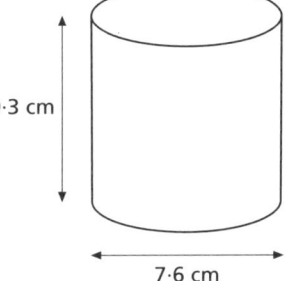

9·3 cm

7·6 cm

3 **Look at this cylindrical mug. It is made of plastic ·5 mm thick (including the base).**

(a)   Calculate the maximum volume of liquid it can hold.

(b)   Calculate the area of the inside surface.

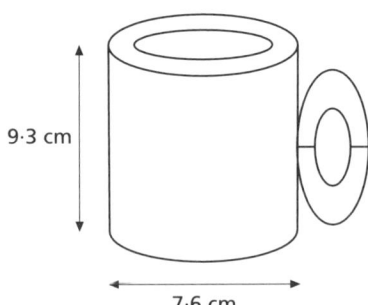

9·3 cm

7·6 cm

4 **A hosepipe 93 m long is made of plastic. The outer diameter of the hosepipe is 5·2 cm. The bore of the hosepipe is 2·9 cm diameter.**

(a)   What volume of plastic has been used in making the pipe?

(b)   When the hosepipe is being used, what volume of water is in the pipe?

5 **Look at the mug in question 3. Imagine it is half full of water.**

A stone with volume 8·3 cm³ is placed in the mug and it sinks to the bottom. How much does the level of the water rise?

      Letts **I See Maths** Book 2

Handling Data: **Probability**

> I rolled a die. This is an *incident.*
> I rolled a die and recorded whether or not it was a 'five'. This is a *trial.*
> I rolled a die and was interested in when the score was 'five'. This is an *event.*

1 Talk about spinning a coin using the words 'incident', 'trial' and 'event'.

2 Talk about a pack of cards using the words 'incident', 'trial' and 'event'.

3 Talk about coloured counters using the words 'incident', 'trial' and 'event'.

4 Think about this event.
I rolled a die and was interested in when the score was 'even'.
These are the outcomes of 7 trials:

$$3 \quad 6 \quad 6 \quad 5 \quad 2 \quad 3 \quad 1$$

(a) Underline the favourable outcomes.

(b) How many outcomes are favourable?

5 Look at this tree diagram for these successive events.
First event: rolling a die and getting an even number (E)
Second event: selecting a card from a pack and getting a diamond (D)

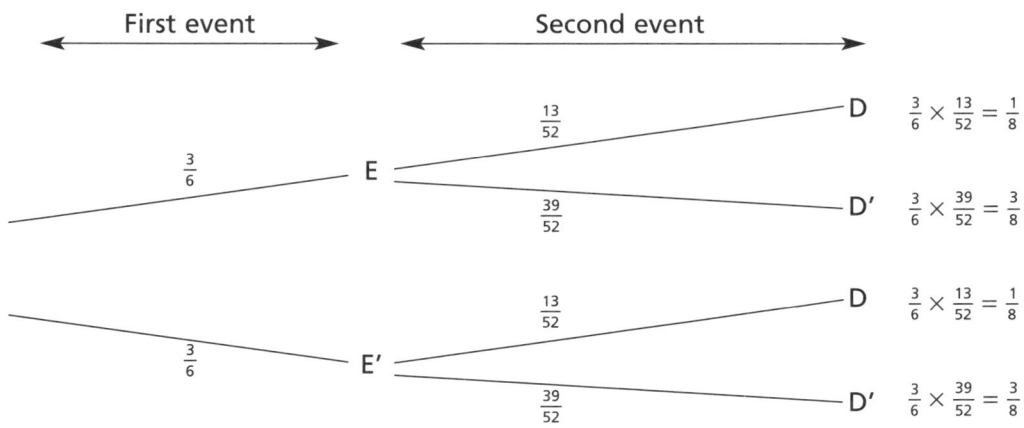

Find the following probabilities.

(a) $P(E)$ (b) $P(E')$ (c) $P(D)$ (d) $P(D')$

6 Write down the probability of getting a favourable outcome to both of these two successive events.
First event: rolling a die and getting an even number (E)
Second event: selecting a card from a pack and getting a diamond (D)

Worksheets

Name ....

Class ....

Date ....

Handling Data: **Probability experiments**

$P(X)$ means 'theoretical probability of event X'. $f_o(X)$ means 'observed frequency of event X'.
N means 'number of trials in an experiment'. $f_e(X)$ means 'expected frequency of event X'.

1 The theoretical probability of getting a 'diamond' by making a random selection from a pack of cards is $P(D) = \frac{13}{52} = \cdot25$.

Do your own experiment with a pack of cards for the following event D.
Select a card at random and see if it is a diamond.

(a) Complete 25 trials. Calculate $f_o(D)$. Calculate $\frac{f_o(D)}{N}$.

(b) Calculate $f_o(D)$ and $\frac{f_o(D)}{N}$ for 50, 75 and 100 trials.

(c) Calculate $\frac{f_o(D)}{N} - P(D)$ for $N = 25$, 50, 75, and 100, and comment on your results.

(d) Combine your results with a friend's results to calculate:

$\frac{f_o(D)}{N} - P(D)$ for $N = 125$, 150, 175, and 200.

2 Look at $\frac{f_o(A)}{N}$. **Repeat (a) – (f) 20 times!**

(a) Tell yourself: $\frac{f_o(A)}{N}$ is the observed frequency of event A.

(b) Tell yourself: N is the total number of trials.

(c) Tell yourself: N is the total frequency.

(d) Tell yourself: $\frac{f_o(A)}{N}$ compares the observed frequency with the total frequency.

(e) Tell yourself: $\frac{f_o(A)}{N}$ is the relative frequency.

(f) Tell yourself: the relative frequency $\frac{f_o(A)}{N}$ is an estimate of the probability $P(A)$.

3 **Do your own experiment with a die for the following event W.**
Roll a die and see if the score is a prime number.

Complete 50 trials, and use your results to estimate $P(W)$.

4 **Professor Amanda Blink has spent the last 30 years walking from her home to the university. During that time she has been interested in two events.**
Event R: It is raining today on my way to work.
Event U: I have forgotten my umbrella today.

She has calculated: $\frac{f_o(R)}{N} = \cdot34$ $\frac{f_o(U)}{N} = \cdot73$

She is wondering about the probability of getting wet in three weeks' time.
Estimate $P(R)$ and $P(U)$, draw a tree diagram and write to her with some advice.

 Letts **I See Maths** Book 2

Name ....

Class ....

Date

Handling Data: **Tree diagrams**

Use the data provided to complete each of these tree diagrams.

1 $P(X) = \cdot 3$ $P(Y) = \cdot 8$

First event ←→ Second event

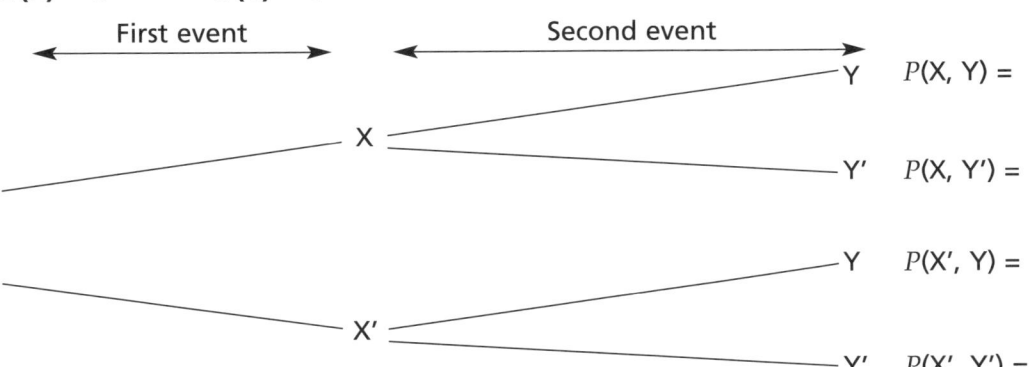

X

Y $P(X, Y) =$

Y′ $P(X, Y') =$

X′

Y $P(X', Y) =$

Y′ $P(X', Y') =$

2 $P(X) = \cdot 62$ $P(Y) = \cdot 04$

First event ←→ Second event

X

Y $P(X, Y) =$

Y′ $P(X, Y') =$

X′

Y $P(X', Y) =$

Y′ $P(X', Y') =$

3 $P(X) = 23\%$ $P(Y) = 64\%$

First event ←→ Second event

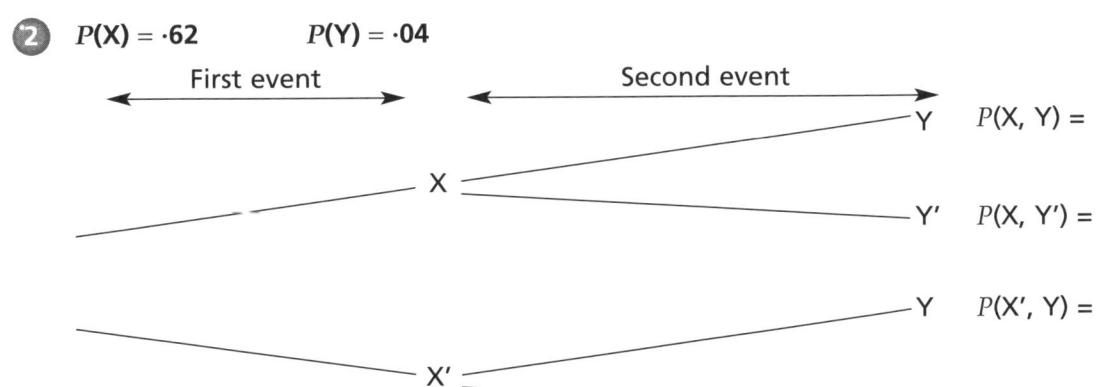

X

Y $P(X, Y) =$

Y′ $P(X, Y') =$

X′

Y $P(X', Y) =$

Y′ $P(X', Y') =$

W o r k s h e e t s

Name ....

Class ....

Date ....

Handling Data: **Box-and-whisker diagrams**

> The five number summary includes:
>
> the highest value of the variable   the lowest value of the variable
>
> the lower quartile   the median   the upper quartile

1 **Draw a box-and-whisker diagram for this five number summary:**

the highest value of the variable = 171   the lowest value of the variable = 155

the lower quartile = 162   the median = 165   the upper quartile = 167

2 **Look at this box-and-whisker diagram, and complete the five number summary.**

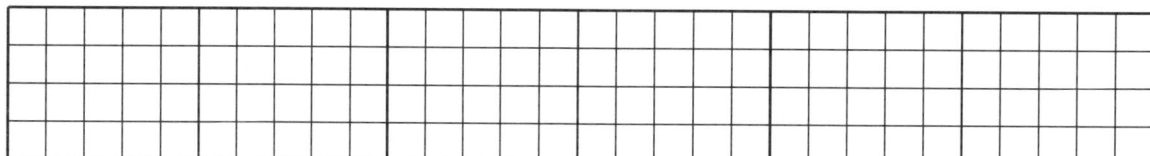

7   9   16   21   28

3 **Examine this frequency table.**

x	7	9	10	13	14	15	17	19	22	24
$f(x)$	1	3	4	6	9	7	10	5	3	1

(a) Work out the five number summary.
(b) Draw a box-and-whisker diagram.

4 **Invent box-and-whisker diagrams for population A and population B.**
- Population A has the same median as population B.
- The range of population A is twice that of population B.
- The upper quartile of population B is twice that of population A.
- The lower quartile of population B is twice that of population A.

    Letts **I See Maths** Book 2

Worksheets

Name ....

Class ....

Date ....

Handling Data: **Stem-and-leaf diagrams**

1 Look at this stem-and-leaf diagram for values between 340 and 370.

stem		leaf
34	8 5 5	5 5 8
35	5 0 1 2 3 3 4 4 5 9 5 7 6 7 8 3 9 6	0 1 2 3 3 3 4 4 5 5 5 6 6 7 7
36	1 0 2	0 1 2

(a) Calculate: $Q_1 =$ $Q_2 =$ $Q_3 =$
(b) Calculate: Range =
(c) Calculate: Inter-quartile range =

2 Look at this population.

26·8 26·3 26·9 26·5 25·8 26·0 27·1 26·1 26·3 26·4 26·4 26·5 26·9
25·5 26·7 26·6 26·7 27·0 26·6 27·2 25·5 25·5 26·2 26·3

(a) Construct a stem-and-leaf diagram.

(b) Calculate: $Q_1 =$ $Q_2 =$ $Q_3 =$
(c) Calculate: Range =
(d) Calculate: Inter-quartile range =

3 (a) Invent a stem-and-leaf diagram for a population with:
   $Q_1 = 35$ $Q_2 = 64$ $Q_3 = 73$ Range = 77   Inter-quartile range = 38

(b) Invent a population that fits your invented data.

Handling Data: **Reasoning about the mean**

1 **Think about these two samples.**
Sample A: $\bar{x} = 4$, $f(x) = 9$ Sample B: $\bar{x} = 6$, $f(x) = 7$

(a)   For Sample A, calculate $\Sigma x f(x)$.
(b)   For Sample B, calculate $\Sigma x f(x)$.
(c)   Combine Sample A and Sample B. Calculate $f(x)$ for the new sample.
(d)   Combine Sample A and Sample B. Calculate $\Sigma x f(x)$ for the new sample.
(e)   Combine Sample A and Sample B. Calculate $\bar{x}$ for the new sample.
(f)   It would be wrong to think that the mean of the new sample should be 5.
      Why might you think it is 5? Why is it not 5?
(g)   Sample A is increased so that $f(x) = 10$. Call this enlarged sample Sample C.
      For Sample C, $\bar{x} = 5$. Combine Sample B and Sample C. What is $\bar{x}$ for this new sample?

2 **Nine boys bought apples. Seven girls bought apples.**
The mean number of apples bought by the boys was 4.
The mean number of apples bought by the girls was 6.

Discuss these statements and decide if each one is true or false.
(a)   The mean number of apples bought by the 16 people was 5.
(b)   The person who bought the most apples must have been a girl.
(c)   Each of the girls bought more apples than any boy.
(d)   At least one girl bought more apples than any boy.
(e)   The total number of apples bought by the boys was 36.
(f)   The variable is 'people'.
(g)   The variable is 'apples'.
(h)   The variable is 'number of apples'.
(i)   Another boy arrives carrying apples. He joins the boys and notices that the mean
      number of apples for the boys is now 5. The mean number of apples for the 17
      people is 5·41 .

3 **Complete these grids.**

Sample 1	x	$x - \bar{x}$
D	2	
E	5	
F	4	
G	7	
H	3	
I	4	
J	6	
K	2	
L	3	
	$\Sigma x =$	$\Sigma(x - \bar{x}) =$

Sample 2	x	$x - \bar{x}$
M	8	
N	5	
O	7	
P	7	
Q	1	
R	9	
S	2	
	$\Sigma x =$	$\Sigma(x - \bar{x}) =$

Worksheets

Letts I See Maths Book 2

Handling Data: **Estimated mean**

Data sets are often presented in *frequency* tables rather than as a long list of values. Frequency tables are convenient because it makes it easier to understand the data; for example, the number of occurances of a particular value of the variable. When there is a very large number of values of the variable it is convenient to use *grouped frequency tables*: they also make it easier to make sense of the data.

1 Look at the frequency table in Figure 1, and look at the grouped frequency table for the same data set.

If we use the frequency table, we can work out an accurate value for the mean. If we only had the grouped frequency table, we could only estimate the mean because we do not know the exact value of the variable in each group. We make the estimate by pretending that each value of the variable in a group has the mid-value for that group.

(a) Use the frequency table to calculate an accurate value of the mean.
(b) Use the grouped frequency table to calculate an estimate of the mean.

2 Look at Figure 2.
(a) Use the frequency table to calculate an accurate value of the mean number of words in a sentence for each book.
(b) Use the grouped frequency table to calculate estimates of the means.

Figure 1 Frequency tables for population: heights of members of Hopegate Sports Club

x	f	x	$f(x)$
155	2		
156	0		
157	0	155 – 159	3
158	1		
159	0		
160	1		
161	1		
162	1	160 – 164	8
163	3		
164	2		
165	3		
166	2		
167	2	165 – 169	10
168	1		
169	2		
170	1		
171	1		
172	1	170 – 174	3
173	0		
174	0		

Figure 2
Frequency table for two samples (Variable x is number of words in a sentence.)

	x	3	4	5	6	7	10	11	12	14	15	16	17	18	19	20	21	22
Book 1	$f(x)$	4	2	2	1	2	1	1	0	2	2	1	2	0	0	1	3	1
Book 2	$g(x)$	0	1	0	1	0	1	1	0	1	2	0	0	3	1	0	0	0

Grouped frequency table (Variable x is number of words in a sentence.)

	x	0 – 5	6 – 10	11 – 15	16 – 20	21 – 25
Book 1	$f(x)$	8	4	5	4	4
Book 2	$g(x)$	1	2	4	4	0

Letts I See Maths Book 2

Worksheets

Handling Data: **Correlation 1**

What relationship exists between height and weight? Taller people do tend to be heavier. But we do not expect the tallest person to be the heaviest, the second tallest to be the second heaviest, and so on. When we draw a scatter graph for the two variables height and weight, we can see that there is some sort of association, or correlation, between the two variables – but can we measure it? Yes, we can.

When we measure quantities like length we use a measuring instrument and we use **basic units** like 'metres'. When we measure quantities like speed we have to use a formula (speed = distance ÷ time) and we use **derived units** (like metres per second). When we measure probability we use a formula ($P(A)$ = number of favourable outcomes ÷ number of possible outcomes) and we obtain a **pure number** without units (it is a ratio). When we measure correlation we also use a formula and obtain a pure number.

You will be introduced to a measure of correlation (in Worksheets 45 and 46) called Pearson's r (named after a scientist called Karl Pearson who worked out a way of measuring correlation in 1896). He called the measure 'r' (We do not know why!). At least, it is called **'r'** when you deal with a **sample**; but when you deal with a **population** you use the Greek letter 'ρ' (we pronounce it 'rho').

You know that probability must be a value between 0 and 1 (we write $0 \leq P(A) \leq 1$). Well, with correlation, r cannot be less than ⁻1 and it cannot be more than 1 (we write $^-1 \leq r \leq 1$).
- Positive correlation means high values of x tend to be associated with high values of y and low values of x tend to be associated with low values of y.
- Negative correlation means high values of x tend to be associated with low values of y and low values of x tend to be associated with high values of y.
- r = 1 or ⁻1means perfect correlation; r = 0 means there is no correlation.

When we draw a scatter graph, the line of best fit always goes through $(\bar{x}, \bar{y})$, and in the examples below its gradient is the value of the correlation coefficient.

You will need some practice in drawing lines. Complete this set of sketches.

1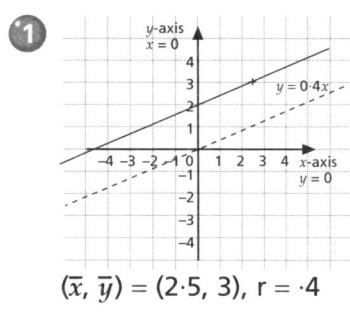

$(\bar{x}, \bar{y}) = (2\cdot5, 3)$, r = ·4

2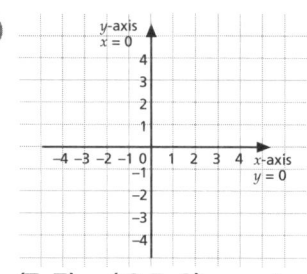

$(\bar{x}, \bar{y}) = (^-2\cdot5, 2)$, r = ·4

3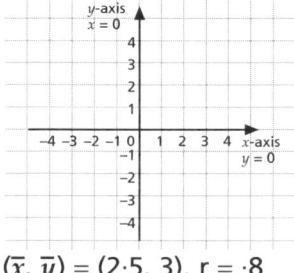

$(\bar{x}, \bar{y}) = (2\cdot5, 3)$, r = ·8

4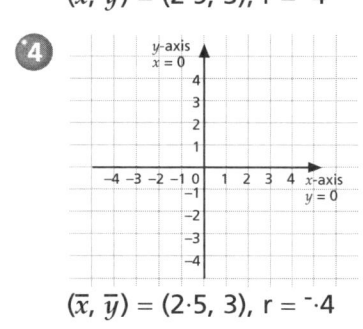

$(\bar{x}, \bar{y}) = (2\cdot5, 3)$, r = ⁻·4

5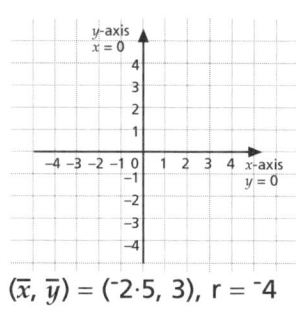

$(\bar{x}, \bar{y}) = (^-2\cdot5, 3)$, r = ⁻4

6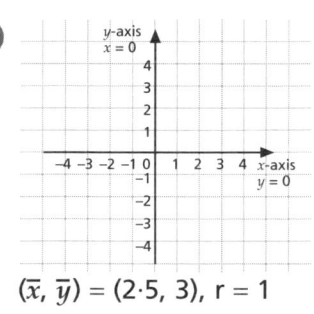

$(\bar{x}, \bar{y}) = (2\cdot5, 3)$, r = 1

Worksheets

Letts I See Maths Book 2

Name ....

Class ....

Date ....

Handling Data: **Correlation 2**

Study these bi-variate distributions and their scatter graphs.

Figure 1		Figure 2		Figure 3		Figure 4		Figure 5	
x	*y*	*x*	*y*	*x*	*y*	*x*	*y*	*x*	*y*
2	3	2	4	2	13	2	17	1	6
4	5	6	2	6	17	5	14	4	11
5	6	7	8	8	8	6	13	5	2
7	8	8	12	8	15	8	11	6	7
8	9	11	5	9	5	10	9	9	5
9	10	11	11	9	11	11	8	9	14
10	11	12	8	12	12	12	7	11	11
11	12	12	15	13	8	13	6	13	11
14	15	14	17	14	2	14	4	14	17
16	17	18	13	18	4	17	2	18	9
mean *x*	mean *y*	mean *x*	mean *y*	mean *x*	mean *y*	mean *x*	mean *y*	mean *x*	mean *y*
8·6	9·6	10·1	9·5	9·9	9·5	9·9	9·1	9·0	9·3
r = 1·0		r = 0·7		r = ⁻0·7		r = ⁻1·0		r = 0·5	

For each scatter graph, check that the line of best fit has gradient equal to r and passes through $(\overline{x}, \overline{y})$.

Figure 1

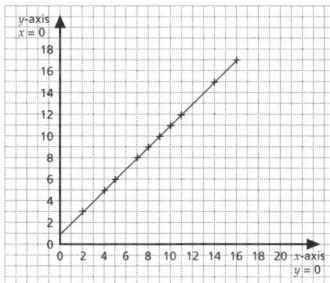

Figure 2

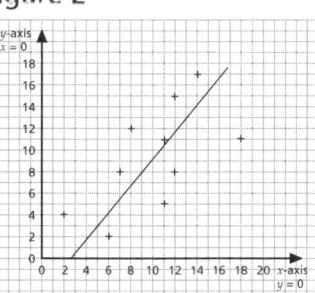

Figure 3

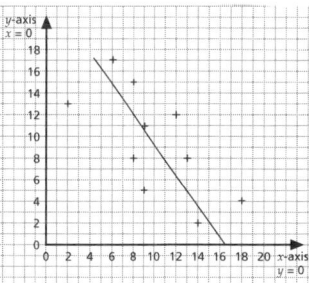

Figure 4

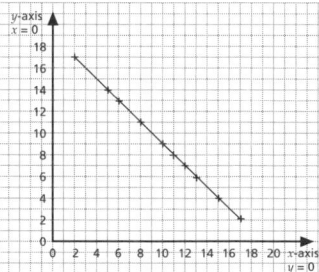

Figure 5

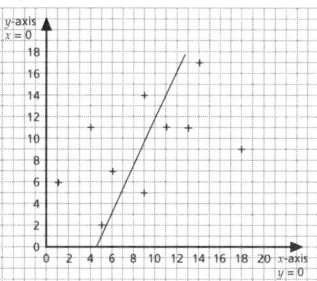

Worksheets

Name ....

Class ....

Date ....

Handling Data: **Pearson's r**

1 **Look at the data set in the grid below. Ten students had two maths tests.
The results for these two tests form a bi-variate distribution.**

(a) Enter the bi-variate data into a spreadsheet and use it to calculate the correlation
coefficient Pearson's r.

(b) Look at the formula for calculating Pearson's r. Check the calculation in the grid using
a calculator.

(c) Do a similar calculation for one of the bi-variate samples from Worksheet 45.

Calculation of Pearson's r

Formula for Pearson's r: $r = \dfrac{\Sigma(x - \bar{x})\,(y - \bar{y})}{\sqrt{\Sigma(x - \bar{x})^2\,\Sigma(y - \bar{y})^2}}$

Student	First test x	Second test y	$x - \bar{x}$	$y - \bar{y}$	$(x - \bar{x})^2$	$(y - \bar{y})^2$	$(x - \bar{x})\,(y - \bar{y})$
A	37	75	⁻1·2	⁻2·6	1·4	6·8	3·1
B	41	78	2·8	0·4	7·8	0·2	1·1
C	48	88	9·8	10·4	96·0	108·2	101·9
D	32	80	⁻6·2	2·4	38·4	5·8	⁻14·9
E	36	78	⁻2·2	0·4	4·8	0·2	⁻0·9
F	30	71	⁻8·2	⁻6·6	67·2	43·6	54·1
G	40	75	1·8	⁻2·6	3·2	6·8	⁻4·7
H	45	83	6·8	5·4	46·2	29·2	36·7
I	39	74	0·8	⁻3·6	0·6	13·0	⁻2·9
J	34	74	⁻4·2	⁻3·6	17·6	13·0	15·1
		total:	0·0	0·0	283·6	226·4	188·8

$n = 10$ mean x = 38·2   mean y = 77·6

$r = 0.75$

Worksheets